# Disquieting Gifts

# Disquieting Gifts
## Humanitarianism in New Delhi

Erica Bornstein

Stanford University Press
Stanford, California

FOUNDATION®
BOOKS

Delhi • Bengaluru • Mumbai • Kolkata • Chennai • Hyderabad
Pune • Thiruvananthapuram

Published by
**Cambridge University Press India Pvt. Ltd.**
under the imprint of Foundation Books
Cambridge House, 4381/4 Ansari Road, Daryaganj, **New Delhi** 110 002

**Cambridge University Press India Pvt. Ltd.**
C-22, C-Block, Brigade M.M., K.R. Road, Jayanagar, **Bengaluru** 560 070
Plot No. 80, Service Industries, Shirvane, Sector-1, Nerul, **Navi Mumbai** 400 706
10 Raja Subodh Mullick Square, 2nd Floor, **Kolkata** 700 013
21/1 (New No. 49), 1st Floor, Model School Road, Thousand Lights, **Chennai** 600 006
House No. 3-5-874/6/4, (Near Apollo Hospital), Hyderguda, **Hyderabad** 500 029
Agarwal Pride, 'A' Wing, 1308 Kasba Peth, Near Surya Hospital, **Pune** 411 011
T.C. 25/ 2731 Lukes Lane, Ambujavilasam Road, **Thiruvananthapuram** 695 001



This edition has been published by Cambridge University Press India Pvt. Ltd. by arrangement with Stanford University Press.

First South Asia Edition 2013

ISBN 978-93-82264-63-7

Published by Manas Saikia for Cambridge University Press India Pvt. Ltd.

Printed at Bhavish Graphics, Chennai

*For my parents*
*and for Elijah and Aneesh*
*for the freedom of being in relation*

# Contents

# Foreword

IN *DISQUIETING GIFTS*, Erica Bornstein both observes and makes her way within the interlocking social networks that mediate between global registers of humanitarianism and what she calls the "business of everyday life," which is itself shaped by pressing material needs, culturally inflected impulses, and changing historical conditions. Her point of orientation is New Delhi in an economically liberalizing India that has come to embody a set of contradictions in which the logics of human rights, democratization, and free markets have underwritten the emergence of a real middle class (not to mention a class of now-famous technology entrepreneurs) without providing clear answers for India's enduring poverty. Despite having one of the fastest growing economies in the world, there is a massive gap between the institutions that comprise social welfare bureaucracies and the sheer magnitude of need, especially in India's cities. As Bornstein explains, this gap—which opens up as much between the promises of economic liberalization and its consequences as between the state and its inefficiencies—is being filled by several different kinds of social, political, and religious philanthropy. Much as religious and moral mutual aid organizations rushed to the assistance of the passive victims of the Industrial Revolution (think Manchester in the 1840s), so too in contemporary urban India, where both neighbors and outsiders take it upon themselves to try to alleviate the experiences of vulnerability and suffering through a thousand "small gestures," as Bornstein puts it—culturally articulated actions that are often "spontaneous, informal, unmediated, and habitual."

This book is both a deeply reflective and deeply personal ethnography of these overlapping cultures of giving and receiving, one that also illuminates a central paradox of the contemporary life of human rights. As Bornstein notes, as elsewhere, the discourse of human rights made its mark in India during the early years after the Cold War. Transnational human rights nongovernmental organizations and intergovernmental agencies played their part in shaping national debates through which endemic social and economic problems were reinscribed within an ethical grammar that provided new grounds for self-reflection and social and political action. Key to this grammar was an account of the abstract human person that suggested a radical normative equality. Moreover, much like earlier cosmopolitan ethics, the rhetoric of the newly reinvigorated ethics of human rights suggested a stark and unmistakable ethical hierarchy: one's primary and most enduring commitments should be to the whole, all humans, as expansive and utopian as this moral ideal might be. Smaller circles of commitment were treated with ever-increasing degrees of suspicion so that by the time one's obligations were circumscribed by, say, the boundaries of neighborhood or extended family, one's ethical position had become dangerously untenable.

This is the double-layered nexus that interconnects both international human rights—primarily as law and political institutions—and humanitarianism: a horizontal conception of the person that is all-inclusive and the equally horizontal ethics that it implies. But here is where the nexus between the two breaks down. The success or failure of human rights compliance very much depends on the state, which means that the nation-state is responsible for reforming society and creating institutions for moral education that ultimately, and paradoxically, are meant to transcend the state. It is not surprising, therefore, that well beyond the constraints of both economics and neoliberal political ideology a chasm continues to separate a state like India from its human rights obligations to the most vulnerable of its citizens. But as Bornstein demonstrates, the international and transnational institutions of humanitarianism—while animated by a similar global ethics—are not constrained in the same ways. They constitute an important part of what she calls the "global economy of giving," and they are less concerned with the long-term programmatic dimensions of the post–Cold War normative revolution of which human rights is in the vanguard. Instead, their concerns are more immediate, simpler, defined by the most pressing of material needs: bodily security, food and water, medical care, shelter. And perhaps more importantly, the global economy of giving is also constituted by national, regional, and local institutions and actors, whose motivations for giving might or might not harmonize with the global ethics of their transnational counterparts.

Even more consequential for our broader understanding of the relationship between human rights and humanitarianism is Bornstein's analysis of the tension between the kinds of expectations that surround giving and those that surround rights-claiming in India. Indians are informed—by both the state and global institutions—that they are rights-bearers who are entitled to make legitimate claims on various institutions of the state. But as elsewhere, effective rights-claiming is for most a practical impossibility. Instead, people must rely on the social and religious networks of obligation to meet what John Burton has described as basic human needs. Although participation in these networks does not, as Bornstein explains, give rise to rights-as-entitlements in the strict sense, the results are more immediate and usually more visceral. And these networks of giving do something else that rights-claiming cannot: they reaffirm the value and meaning of quite local categories of belonging—those that people actually inhabit. This is what makes Bornstein's study of humanitarianism so "disquieting" for both scholars and practitioners of human rights: giving cannot be compelled or legislated by the state; it takes places within social networks that value relationality over the individual; the humanitarian impulse does not usually ground broad programs for social change; and yet the rhythms of giving and receiving are what define for many people the expected—and thus organic—practice of everyday life.

*Mark Goodale*
*Series Editor*
*Stanford Studies in Human Rights*

# Acknowledgments

ETHNOGRAPHIC BOOKS take a long time to write, and this one is no exception. Far from a solo endeavor, it has been formed through conversations with colleagues, friends, and family that have kept me fed, grounded, and critical. My son, Elijah Aneesh, has been a constant reminder of what matters most.

The book began with a fellowship at the Society for the Humanities, Cornell University, in 2003–04, a year sustained by conversations with Shelley Feldman, Dan Gold, Ann Grodzins-Gold, Steven Miller, Hiro Miyazaki, Max Pensky, and Jessica Winegar.

Research in New Delhi during 2004–05 was funded by a fellowship from the American Institute of Indian Studies, which was funded by the National Endowment for the Humanities. My ethnographic work in India would not have been possible without this grant, and I am grateful to AIIS and NEH for their generous support. In India, family made New Delhi a home: Babuji (late), Mummy, Bhavna, Dunny, Chillu jijaji, Dammo didi, Sunny bhaisaib, Bhabi, Anku, Goldie, Kishi, and Mr. and Mrs. Kapur. Thanks also to my driver, Bittu Chauhan; my research assistant, Disha Tiwari; and friends and colleagues: Jane Birch, Jacky Bonney, Mahesh Tiwari, Jitendra Uttam and Lena Pulenkova. I am grateful to all of the institutions and individuals that indulged my persistent requests for interviews, answered my questions, and hosted participant observation of their charitable, philanthropic, and humanitarian activities. At the University of Delhi Department of Anthropology, Dr. P.C. Joshi was always ready to engage in critical and dynamic conversation and I appreciated his steady enthusiasm. An audience in the department debated what is dān in Delhi and reinvigorated its importance for me as a contemporary topic.

When I returned to the United States in 2005, colleagues at the University of Wisconsin–Milwaukee generously welcomed me and made Milwaukee a home. The Department of Anthropology and the Program in Global Studies at UWM have consistently supported my research and teaching on humanitarianism and human rights.

A Resident Scholarship at the School for Advanced Research during 2006–07 through the Social Science Research Council offered the greatest gift—of time! In addition to some serious writing, I will never forget our Wednesday seminars, weekly hikes, and all around good intellectual companionship with the other fellows and SAR staff. The deep friendships formed during that year still continue. Thanks to Rebecca Allahyari, James Brooks, Cam Cocks, Noenoe da Silva, Eric Hanstaad, Barbara Rose Johnston, Nancy Owen-Lewis, Graham St. John, and Julie Velazquez-Runk.

In 2009–10 a fellowship at the Center for 21st Century Studies, University of Wisconsin–Milwaukee, made another year of writing-in-dialogue possible. Thanks to Jennifer Johung, Nan Kim, Jason Puskar, Manu Sobti, Deborah Wilk, and Merry Wiesner-Hanks.

As I was writing this book, family, friends and colleagues shared meals, kept my sense of humor alive, read drafts of chapters, and initiated other collaborative projects. Thanks to Aparna Datey, Angela Davies, Harri Englund, Meena Khandelwal, Liisa Malkki, Monika Mehta, Omri Elisha, Peter Redfield, Arijit Sen, Mark Sidel, and Vaishali Wagh. Lisa Silverman heroically read the penultimate draft on short notice. Manu Sobti generously provided the beautiful photo for the book cover. I thank JoAnn Bouikidis and Melania Dessoubret who worked as my undergraduate research assistants at UWM. And I am grateful to my parents, Gloria Bornstein, Paul Bornstein, and stepfather Yasuo Mori, for their ongoing encouragement.

Audiences at universities and conferences where I presented my work helped me think through sections of the book. Jonathan Benthall, Didier Fassin, Kathryn Libal, and an anonymous reviewer read drafts of the manuscript at various points, offering insightful suggestions for revision. Thanks to staff at Stanford University Press—editors Kate Wahl, Joa Suorez, and Carolyn Brown, and copyeditor Jessie Dolch—for making the book better.

I would not have considered going to India if my life had not intertwined with my husband Aneesh's. Although I don't hold him responsible for the contents of this book, he has been a provocative interlocutor in the adventure that it has become and deserves an award for reading too many drafts to count.

# Disquieting Gifts

# Prologue

LIKE THE STRANGER described by Georg Simmel (1908) who "comes today and stays tomorrow," anthropologists are a perpetual synthesis of wandering and attachment, simultaneous nearness and remoteness. Anthropologists embody a particular social relation distinguished by membership in a group to which they do not belong. Simmel writes that the stranger "is near and far at the same time, as in any relationship based on merely universal human similarities. Between these two factors of nearness and distance, however, a peculiar tension arises, since the consciousness of having only the absolutely general in common has exactly the effect of putting a special emphasis on that which is not common" (1971 [1908]: 148). The position of the anthropologist and the stranger can be one of confidante—the stranger "often receives the most surprising revelations and confidences, at times reminiscent of a confessional, about matters which are kept carefully hidden from everybody with whom one is close" (145). As anthropologists enter and leave communities, they span boundaries of difference to understand specific "others" and write about their experiences in terms of more general human questions. In the field, anthropologists engage in meaningful relationships that may overflow the boundaries of their research. Those who welcome anthropologists into their worlds—whether informants, friends, or families—do it deeply, personally, emotionally, and temporarily.

Anthropologists dwell in the field, with families of their own and with host families who have embraced them.[1] Unlike children adopted cross-culturally who are fully and permanently integrated into their new families, anthropologists adopted by their host families are adults who leave their field site and at times return. Membership in communities (and families) formed by anthropological relations is partial and may be temporary. Yet relationships created by anthropologists with their hosts are also forms of membership, and membership in the field remains an anthropological ideal.

When I began my ethnographic research in India, much had changed in my life since my previous ethnographic experiences to alter my perspective on fieldwork (Bornstein 2005, 2007). With my research in Zimbabwe complete, I embarked upon the project that constitutes this book on charitable giving in New Delhi with the aim of examining Hindu teachings of charity and the lived practices of humanitarianism in religious and secular contexts. Research in India had emerged out of an interest, developed in Zimbabwe, on how global, humanitarian practices of child sponsorship both transformed and were transformed by local contexts. Building on insights from my work in Zimbabwe, but aware of the radically different cultural and religious context of India, I chose New Delhi as a field site partly because my husband, a sociologist, conducts research in India. He also happens to be Indian. Furthermore, during the years between my research in Zimbabwe (1996–97) and my research in India (2004–05), we had a child, and the political climate of Zimbabwe made it a less likely choice for fieldwork with a family.

In India, I was suddenly thrust into an affinal family setting of which I was a new member. The people through whom I learned about north Indian kinship were my affinal relations, and the anthropological fantasy of "fitting in" became immensely real. Despite this built-in membership, culture shock was painfully apparent, and my Hindi was rudimentary. My husband was returning home, and everything was conducted in Hindi. The cleaning lady, the cook, the maid, my mother-in-law (who came to visit and stayed), and some of the wives of my husband's friends spoke only Hindi. My son, who was three years old at the time, spoke Hindi. I had not expected the transition to the field to be such a rupture. I was emotionally and culturally at sea. For instance, most middle-class Indians either have extended families or nannies (*ayas*) to care for young children, but since my husband is the youngest in his family, his elderly parents required care of their own, and other relatives were unable to help. It took us one month to find a preschool that would provide full daycare. The school we selected was in the center of New Delhi, a half hour's drive from the southern part of the city where we lived. At first, I considered family a distraction from my ethnographic work at temples and humanitarian nongovernmental organizations (NGOs), but I soon found that the people I met through my son and his school shaped my understanding of giving, charity, and humanitarianism. At the school I was introduced to donors and became involved in charitable efforts. I quickly learned to notice opportunities as they presented themselves, often at unexpected moments.

Despite the built-in relationships of my Indian family, or perhaps because of them, my field experience unfolded in Delhi with a great deal of confusion. In the spirit of anthropological mistakes that shed light on the practice of fieldwork itself, I offer an example of an encounter that was particularly awkward though instructive in which I became confused as to whether I was an anthropologist or kin.

My husband, his brother, and I went to the train station in New Delhi to meet my eighty-four-year-old father-in-law, Babuji, who had come from Kanpur to stay with us and have surgery. He was traveling with his servant, Rajol. The platform overflowed with people, and a sea of greetings, welcomes, and reunions surrounded us, along with luggage, shoving, and the smells of multitudes. Our party decided to split up and search for Babuji and Rajol, as we didn't know in which train car they had traveled. I scanned the crowd, looking for the two familiar faces. Yet I was searching with an anxiety beyond that of a daughter-in-law preparing to meet her father-in-law, to obey customs of hierarchy, age, and gender in India, as I had learned to do—to behave properly. I was also searching with the anxiety and excitement of an anthropologist. I, the ethnographer, watched Indian families as they greeted each other. I watched out of ethnographic curiosity—what do *they* do?—and out of a kind of personal desperation—what do *I* do? I knew that younger family members were supposed to genuflect and touch the feet (*charan-sparsh*) of a respected elder and then . . . what had I seen in Hindi films? Some specific gesture of touching the feet with your right hand, and then, touching your own forehead . . . or chest? I scanned the crowd for a model pair to help me recollect the movements of my kinship choreography. I watched to learn, urgently trying to decipher the code—the winks, blinks, embraces. Where was Clifford Geertz when I needed him? Multiple greetings later, eyes dry from absorbing visual cues and looking for Babuji and Rajol in the crowd, I spied Rajol. We greeted each other with a joyous "Namaste!" No genuflection necessary, as he was Babuji's helper. I bowed my head, and he pointed in the direction of Babuji, who was sitting on his suitcase, a few rail cars away on the train platform, waiting for us in his white khadi. I moved quickly to him and touched his feet. Hands to chest, forehead, and then the greeting, "Namaste." I had recollected the movement, absorbed it, embodied it, and performed it. I was proud of myself. Babuji stood and greeted me with a reciprocal "Namaste." He did not mention my greeting; he had not noticed it. Although I was a foreigner, I was kin, and I had done what was expected of me. I blended into the surroundings. I was taken for granted, foreign no longer. Yet I was confused; the glitch between performing daughter-in-law and ethnographer was a skip in a recording, a trip in a song that apparently only I had heard. I was related; I was not foreign. Although I was as culturally lost as I have ever been in any field setting, I was no longer just an ethnographer; I was kin. More importantly, I was mortified by this private dissonance. That I had considered myself an ethnographer and *not* kin even for a moment exposed a distance, an instrumental formality that only I could perceive but that was inappropriate in the context of my Indian family.

As the year progressed in New Delhi, I made efforts to consciously evaluate my fieldwork, and I found that my desire for intimacy with local informants and new affinal family created a particular problem. There were limits to how far I could go to observe local practices. For example, we hired a woman to assist in the kitchen and watch our son in the evening after his school had ended. We agreed to give her a meal each night, and I announced that she would eat the meal at the table with us, the family. My Indian relatives were at first shocked and perhaps even horrified by this pronouncement, but they were willing to go along with my social experiment. "Why not?" said my brother-in-law after some discussion; it seemed like the correct, progressive thing to do. I was put in the position of being the American with new ideas, and my Indian family was curious and accommodating. However, after a month of joining our dinner table, the maid stopped listening to me. Perhaps my progressive ideas confused her. Maybe she really thought she was part of the family, rather than a wage-earning employee, and thus an equal. She refused to do things I asked her to do and preferred instead to look at pictures in the newspaper. Eventually, I became so frustrated with the situation that I wanted to fire her. My Indian relatives protested: one does not hire and fire people so easily. Even domestic help is not a loose social connection; they become part of the family. Relationships such as these were not simply transactional—as easily dissolved as they might be in the United States, which was my point of reference for both kin and staff (and my Indian family, including my husband, used to laugh when I called the help "the staff"). Not only did I get it all wrong, I was breaking all the rules in what turned out to be a costly mistake. Amidst great protest and in a dramatic scene in front of the entire extended family, I fired the maid.

The closeness of my family, and the codes of conduct that it dictated, altered my daily decisions; it impinged on the quiet, private time that I found necessary and productive for writing up field notes. With little time to write down the events of the day, I found myself waking up in the middle of the night to slip away to my computer and reflect on events. Field experiences and interviews began to stack up in piles of notes and digital computer files. Unreflected, the experiences built to the point of conceptual overload. Moreover, the family that I had become a part of put emotional and moral constraints on the content of my writing. Ethnographic writing always risks alienating informants, but in India such alienation would mean social death, with long-lasting repercussions extending beyond field experience to my relationships with my husband, our son, and our extended family. My anthropological "host family" *was* my affinal kin. True, I did learn a great deal about kinship in New Delhi through family, but the calculated distance that structured my earlier experience of field research in Zimbabwe was no longer present or possible. A number of informants whom I interviewed were in some way or another connected to family, further embedding me in a web of social relationships.

One could argue that family is important in India and that I was learning this social fact firsthand.[2] I met Indian anthropologists, and we discussed how, in interviews, we found ourselves discussing our families as a point of reference, a calling card, before people would begin to talk to us. On a few occasions, I used the name of my father-in-law to gain access to informants through lineage and belonging. I learned that once I was located in relation to kin, my credibility was enhanced. My membership in an Indian family, even if by marriage across cultures, became essential, and I soon had the feeling that no one would talk to me unless I could first prove I was connected to someone recognizable. More than once, family connections facilitated finding informants. I did some letter writing and self-introductions, and I benefited from introductions by obliging colleagues who knew Delhi well; but in most cases, once an initial contact was made, discussions of family almost always ensued. It mattered to whom one belonged.

In addition, the types of field sites I began to work in presented new ethnographic challenges. In Delhi, unlike my earlier work (Bornstein 2005), I studied some NGOs, but they were not my primary focus. I sought to widen my purview to include philanthropists, priests, temple devotees, individual donors, volunteers, and any other social instance of charitable giving. Much activity was going on that did not fit into an institutional frame, and once my vision adjusted, I took note. I started looking and listening for instances of philanthropic practice wherever I found myself—often places to which my family took me instead of active research locations I sought on my own. I witnessed philanthropy at home where families supported their maids and other domestic helpers, who clearly did not have the systemic support of either a formal economy or institutions such as NGOs. For example, we paid an extra month's salary to help our cook, whose nephew fell from a roof at home (he miraculously recovered). Informal forms of charity happened frequently in everyday life—an important contrast to more formal, institutional, and distanced forms of humanitarian assistance. Another example was my son's school, which was involved with philanthropic activity. After the devastating Indian Ocean tsunami of December 2004, the school linked itself to NGOs that were coordinating relief programs, and soon my commute to my son's school became research. It was fieldwork that found me. Perhaps this happened during previous ethnographic experiences, but earlier I had felt as if I had to seek it out.[3] At first I had difficulty maintaining research momentum in Delhi at sites I selected on purely intellectual grounds: temples, NGOs, charitable organizations. Soon, I let life lead my fieldwork.

In New Delhi, I was drowning in anthropological riches, especially on weekends. Many informants invited me to events—rituals, weddings, and celebrations—but because of my own family obligations and responsibilities, I could not attend most of them. It was impossible to be part of the families of "others" in quite the same way. So I started developing alternative research strategies. My research had shifted toward a focus on orphans and orphanages, which were significant sites of giving, charity, and philanthropy. However, I found it painful to go to these orphanages. My emotional resistance mounted, and I dragged myself around Delhi, trying to conduct research. It was not until I recognized the problem as one of emotional isolation that I figured out how to address it. I met women from the United States and Britain living in Delhi who had been in the city for some time, or had just arrived there, but were also looking for meaning in the bustle of the metropolis where their husbands worked. We met at a hotel where a membership organization for expatriates gathered weekly. I originally joined, as an anthropologist, to meet wealthy foreign philanthropists. I was hoping to contrast foreign charity with Indian practices of *seva* (service) and *dān* (which I will explain shortly, but roughly, donation). Instead, I found friends who wanted to get involved with charitable organizations but did not know where to start. The sharp economic contrast between the expatriates and pockets of poverty in Delhi was something they wanted to do something about. When they heard I was studying orphans and charity organizations, they became interested and I invited them to join me. My research started humming. I took my friends along to visit and tour charitable organizations. Some of them wanted to volunteer, and I matched them with organizations. I felt productive, if not in field notes, then in a social world. The topic of my research was swirling around me. It was only when I could incorporate into my research multiple aspects of my own identity—anthropologist, ethnographer, humanitarian, Jewish foreigner living in India, and affinal member of an Indian family—that ethnographic practice seemed in harmony with living. Only then could I dwell in the field, and only then could I really do fieldwork.

In India I did not have the option to maintain distance between my anthropological and affinal roles. Yet, while my father-in-law praised me for being so much like a native daughter-in-law, for doing seva, I was at first troubled by the tension between my ethnographic desire to belong to my family and their sudden embrace that canceled ethnographic distance. To live in or inhabit a culture or place, one must abandon the objective distance required to systematically, instrumentally, and diligently record daily behavior; yet without this documentation, this data, there is no ethnography. In India I had multiple roles. I was an anthropologist, daughter-in-law, wife, and mother—all roles that I interpreted and reinterpreted according to ideas of "correct" behavior by my "host family," which was also my affinal family. But what does this mean when you cannot stop inhabiting the field, when your socially adopted relatives become your real (in my case, affinal) relatives, and when you can no longer defamiliarize yourself from the ethnographic site in order to write an ethnographic account? Although the category of "native anthropologist" has been well interrogated (Narayan 1993), even this did not correspond to my situation. Previous scholarship on research subjectivity did not offer a ready answer.[4] It became apparent that my idea of ethnographic distance was at odds with my integration into family life in Delhi where, even though I was obviously not a "native ethnographer," I did, through affinal relations, become part of the field and embraced.

How ethnographers live in the field has much to say about fieldwork itself. In India, because I was an affinal member of an Indian family, "fieldwork" was integrated with life almost by necessity. Ethnographic immersion no longer became a choice or a task that I could avoid. As a result, I was connected to the field in ways I had not anticipated, and I sometimes found myself longing to escape, as many people may wish to do from their own families. Families can be claustrophobic, like the field. But one can leave the field; there is a built-in escape: anthropologists can come and go from the social obligations of field relations in ways they may not be able to at home. Yet in India I was not only conducting research, I was living. Surrounded by and conscious of my webs of affiliation, my relationships in Delhi were rich and I was not disappointed. I did not expect to befriend or to be included in the lives of many of my informants. I did not expect to have lasting relationships with all but a few. Yet, in Delhi, I was in relation; I was part of the field in a way that I wish I had known earlier how to be.

Relationships in the field involve loyalties that tempt a complete immersion, represented ultimately by the imagined possibility of "going native" (which is obviously problematic and extensively critiqued). Whereas now no one assumes one will go native, there remains an anthropological ideal of membership—that one will be accepted by and integrated into, or even initiated into, the groups and sites where one works. Relations of friendship, love, parenthood, and affiliation fill fieldwork. Our field families are often "families we choose" (Weston 1991), sometimes in relation to our own families that we have chosen to cross the globe in order to flee. My intent is to stress that in anthropological fieldwork, models of membership are useful, and here I include honorary or symbolic membership. These relationships affirm the moral grammar of ethnographic engagement: "I was there"; "I am responsibly socially connected and maintain obligations toward my host family and informants"; "I am still part of the community despite cultural and/or physical distance"; and "I lived with them." Speaking to the complex experience of fieldwork, membership is a useful notion in anthropology. That we can even attempt to create a "bridge to humanity" through our ethnographic fieldwork (Grindal and Salamone 2006), by forming meaningful and at times temporary relationships with those radically different from ourselves, is an ethically challenging and compelling endeavor.

This ethnographic meditation sets the ground for the relational grammars of rights, giving, and humanitarianism that are the subject of this book. Humanitarianism—giving to strangers—is distinguished from the care of kin, and in order to make this distinction, one must know to whom one is related. One overarching theme of this book is the tension between giving to strangers and giving to kin. Although boundaries of affiliation may orient moral directives to give, it is difficult to classify giving to kin as a humanitarian act, although it is no less valid. Relations of affiliation, such as families, define to whom one belongs, within which group one has rights, and to whom one is socially responsible. One could say, more broadly, that such affiliative relations structure obligation and responsibility in urban India. With fluidity that surpasses distinctions of kin and caste, affiliative relations in Delhi may also be articulated through where one lives (in north, south, east, or west Delhi), the language one speaks (Hindi, Urdu, or English), the city of one's birth (Allahabad, Lucknow, or Delhi), or one's religious identity (Hindu, Muslim, Christian, Parsi, or Jew), among other associations. Each of these identities asserts group membership and provides referents for giving, helping, and other forms of humanitarianism.[5]

# Introduction

FROM EARTHQUAKES TO TSUNAMIS, from AIDS to hunger, our moral horizon is increasingly global. Televised images of catastrophes around the world make it difficult to ignore remote suffering as distinct from one's immediate concerns. All disasters, in an important sense, are global, and as such, our attention is drawn, justifiably, to the victims of misfortune. Yet the story often fails to include the other side of the equation—those who want to help the victims: poor students sending money for those in need, activists struggling to help the injured, wealthy philanthropists seeking to make a difference. The subtle shades of humanitarian efforts—differentiated by varied imperatives, impulses, and systems of obligation and assistance—remain less visible. Alongside the heroic efforts of professional aid workers and the dramatic suffering of disaster victims are those who provide care inaudibly, without recognition and without status.

Humanitarianism occurs in particular settings, and it is in such a setting that my story unfolds. Winter morning sun warmed me and a sari-clad widow in white as she sorted biscuits for tea. Hundreds of girls would partake of tea that January morning in 2005, with biscuits provided by an anonymous donor. The woman had been working and living at the Hindu reform orphanage in south Delhi for the thirty-five years since her husband had died. Although the orphanage was a residential school for girls, primarily supported by donations of sponsors who paid for their education, it also received assistance from the Government of India (GOI), and relied on the labor of destitute women, as well as on the efforts of volunteers, who, inspired by religious piety, gave their time. The orphanage was at once a realm of Hindu dān, a form of nonreciprocal giving that does not demand a return; a site of state welfare, where citizens enjoyed certain rights; and a place where volunteers responded to social obligations and the impulse to help others. Destitute women lived with the girls and oversaw their care. Volunteers arrived weekly to distribute food and drop off clothes. Some visited regularly to care for the cows that provided milk for the school. Others made monthly payments to sponsor a girl's education, or eventually to sponsor her wedding. The orphanage was not a permanent home for many of the girls; most had a living parent who had placed them in the institution because of poverty. One could interpret the institution as a form of state-sponsored social welfare. The girls, as citizens of India, had rights and entitlements; it was the obligation of the state to care for its citizens. Yet the volunteers who donated their time did not fit into this frame. They practiced what in India is called *seva* (service). The sponsors who supported a girl's education or wedding did so through the Hindu lens of dān. As to the women who worked at the institution, some were welfare recipients who took refuge at the orphanage school, and others had renounced their families to serve society.

Most scholars of economic development, philanthropy, and humanitarianism would agree that sponsoring the education of an orphan or giving to beggars on an urban street is not usually considered to be in the same category as the institutional complex of international humanitarian aid. Yet the two forms are linked through the gift—connecting those who are excluded from resources with those who are willing and able to actively engage. One aim of this book is to dissect how social acts often academically considered to be in separate realms—of development, charity, and humanitarianism—are part of a larger universe of giving marked by notions of global citizenship, relations of social obligation that entail rights and entitlements, and sacred conceptions of religious donation. The subjects of this book are engaged in the contemporary practice of helping others in New Delhi, India, situated against a backdrop of the global economy of giving. Their efforts contrast with those of professional aid workers who adamantly assert, "We don't do charity." The subjects of this book are Indians and foreigners who attempt to alleviate suffering as activists, volunteers, professional NGO workers, and citizens who give spontaneously, religiously, and/or impulsively. Expectations surrounding humanitarianism for urban Indians and non-Indians differ, of course, but they intersect in the charitable sector of global India. This book is about humanitarianism as a transnational form *in* India; it is not about Indian humanitarianism.

Intentions of giving may not translate across groups, especially as prestation is embedded in and defined by particular social logics. In the United States, for example, a "thank-you" is expected in exchange for a gift. Imagine giving a gift to a child. What is the anticipated normative behavior? It may include the child opening and publicly appreciating the gift and expressing thanks with sincerity. How many times have I heard at a child's birthday party, "Say thank-you, nicely"? How many times have I provided the same pedagogical directive to my own son? The trend is exaggerated by the proliferation of thank-you cards that perfunctorily follow attendance at children's birthday parties. This norm is perpetuated in the immediate letter of thanks one receives after donating to a charity. With online donations possible through the Internet, the speed with which thank-you letters arrive almost threatens the potential for social obligation to accrue. Meanwhile, thank-you letters are tax receipts that gain legal lives of their own.

In the context of simple gifts (rather than humanitarian aid), different cultural codes define giving. One could say, rather generally, that in New Delhi it is considered rude to open a gift in front of the giver. There is no Hindi word for "thank-you." Its counterpart, *dhanyavad*, is a relatively recent translation with a short cultural history. One explanation is that saying "thank-you" in the Indian context threatens to turn social relationships into transactions, which obliterates the possibility of social obligation. Imagine the difficulty of translation this poses for foreigners in New Delhi and, one can deduce, for Indians in other parts of the world. For instance, in Delhi a British friend complained to me about her driver, about whom she was perplexed. She repeatedly gave him what she considered gifts—of clothing, extra money, and food—yet she considered him rude and ungrateful for not saying "thank-you." I explained to her that his appreciation might have been expressed in a different manner, such as through action, perhaps by putting an extra shine on her car, which she may not have noticed. Moreover, in his cultural logic these gifts were expected and taken for granted. They were not extra-ordinary acts. In fact, the driver may not have perceived them as gifts at all: they were relational obligations. It was her duty as his employer to give gifts, and their hierarchical relationship was strengthened through these gifts of obligation, which were so unremarkable that they did not require any comment.

Another example of the challenge inherent in the cross-cultural translation of gifts will clarify the distinction I am making. During my fieldwork, my mother-in-law (who is Indian) was living with us in south Delhi. She expressed her motherly love by making tea for me as I sat at my desk and typed up field notes after a day of interviews. Each time she brought me tea, I would say, without thinking, "Thank-you." How nice it was to have someone bring me tea! However, my appreciation was a source of confusion for her because thanks are not commonly expressed in India. Soon she was bringing me tea and saying "thank-you" to me as she set the tea on my desk. After a year in Delhi, I began to see the depth of this mistranslation: in India, donors are grateful to recipients for receiving their gifts. You may say this conceptual stretch is too vast—from children's birthday parties; to thank-you for tea; to philanthropy, humanitarianism, and social welfare. You may exclaim that comparing the micro-practice of giving gifts to humanitarianism poses a logical fallacy of scale. But if you bear with me, I hope to make larger social processes visible through the detailed ethnographic accounts of daily life, showing how gifts to beggars and donations to organizations are infused with cultural codes that structure the expectations and experiences of giving.

Theoretically, my research is inspired by a debate surrounding Marcel Mauss's classic work *The Gift* (1990 [1950]). For Mauss, the gift involves social contracts and reciprocity; every gift demands a "return," and in this manner gift exchange is, by nature, reciprocal. Giving manifests social solidarity, for it is through the exchange of gifts that individuals are hierarchically connected to a larger society (also see Bourdieu 1977: 1–30). However, scholarship on giving in north India in traditional settings such as village prestation (Raheja 1988), funerary priests (Parry 1994), and Jain mendicants (Laidlaw 1995) has challenged Mauss's assumption of the reciprocal nature of giving. In north India, those who give strive to release themselves from any future contact (Parry 1986; Laidlaw 2000). With dān, no social obligations are incurred.[1] Jacques Derrida (1992) weighed in on this debate and argued that Mauss mistook the concept of exchange for the gift: the only real gift is one that can be neither identified nor returned. The minute one acknowledges a gift, it is no longer a gift; the ultimate gift, for Derrida, is the gift of time.

While Mauss's concept of the gift offers a basis for relations of social obligation, Indian ideas of dān are precisely the opposite. Mauss's concept requires a return, whereas dān is a gift that is not reciprocated. Dān is a liberating mechanism that releases the giver of social obligation and eventually frees the giver of the constraints of the material world.[2] As I set out to examine the difference between the Maussian gift and Hindu dān, my ethnographic research centered on an eclectic group of informants that included Indian philanthropists; employees of transnational foundations; Indian NGO directors and employees; Indian and expatriate volunteers who cared for children in orphanages and slums, provided tsunami relief, and devoted time to development programs; Indians who built schools for slum-dwellers and the disabled; and Hindu temple priests and devotees who donated to Hindu temples and their associated charitable medical clinics.

Giving may well be an ethos of our time. Humanitarianism is a form of the gift; although not a right, it may be considered a duty or righteous action. The humanitarianism I write about occurred in the capital city of New Delhi, in an India aiming to configure itself as a global superpower and a benefactor in the geopolitics of aid. Amidst this transnationally oriented national identity was also the reality that with increased wealth, existing poverty came to be seen anew in stark relief. As the GOI began to liberalize its economy in the early 1990s, issues of inequality and social welfare entered a transitional period during the next decade. In 2000, the Charities Aid Foundation documented that India had close to one million voluntary organizations registered as trusts, societies, trade unions, or charitable companies (CAF India 2000; Sen 1992; Tandon 2003). It also had the largest number of voluntary organizations in Asia. It was in this context that Indians and expatriates alike found themselves compelled to engage with the urgency of social welfare. While some of this engagement was formally registered with the GOI, much of it was spontaneous and undocumented. This diverse context of donation in the political capital is also categorized according to those who practice it as charity, philanthropy, or humanitarianism.

Contemporary India is a globalizing nation of technological innovation, shining skyscrapers, and new wealth—but also of vast poverty. Although giving is a symbolic platform upon which many claim firm ground, in addition to those who assist the needy are those who do *not*, those who ignore suffering and despair in the name of hierarchical relations of destiny, chance, circumstance, and fate. In India, poverty is part of life—if not yours, then of others in close proximity. People engage with need, broadly defined, in daily life at the interstices of formal, accounted-for charity, manifest in the work of NGOs registered with the state, and informal giving, much of which is constituted by religiously motivated donation.[3]

The significance of humanitarian activity is evident through its extensive media coverage, the copious transnational humanitarian organizations that toil in emergency contexts, and the force of voluntary efforts that are international in scope. However, one may still ask what humanitarianism looks like for those who practice it. Why do people engage in philanthropic activity, and what sorts of ethical and political dilemmas do they encounter? How do they make sense of their work? I hope that readers will read this book as encouragement to pay attention to the impulses that inspire people to engage in humanitarian action instead of solely paying attention to outcomes. I realize this is somewhat controversial, as most people aiming for social change, whether through philanthropy, development, or humanitarianism, reach toward specific results. Yet, as historians (Haskell 1985a, 1985b) and philosophers (Foucault 1973) have noted, different historical moments offer varying conditions for action. Specific eras articulate what makes something thinkable and possible at a particular time. For example, the relation of capitalism to humanitarianism, as Thomas Haskell (1985a, 1985b) has noted, is a particularly fruitful conjunction that emerged in the eighteenth century. The growth of development as a project in the wake of World War II also had much to say about its own time, with metaphors of construction articulating aims to rebuild a world broken by war and transformed by colonies declaring independence from imperial rule. Building nations and supporting economies seemed pertinent causes of that era. Now, many readers will agree, development has lived past its prime. Some theorists (Sachs 1992; Rahnema and Bawtree 1997) have pronounced it dead, although many in the "developing" world (or, the "global south") still clamor for resources promised through its institutions. Some call development a right.

Economic development is currently being met by an older form of helping: philanthropy, which is taking on a new valence with the emergence of technologies, such as the Internet, that facilitate a gift going to a needy stranger across the globe. And it is not just the Internet that signals such a shift. Some scholars go as far as advocating direct cash transfers to the poor, bypassing NGOs and government institutions altogether (Hanlon, Barrientos, and Hulme 2010). Cell phones in rural Bangladesh make it possible for women to benefit from microenterprise programs; airplanes take volunteers to remote sites in times of disaster—all responding to the new urgency of the gift. Perhaps humanitarianism and philanthropy—the gift of an individual to a cause—have become the new development.[4] As much as development-inspired teleological metaphors of construction, humanitarianism inspires metaphors of repair: saving others, rescue, and other immediate or impulsive responses to violence, disaster, and human misery. Humanitarianism is urgent and relevant right now, in our world. It has an intensity of purpose that compels university students in Wisconsin, where I live and teach, to donate to strangers halfway around the planet at the click of a mouse and, more importantly, to march into my office each semester and inquire how they can volunteer, and eventually work, for an NGO overseas.

For many students, the work of humanitarianism consists of abstract policy initiatives undertaken by governments and international organizations. They cannot often connect their own experience working on humanitarian issues with the broader picture of global humanitarian aid. In the courses I teach and in this book, I aim to address this translation. Voluntarism is a classic component of a coming-of-age ritual that has become popular in American higher education. Building on American civic and associational engagement and its link with character building, many students engage in voluntarism in order to have something that appears worldly and morally good on their resumes. However, the current population of university students are of a new generation. They have grown up during the era of globalization. They are not activists, yet they want to engage with the world and change it. In state universities such as the one where I teach, these students are neither worldly nor privileged; yet they perceive a need for global engagement. Majoring in anthropology or global studies, their motivation hovers among curiosity, impulse, and obligation. While perhaps utopian or naive, this desire for global engagement is particularly dynamic. University students today have their fingers on their iPads and their cell phones to their ears. Some might say that, glued to their computer screens, they are out of touch with the types of grave social concerns that compel humanitarians to work for Oxfam, World Vision, or a community-based organization. However, these students desire engagement with humanitarian issues of philanthropy and development, and they are not satisfied with existing institutions. They, like the subjects of this book, donate, volunteer, and work temporarily for humanitarian causes.

Helping others in need has touched a nerve among young people today. I have come to realize that engaging with global charity and humanitarianism has become, for some, a way of engaging with a world in dramatic flux. Students long to work for an NGO, to have an internationally oriented internship, to get "global experience." NGOs become portals for entry into an international arena. "How can I volunteer?" some ask; others return from Rwanda or China, having had their worlds cracked open through their experiences. Perhaps helping others is a form of ritual passage for global citizenship in a global age (see, for instance, Kristof and WuDunn 2009). Maybe it is a new version of adventure, an echo of earlier colonial missions and travels. In any case, these adventures are purposive and productive. They are temporary, yet they have lasting effects. These stints, or shocks, in extreme circumstances, put the lives of the privileged in relief. Some might argue that charity is a means for reproducing inequality, and that only those who are well off have the luxury of travel. This may be so, yet we come full circle to a philanthropic mode. From development, we have returned to philanthropy, and this, I argue, is not a regressive move. Rather, it marks a moment in history when charity has become urgent again—like the moment at the turn of the twentieth century when philanthropy became scientific and foundations were established (see Howe [1980] for the United States; see Jurgensmeyer and McMahon [1998] for India). We now find new forms emerging. Hybrid, transnational, cosmopolitan, and ad hoc, many of these forms are underground, undocumented, and discounted by those whose eyes focus solely on institutions. Much of the charitable activity I document exists alongside institutions and may even be collaboratively part of their efforts.

Unfortunately, we live in a world in which disasters seem to be the norm. From the Indian Ocean tsunami of 2004, to Hurricane Katrina in 2005, to the Haitian earthquake of 2010, to the Japanese tsunami of 2011, humanitarian emergencies are recurring phenomena that challenge the world to assist. Craig Calhoun uses the term "emergency imaginary" (2008: 73–97) to reference the growth in complex humanitarian emergencies worldwide since the Cold War and the capacity for comprehending these emergencies as a counterpoint to global order (also see Barnett and Weiss 2008: 24). Writing on the subject began in political science, with a focus on large institutions, foreign policy, and international relations (see, for instance, Barnett and Weiss 2008; Minear 2002; Weiss and Collins 1996; an exception is De Waal 1997). Some anthropological work on the aid industry focuses on aspects of economic development (Bornstein 2005; Stirrat 2008) and global governance (Mosse and Lewis 2005). Humanitarian practitioners (Terry 2002) and public intellectuals (Hancock 1989; Rieff 2002; Sontag 2003) have offered stringent critiques of the aid industry, often with an insider's knowledge of the complexity of humanitarian endeavors. These critiques emphasize the murky arena of humanitarianism in practice—a gray area beyond the polarized good and evil of more superficial accounts found in aid industry marketing materials aimed to solicit donations. Some are more hopeful about possibilities for social change resulting from humanitarian work (Kristof and WuDunn 2009). More recently, works have focused on the relationship of humanitarianism and armed conflict (Duffield 2001; Fassin and Pandolfi 2010; Pandolfi 2011; Goodhand 2006; Hoffman and Weiss 2006).

Within this quickly expanding literature is a new body of anthropological work in critical humanitarian studies (for example, Bornstein and Redfield 2011; Fassin and Pandolfi 2010; Feldman and Ticktin 2010; Lakoff 2010). While the work in academic disciplines of political science and international relations tends to emphasize large-scale NGO and state interventions, anthropologists write about humanitarian engagement as it is lived, focusing on immigration asylum in France (Fassin 2005; Fassin and D'Halluin 2005; Ticktin 2006); Médecins sans Frontières (Fassin 2007; Redfield 2005, 2006), trauma and rights (Fassin and Rechtman 2009), refugees (Feldman 2007; Malkki 1996), Islamic charities (Benthall 1997, 1999; Benthall and Bellion-Jourdan 2003), and the military-humanitarian apparatus (Pandolfi 2003). For an overview of the anthropology of humanitarianism, see Minn (2007) and Redfield and Bornstein (2011).

This book focuses on unofficial and ad hoc humanitarian work, largely composed of people who find themselves in circumstances that compel them to initiate humanitarian projects. It addresses the tremendous amount of humanitarian activity that is currently off the radar of more formal humanitarian organizations (by some estimates, 77 percent of donations in New Delhi are unofficial and undocumented [Sampradaan Indian Centre for Philanthropy 2001: 48]). The people in this book—positioned at the intersection of formal accounted-for charity manifest by NGOs registered with the state and the informal practice of donation and voluntarism—are Indian volunteers, foreigners who travel to India to engage with suffering, and diasporic Indians who have lived abroad and return with the desire to help their homeland. Those who engage in humanitarianism do so with varied intentions, desires, and outcomes. Difficult to classify and difficult to ignore, variation is key.

Each chapter of this book explores a theme through specific cases, or portraits, of people engaged in humanitarian endeavors. Chapter 1, "Philanthropy," examines how the fleeting impulse to give to immediate others in distress is tempered by its regulation. Whereas impulsive philanthropic giving allows no claims on the donor, welfare-oriented giving transforms recipients into claimants with rights. The chapter analyzes how some contemporary practices of philanthropy in India are related to sacred conceptions of dān. When scriptural ideas of disinterested giving intersect with contemporary notions of social responsibility, new philanthropic practices are formed that highlight the tension between the immediate impulse to end suffering and the social obligation to create a just society. It is a tension between giving away to proximate strangers in need, and giving to organized charity that is regulated by accounting systems. NGO and government efforts to regulate one of the most meritorious forms of dān, *gupt dān* (anonymous dān), articulate a critical issue in philanthropy and a scriptural concern of dān: the tension between the urge to give without attachment in response to immediate suffering and the social obligation to find a worthy recipient for the gift. The chapter is structured around three portraits: a family who gave dān daily out of their home, a woman who started an orphanage and sponsored the education and welfare of needy children, and a man who built a temple and an associated school for girls. These three cases of philanthropy question who deserves to receive assistance, and why.

In addition to the dynamic tension between giving to immediate others and giving to society, those who give are concerned with finding suitable recipients for their gifts. Chapter 2, "Trust," deals with this. The response to the 2004 tsunami disaster in India was a moment in which tensions of aid provision became public discussions of truth. Prime Minister Manmohan Singh's decision not to accept aid from the United States was in harmony with a new positioning of India as a nation ripe for investment and not in need of charity. Parallel to this public statement was an outpouring of media reports of corruption and inefficiency as well as the difficulties that local government and NGOs faced in their efforts to reach those in need of aid. Chapter 2 draws on the activities of schools raising money for tsunami relief, NGOs delivering charitable goods, and print media coverage of six weeks following the tsunami to show how rational modalities of accountability and calculation did little to assuage distrust in the NGO industry. Behind public demands for accountability and transparency in aid lay a simultaneous distrust of the charitable aid sector and a dependency upon it. The efforts of NGOs mirrored larger struggles about how money should be spent and tracked, how need was identified, and what constituted a worthy charity. This chapter explores how noninstitutional forms of social welfare—unregulated by NGOs and the state—intersect with institutional ones through two case studies: a wealthy school and its relationship with a slum school, and an American doctor who provided cash deposits to sponsor medical care for four HIV patients in India. In both of these cases, we see how suspicion and distrust may function as a social audit when it comes to providing humanitarian support.

Suspicion is not only directed toward individuals and institutions such as NGOs and the state that are involved in disaster relief. It also enters the discourse of care for abandoned children and frames the potential adoption of orphans in New Delhi. India has some of the most stringent adoption laws in the world, and given these legal constraints, orphans, the topic of Chapter 3, are important targets of humanitarian activity and value. Orphans are protected, saved, and managed by humanitarian institutions and the state. As this chapter suggests, transnational adoption, which ultimately transforms an orphan's status as a member of a new family and new nation, is far from the only possible outcome for abandoned children. Other contexts of their care include orphanages and "social adoption," according to which the state remains the legal guardian and an individual (or family) economically supports an orphan's education and care. Taking as its locus specific laws governing the adoption of orphans by Hindus, Muslims, and Christians, Chapter 3 explores how in India, when children are orphaned, they literally become children of the nation. Although an orphan's religious or other identity may not be clear, the extensive legal procedures for adopting orphans differ according to the adoptive parents' nationality and religious identity. Most orphans in India are not adopted. Instead, they remain in orphanages, sponsored by the GOI and supported by donors who pay monthly for their education, upkeep, and eventually (if the orphan is a girl) for their marriage. This chapter focuses on the reasons why orphans serve as good recipients of gifts, and why orphanages are pure sites for those gifts, highlighting the work of one reform Hindu orphanage in Delhi that housed adolescent girls and employed destitute women as their caretakers.

In contrast to the welfare work of transnational NGOs or the efforts of the Indian state, Chapter 4, "Experience," continues the book's focus on humanitarian efforts that often go undocumented, this time through the work of volunteers. Unlike service to society (*samaj seva*) and donation (dān), volunteering in its organized form is relatively new to India. The bounded experience of volunteering brings the giver closer to the afflicted, the poor, the suffering, and the needy, if only for a short time. As such, volunteering also has the potential to provoke an emotional crisis of experience for those engaged in it. Although volunteering speaks to the potential of civil society, it is largely practiced because of the potential for a transformative experience for the volunteer. In this way, volunteering differs from other humanitarian forms of practice—such as financial donation and professional aid work conducted by NGOs—in that it is undertaken as a leisure activity outside the productive realm of wage work. It is also a particularly powerful phenomenon that is gaining global currency. This chapter compares four groups attempting to organize volunteers to examine how some people seek out this dramatic experience and then try to encourage others to do the same. The first group is a pilot program that recruited students from Delhi's top universities to volunteer over the summer with NGOs in rural India. The second is a group of young urban Indians who volunteered at an orphanage in a slum. The third is an ad hoc group of expatriate women who met to hold orphans at Mother Teresa's Missionaries of Charity welfare home for children. And the fourth features two women: one an Indian who renounced her life of prosperity to start a school for disabled children in rural Rajasthan, and the other a young British volunteer who found herself seeking meaning while working in a lucrative career in the banking industry. These four groups differ in the type of experience of volunteering they provide, but the expectations of experience they elicit are central to all.

Chapter 5, "Empathy," explores the role of empathy in humanitarian efforts and engages with the Maussian theme of gifts and obligations: to known others, such as kin, and to abstract others, such as strangers and society. Much has been said about the capacity for the liberal imagination to provoke empathy, and for this to inspire altruism. I argue that there are other forms of empathy that cannot be understood through the framework of liberal altruism. I present a concept called "relational empathy," which I elaborate through four ethnographic cases that sit on a spectrum and challenge the empathy-altruism thesis: a group of volunteer knitters who distributed sweaters and organized a party for slum children in New Delhi; a foreign volunteer who found herself in Delhi longing for community through voluntarism; an Indian man who started a school in his home for the children of urban laborers; and a British nurse who worked in a leper colony for fifteen years in Andhra Pradesh. Whereas the first two cases fit within the bounds of the empathy-altruism thesis, the third and fourth cases provide a challenge. Liberal empathy seeks to assist abstract others in need; relational empathy turns strangers into kin.

Finally, a brief epilogue provides an overview and summary of the book, exploring the circumstances under which humanitarian acts can veer into the realm of rights and entitlements.

Chapter 1

# Philanthropy

*Shat-hast samāhār sahasra-hast sankir.*
Collect with a hundred hands and give away with a thousand.
*Vedic sūkti*

IN 2005, as I sat in a car in New Delhi with my son, who was three years old at the time, a woman in tattered clothes ran up to us and begged for money to buy medicine for her son, who was slumped over the shoulder of a man a few cars down the road. Just beyond the hysterical woman, I caught the eye of an auto-rickshaw driver in the next lane, and he shook his finger as if to say, "Don't give money to them." I followed his social directive, the light changed from red to green, and the woman ran toward another car. My son often tried to talk to beggar children who tapped on our car windows. The immediacy of his response was visceral and emotional, not filtered through moral judgments and political frames, as were my attempts to theorize poverty and charity. Both my son and I worked to find ways to understand what we saw on the street. However, whereas my son focused on the moment of confronting others in need, and the impulse to respond, my vision was clouded by the sinking feeling that I must do more than identify the problem. There must be solutions. I could not notice suffering and then drive away without trying to put it into a web of causality: Why were they destitute? What could be done?

This scene illustrates how the fleeting impulse to give to immediate others in distress is tempered by its regulation. Philanthropy is an impulse—a focus on the kindly desire to end misery and suffering—yet it does not offer any rights to its recipients, who can make no claims on donors. As George Herbert Mead argued, the impulse to give "is at times deprecated by charity organizations, which desire to bring the impulse under rational control" (1969 [1930]: 133). The impulse of philanthropy is spontaneous and has its own beauty; when giving is unregulated, it becomes deeply moving, an act of freedom.[1] Yet this poignant impulse to relieve suffering threatens rationalized charity and social welfare that focus on the long-term alleviation of need. Just as impulses do not focus on results, impulsive philanthropy is condemned as being outside of reason.

## Giving, Reason, and Religious Ethics

In *Economy and Society* Max Weber discusses instrumental reason in the context of social action more broadly (1978: 24–26). For Weber, social action is action oriented toward the behavior of others and falls into four ideal types: (1) instrumentally rational (*zweckrational*)—using expectations of results as the conditions and means for attaining calculated ends; (2) value rational (*wertrational*)—valuing action for its own sake regardless of the possibility of successful outcomes; (3) affectual—determined by feeling states or emotions; and (4) traditional—determined by habit. Weber argues that instrumentally rational action, when the ends, the means, and the results are rationally weighed, is incompatible with action that is either affectual or traditional. Value-rational action is also irrational. The more one orients action toward a value for its own sake, "to pure sentiment or beauty, to absolute goodness or devotion to duty" for example, "the less is he influenced by considerations of the consequences of his action" (26).

Giving may fall into one or more of these ideal types. For example, in New Delhi, dān may have religious value for its own sake and thus be categorized as value rational. The impulse to give is one of immediacy and empathy and in this manner is affectual. Dān may also be considered a duty or a habit and thus fall under the rubric of traditional rationality. When a gift is regulated, it becomes instrumentally rational. Although classical dān cannot be instrumental in the Weberian sense because giving dān involves releasing oneself from the gift, contemporary dān becomes instrumentally rational when it is facilitated by NGOs regulated by the state or when donors receive tax benefits for their donations. As we will see, dān is difficult to categorize; this prompts an updating of Weber's theory and suggests that differences in social action may arise from different realms of participation. The same act of dān may be reconstructed differently in varied domains of action: affectual (dān to beggars and those with physical ailments), traditional (dān to mendicants), religious (dan to Brahmin priests), and instrumental (dān as a form of social welfare). Giving dān in these domains is not mutually exclusive. One may give dān with religious rationality or with instrumental rationality to beggars and to mendicants as well. The cases explored in this chapter demonstrate how, in the context of social welfare, impulsive forms of dān threaten to disrupt the regulation of instrumentally rational giving. This occurs as the logic of capitalism attempts to regulate the gift.

In addition to differentiating forms of social action, Weber explored the relation of alms giving and religious ethics (1978: 581–89). The giving of alms is an aspect of ethics in many religions: for instance, in Islam it is one of the five pillars of the faith (*zakat*); in Hinduism, Buddhism, Confucianism, Judaism, and early Christianity, it is considered "good work." Correlatively, in all of the religions I have mentioned, the impersonal and economically rational pursuit of wealth is considered ethically irrational and is often denounced as greed. Although there is space for charitable sentiment in relationships between people, there is no possibility of caritative relationships between those defined by purely instrumental economic relationships, such as between a bank loan officer and a mortgagee (Weber 1978: 585). For Weber, the instrumentally rational world of purely economic activity is against charity. Moreover, as much as the inner-worldly asceticism of Protestantism offered ideals that justified the rational accumulation of wealth, Weber suggests that the religious ethics of Calvinism also destroyed unsystematic alms giving and ended benevolent attitudes toward beggars. If one interprets the idleness of a person who is capable of work as that person's fault alone—with salvation demonstrated through one's vocational capacity—those unfit for work in the Calvinist ethic, such as orphans and the disabled, are to be approached instrumentally. Such a systematic approach to charity is considered a rationalized enterprise that contrasts the erratic and impulsive giving of alms.

Giving is of central importance to all "other-worldly religions," but it is neither a monolithic nor a static social institution (Weber 1993; Parry 1986, 1994; Silber 2000, 2002). Romila Thapar, writing on the political economy of *dana* (dān) and *dakshina* in ancient India, correlates changes in giving practices to shifts in power and land use (1984: 105–21). Following Thapar, I am not concerned with whether or not a particular religious practice is true, worthy, or effective; rather, my concern is with how it is practiced as part of a changing social world. Like transformations of giving practice in ancient times, contemporary humanitarianism—as a manner of giving—can be understood through the discourse of donation and dān (which entail renunciation) or of rights (which assert group membership).

Dān as a Hindu practice is best understood in relation to historical transformations in other traditions of religious giving. This wider umbrella will provide a referent for understanding what makes dān unique. In rabbinic Judaism, for instance, tithing for the poor (*zedakah*) emerged as a principle of justice through an "ethicization of gift giving" (Silber 2000: 117). As part of the more general process of developing and interpreting laws that Jews needed to carry out in order to live by God's commandments, the rabbis replaced biblical directives for sacrificial offerings with prayers and transformed zedakah into a divine commandment connected to ideas of righteousness. As a result, zedakah became something to which the poor were entitled. Jewish charity became a collective responsibility, a religiously meritorious social obligation and duty supervised by communal and appointed leaders. Unlike dān, however, zedakah was neither disinterested nor voluntary. As a religious gift, it was a commandment. Giving to the poor was part of religious practice, and as such it was to be carried out on the same plane as other rabbinical directives.

One way to analyze the religious ethics of giving is to identify typologies of appropriate recipients according to a particular doctrine, such as giving to gods, giving to religious specialists, and giving to the poor and needy. Ilana Silber argues that in different religious traditions, one or more recipient groups are dominant (2000: 122; 2002). For instance, she claims that in Hinduism and Buddhism, giving to religious specialists and institutions is emphasized over giving to the poor, whereas in monotheistic religions such as Judaism and Islam, giving to the poor is more prominent. However, Vijay Nath articulates how in addition to religious specialists (such as Brahmins and renouncers), beggars, orphans, and the poor and destitute could also be recipients of dān (1987: 110–19). I found this to be the case in my research in Delhi as well: giving to different recipient populations may overlap. In Judaism, Christianity, Islam, and Hinduism, religious institutions dispense charitable services for the poor, orphans, and the needy. Moreover, historically, Christian monks, Hindu renunciants, and mendicants were deemed a special class of "the poor," although not indigent.

Another way to categorize giving is to determine the relative interestedness and disinterestedness of the gift. For Marcel Mauss (1990 [1950]), the gift is inherently paradoxical: it involves freedom and constraint, interestedness and disinterestedness. Silber suggests that the import lies not in whether the gift is free or disinterested, but in the "emphatic ideological valorization of non-reciprocity" in a particular religious tradition (2000: 127). Judaism and Hinduism both valorize anonymous gifts. In Judaism, this occurs so as not to shame or humiliate the recipient (a Jewish hidden or secret gift is called *matan beseter*).[2] In Hinduism, an anonymous gift is called *gupt dān*, and, as we will see, the motivations behind anonymous donation in Hinduism are tied to ideas of renunciation. The renunciative aspect of dān, and its correlative resistance to regulation, suggests that this may be an important reason why Hinduism, unlike Christianity and Islam, has not seen the extent of growth in global giving through religious institutions.

On the other hand, Muslim-oriented NGOs have successfully integrated zakat into global forms of institutional donation (Khan 2012; Benthall 1999, 2012; Benthall and Bellion-Jourdan 2003). Thierry Kochuyt (2009) argues that zakat inspires social solidarity in what he calls a "community of faith." He writes that "the beneficial effects of the zakat are not restricted to individual receivers and donors only, it is constitutive for the religious community at large and its relation to God" (99). Directives in the Qur'an specify obligations to give zakat to the poor and define the wealth of the faithful as created by God. "A good Muslim is obliged to give because he has received from God," Kochuyt writes. "Consequently charity is not initiated by the believers because their zakat is already a counter-service for what Allah offered them earlier. It is the binding consequence of a reciprocal relation between God and his faithful believers: they give to the needy as God gave to them" (100).[3] Zakat is given to the fellow faithful (in the Muslim community, the *Ummah*)—whether extended family, servants, beggars, or townspeople—and in this way it builds solidarity, marking members of a group. Transnationally, zakat is given to Muslims in need through international charity and humanitarian aid. Some international NGOs such as Islamic Relief provide on their websites the option of selecting "zakat" as a specific type of charitable donation. As Kochuyt points out:

> The wide range of these solidarities shows that the community of the faithful is indeed a transnational body in the making. Although none of these people meet each other face-to-face, the anonymous donor will give to an unknown fellow living in a far away country and all that because he sees himself as a member of an "imagined community." This Ummah exists regardless of actual differences: it is conceived as a deep horizontal brotherhood that serves Islam, in other words the cause of Allah. (106)

Zakat is not attempting to overturn stratification. It is not a leveling of wealth, but it does initiate solidarity between rich and poor. Zakat, like Jewish zedakah, is considered a right.[4] Poor beneficiaries do not have to reciprocate the gift; the giver is purified by giving and in giving receives blessings from Allah (Benthall 1999, 2010).

Dān in Hinduism also outlines particular recipients: priests, Brahmins, the poor and needy, and orphans (Nath 1987). However, unlike zakat, dān is not a reciprocal gift and does not create solidarity with fellow Hindus. In contrast, renunciation structures the practice of dān. *Dana* (in Sanskrit) and *dān* (in Hindi) are words for giving as an aspect of religiosity. Classically, there were six elements of dana (as Vedic concepts): (1) the donor; (2) the donee; (3) the charitable attitude, which reasserts social hierarchy and which Maria Heim (2004) calls "an ethics of esteem"; (4) the subject of the gift, acquired by the donor in the proper way; (5) the appropriate time; and (6) the appropriate place. While dān is an expression of obligation, seva (developed in the Bhakti movement as a form of devotion) is an expression of love (Jurgensmeyer and McMahon 1998). Heim's book *Theories of the Gift in South Asia* (2004) compares Jain, Buddhist, and Hindu ideas of giving in medieval South Asia. As a comparative scriptural overview, she emphasizes the overlaps and influences among the three religious expressions of dān. Unlike Islam, in which there is one scriptural referent (the Qur'an) for zakat, in Hinduism there is no single scriptural source for dān. Even though Heim argues that there is a scriptural distinction between religious giving to worthy recipients for merit (Brahmins, mendicants, renunciants) and giving to the needy out of compassion (which garners less merit), she reminds us that this is also contradicted in some scriptures.

In the contemporary practice of dān in New Delhi, distinctions are even more porous. While I am cautious in using medieval scriptures to help understand contemporary interpretations of religious ideas, a basic comparative philosophical orientation provides the scope of long history for some of these concepts and practices. Although they are regional cousins (Benthall 2005), zakat and dān are distinguished by the influence of renunciation as an orienting directive for dān. Zakat can be given to extended family, but dān cannot. In Hindu, Buddhist, and Jain traditions, gifts to family are treated as social obligations, not dān. One may gain merit (*punya*) from giving dān, but it is not a reciprocal relationship, and there is no single scriptural referent or guide. According to these expressions of dān, liberation and renunciation from the material world are the orienting directives. Dān, as a noninstrumental and nonattached gift, is a sacred directive to give to strangers scripturally regulated by dharma, or duty. The ethical responsibilities of dharma depend on context and circumstances of social location (Jurgensmeyer and McMahon 1998: 264; cf. Ramanujan 1989 regarding "context-sensitive" and "context-free" distinctions). When I met with temple priests to discuss dān, they emphasized this link between it and dharma.[5]

## Dān as a Donation

In Delhi, one does not have to travel far to find a temple. Around the corner from our flat in south Delhi was a street lined with temples and churches. At different times of the day and year, one could hear Hindu *bhajans*, the *azaan* from the Muslim mosque, and Christian prayers sung and broadcast on loud-speakers. I often strolled down the street to reach the local market, passing devotees and beggars waiting for dān. I walked inside some of these temples and interviewed priests and devotees. On one day, my research assistant and I visited the largest temple on the street, which stood majestically on the corner, a fruit vendor positioned in front selling his wares to neighborhood residents. That day happened to be a full moon, and a few people were distributing tea and loaves of bread to beggars who sat on the edge of the street by the temple. My research assistant and I inquired why they were distributing bread, and a woman cheerfully explained that her mother-in-law used to like to distribute food to beggars, and since she was no longer alive, either on a moonless night (*amavasya*) or on a full-moon night (*purnima*) they distributed bread and tea in her memory. This distribution of dān was "to please her soul."

We entered the temple and met with the main priest, who explained in scriptural terms why people gave dān. His responses echoed those I heard from priests at other temples in Delhi:

> Whatever a person earns, he should always donate the tenth part of that; this is because he will get progress in the future. Whatever scarcity or lack is there, it will be overcome so that our children are never lacking. This dān is called *vitran* [swimming/distribution]. Vitran allows for an easier next birth. It makes it easier to cross the celestial river Vaitarni, which can be crossed by only those who have given dān; otherwise, the person will keep diving and drowning in the river. Dān helps in the work of helping others. One and one make eleven. The poor get served in the charitable institution. Every day poor beggars come here for the *prasad* [offerings blessed by the gods] in the morning. Days are fixed when different types of *prasadam* are given because each god has a different day. . . . Every person in this world wants happiness; dān is a form of dharma. People can attain happiness through *tapasya* [discipline]. In *Kalyug* [our age of vice] only dān can offer solace to the soul. The essence of everything is dān. The one who gives becomes the giver, which also stands for God, the biggest giver.

In this short paragraph we have the duty (dharma) to give and the ideas of *samsara* (transmigration of souls), *moksh* (liberation from the cycle of birth and death), and gifts to the poor. Because the giver was merely a medium, he or she should feel no pride in the gift.

In order to impress his point upon me in a language that he thought I might comprehend, the priest used the quotidian example of traffic lights. Dān is not given to kin; it is given to strangers without any expectation or motive, out of duty:

> It is our duty to stop on a red signal and start on green in the same way it is our duty to take care of our parents. This is to ensure that our son will also do the same with us when we will be old. Good happens for every good deed. But to serve any needy and helpless person is a donation or dān. This helps us in our next birth. Like Mother Teresa did service to humanity without any motive. She is equivalent to god. She did both dān and service to humans. In this way she has placed an example in front of everybody. It's our *kartavya* [duty or obligation] to follow her.

The priest may have used Mother Teresa as an example for my benefit, but his interpretation of her work was distinctly Hindu: "service to humanity without any motive," articulating the freedom and renunciation in dān. In this scriptural context, there was no regulatory body that oversaw dān, although religious priests officiated over its reception in temple and ritual settings. Dān is given to strangers, and it does not matter whether recipients are Hindu. What matters is that an attachment or relationship with the recipient does not exist. Religious institutions such as temples may facilitate sacred giving, but religious giving extends beyond the boundaries of these institutions. It intersects with secular contexts of humanitarianism, and this is where, in attempts to regulate the practice of dān (as the gift) by the state, organizations, or individuals, the ethical dynamics of donation are scrutinized.

In some ways dān is like philanthropy, and philanthropy in its ideal sense resembles dān. Classically and scripturally (Heim 2004), dān is a disinterested gift. The *Bhagavad Gita* characterizes such a gift as being offered through desireless action (*nishkām karma*). The following quotation comes from a commentary on and translation of the *Bhagavad Gita* given to me during an interview, which distinguishes between a noninstrumental and an instrumental gift (Maharaj 1972: 248):[6]

> There should be no motive in charity and there should be no aim, direct or indirect. Let those, to whom you give, be such, that they cannot make any return to you. Just as, when shouting towards the sky, there is no reply, or nothing can

> be seen at the back of a mirror, or a ball when thrown on the water does not rebound in one's hand, or just as a wild bull is fed on grass, or an ungrateful person returns no obligation, charity should be without any idea of return. This is the supreme notion of charity.
>
> The inferior kind is that, in which there is some other intention. It is like feeding a cow with the intention of getting milk, or sowing a seed with the intention of selling corn, or inviting relatives with the intention of getting presents, or sending sweets to friends expecting them to return them, or like working for others after they have paid the fees, or giving medical aid, after charges have been paid.

One philanthropist I interviewed articulated that when dān is given with selfish motives, with the expectation of salvation, for example, it becomes polluted: "Any charity, when it is given in the hope of getting to heaven or any hope of welfare beyond this life, that weakens [it] so that it is a little polluted; it is not very good charity." One distinction we can keep in mind is between donations to kin, which are interested and relational (at times reciprocal), and donations to those with whom one has no relation (and who cannot give back).

Religious donations such as dān confer no tax benefit to donors and are currently unregulated by the Indian state (Agarwal and Dadrawala 2004). A special issue of a newsletter for NGOs in India titled *AccountAble* (2005) is devoted to accountability in Hindu dān.[7] I use this example to illustrate that bringing concepts from Hindu scripture to the world of NGOs in Delhi is not an idea of my own. The newsletter translates the Hindi word *dān* into "gift" or "giving" rather than "donation" and contrasts Hindu and "Western" ideas of giving. In the West, the newsletter explains, people remain attached to their donations and are interested in knowing how their money is used. They derive satisfaction from having achieved the purpose of their donations. In Hinduism, in contrast, "donors are required to detach themselves from the object that has been donated. Dān then requires *tyāg*, or relinquishment of all proprietary rights in the property. This tyāg cannot be achieved if we remain concerned with the outcome of our dān."[8]

The *AccountAble* newsletter outlines three scriptural forms of dān as defined in the *Bhagavad Gita*: *sāttvik dān*, *rājasik dān*, and *tāmasik dān*. (These three forms were mentioned by only a very small number of my informants, mostly by pundits in temple settings who were familiar with scripture.) The newsletter defines *sāttvik dān*, associated with purity and spirituality, as one made as a duty after the time, place, and suitability of the receiver are considered: "The receiver should not perform any service or provide any benefit in return. . . . The person making such a dān does not seek *punya*, merit in return. Seeking such punya will transform the dān into *rājasik*. Rājasik dān is made for getting some direct or indirect benefit (whether material or spiritual in return)." This form of dān is associated with materialism and is focused on worldly affairs. The author identifies it as "one of the four Indian approaches to solving political problems" as outlined in the epic the *Mahabharata*. Finally, *tāmasik dān* is "when dān is made to an unsuitable person or without considering time or place." It also includes the instance when dān is made "without showing proper respect or in an insulting manner" (see also Agarwal [2011] for orthodox definitions of dān). The newsletter then explores "Dān in Practice" through four broad categories: "offerings to deities (*nirmalya*), dān to individuals, dakshinā to individuals [fees to priests for services], and dān to institutions." Only dān to institutions raises serious issues of accountability. The first type of dān, *nirmalya*, does not raise concerns about accountability among devotees. The second type to individuals is supposedly for their personal use, although I found this was not always the case, and the issue of worthy recipients did arise. Dakshina is a fee for services so it is not technically dān.

What, the authors of the newsletter ask, is the accountability model in Hindu society that makes sure that dān is used properly? In answer, the newsletter explains: "in our understanding, the emphasis is on proper selection of the donee. If the donee is selected carefully as a worthy recipient, then the dān will be effective. There will be no need to monitor how the funds are actually used." It continues to explain that "Hindu thought encourages gradual detachment from the material world, if one is to achieve *moksh* or release from the painful cycle of birth and death. The act of giving is, therefore, an act of cutting off ties from the material world." Here, the gift is a liberating mechanism. The impulse to give is a release—as opposed to the socially obligated context within which gifts are made meaningful through instrumental social action.

## Instrumental Gifts

Jacques Derrida, in his book *Given Time* (1992), critiques Marcel Mauss for his interpretation of gift giving as reciprocal and socially obligated. Unlike Mauss's conception of the gift (1990 [1950]), which requires a relationship and a return, pure gifts, Derrida argues, are neither regulated by institutional rituals, nor morally obligated. "A gift must not be *bound*" (137), for if it is, it is no longer a gift. He continues: "Laws, therefore transform the gift or rather the offering into (distributive) justice, which is economic in the strict sense or the symbolic sense; they transform alms into exchangist, even contractual circulation" (138). Even alms given with the aim of receiving merit from the gods fulfill qualities of a regulating and distributing principle that counters the purity of the gift. Once the gift contains the expectation of a return, it remains in the realm of debt and credit and is no longer a gift.

Scholarship on giving in India has challenged Mauss's assumption that gifts must by their nature be reciprocal. Those writing about the concept of the "free gift" in north India (Laidlaw 2000; Parry 1986) argue that in this cultural context, people who give strive to release themselves from any future contact. In the Jain setting that James Laidlaw explored, the food given by lay Jains to Jain renouncers is termed dān; the concept of the "pure" or "free" gift exists in practices of mendicancy in which no social obligations occur between givers and recipients. As Laidlaw points out, "the fact that the free gift does not create obligations or personal connections is precisely where its social importance lies" (2000: 618). In addition, he notes the significance of both impulsive and anonymous gifts, which cannot be tied to the giver: "A gift given on impulse is thought to be especially productive of merit: you see a beggar and you give, without stopping to think. Another highly valued gift is one which is given in secret—*gupta-dan*. Giving in secret avoids the immediate reward of an increase in the donor's public status, and people say that because of this the unseen reward which comes as merit or good *karma* will be greater" (297).

The gift given on impulse stands against that which is rendered accountable through instrumental action. The focus on the effects, or one could say results, of giving is an attempt to reign in the impulse to give. Impulsive giving to beggars is not typically placed in the same category as giving to institutions such as NGOs, despite the fact that both forms of donation respond to human suffering. Religious philanthropy, defined here very broadly as a form of dān, thus is distinguished from the legal context of social welfare, with its correlative entitlements bound up with the rights-based regimes of states. Writing on philanthropy and law in India has focused on this economic and legal regulation of the voluntary sector, particularly regarding foreign contributions to NGOs (Asia Pacific Philanthropy Consortium 2007; Dadrawala 2003a; Government of India 2006; Sidel 2004b; Sidel and Zaman 2004; Sidel 2010; Sundar 2010). In these instances, government attempts to regulate resources are simultaneously attempts to regulate civil society. Yet in this context, what happens to the impulse to give?

## Indian Philanthropy

Philanthropy has only recently been seen as a form of instrumentally rational action. "Scientific philanthropy," the systematization and institutionalization of charitable giving (Howe 1980), is linked to the birth of foundations and the emergence of new U.S. millionaires during the Industrial Revolution. John D. Rockefeller, for example, advocated the "scientific benevolence" of giving to organizations rather than to individuals (28). While Rockefeller's benevolence is considered distinctly American and influenced by Christian ideas, my research suggests an alternative explanation, which links Rockefeller's impetus to give toward public welfare to an encounter with the reformist Hindu teacher and guru Swami Vivekananda. A letter in the collected works of Swami Vivekananda documents a brief meeting between Rockefeller and Vivekananda in 1893 at the World Parliament of Religions in Chicago during which the swami told Rockefeller that the money he had accumulated was not his: "He was only a channel and that his duty was to do good to the world—that God had given him all his wealth in order that he might have an opportunity to help and do good to people."[9] According to this document, Rockefeller initiated the first donation to his foundation after this encounter. I contacted the Rockefeller archives in New York and was not able to find this reference in Rockefeller's papers. Nonetheless, the fact that it is documented in India attests to the global, dynamic nature of some of these ideas. Furthermore, a swamiji I interviewed at the Ramakrishna Mission in Delhi repeated the story:

> Swamiji Vivekananda went to meet Rockefeller in Chicago in 1893. Rockefeller was full of ego. Swamiji paid no attention. "You may be a rich man," he said, "but the money you earn, you are not the owner of the money. You are the trustee of the money." Rockefeller told Swamiji he will start a scholarship and said "you will thank me." Swamiji said "you should thank me." If you are the owner of the money, you are a slave. If you are the trustee, you will be god. As a trustee you cannot use it according to your will or sense pleasure."

In India, the social responsibility of wealth has been imagined differently in various eras. In classical Hinduism, helping those in need was considered to be the duty of the individual as opposed to institutions (see Tandon 2002). Modern institutions of philanthropy in India may trace their roots to the social reform movements of the late 1800s when a sharp criticism emerged of Hindu practices (such as polytheism, idolatry, child marriage, and taboos associated with widow remarriage), along with the rise of such voluntary organizations as literary associations and indigenous newspapers. Voluntary organizations were so widespread that they were perceived as a threat by the British Indian government, which in 1890 enacted the Societies Registration Act to provide a legal context for registration and incorporation. During this period, giving was dominated by missionary philanthropy and the philanthropy of the national business sector, which engendered large philanthropic trusts focused on social welfare (Sen 1992; Sundar 2000). Douglas Haynes (1987) has written about how elite merchant businessmen built their social reputations and economic credit through gifts. Their gifting practices in the colonial era shifted from tribute to large-scale philanthropy. This new idiom was meaningful to colonial rulers, who gained social and political capital through philanthropy. Yet even in this context, Haynes notes that "most contributors to secular charities espoused by the British, for instance, continued older forms of religious gifting, usually on a significantly larger scale than in their secular charities" (353). In other words, religious gifting that supported temples, feasts, and religious festivals continued alongside the advent of secular forms of large-scale philanthropy for social welfare such as famine relief (also see Greenough 1982; Sharma 2001).

During the struggle for independence, Mahatma Gandhi launched mass-based voluntary action movements against colonial rule and in the 1920s advocated voluntary effort, or "constructive work," that included activities we would today call "development": "education, sanitation, protection and promotion of *khadi* and village industries to help local handicrafts and artisans, and the fight against untouchability, illiteracy, and consumption of liquor" (Tandon 2002: 7). Gandhi made gifts and service (dān and seva) into social obligations and obligations to society. Gifts went from tribute to philanthropy for the general welfare of all (as in Haynes [1987]). Gandhi also influenced major industrialists such as the Birla family, who built temples, schools, and hospitals (Jurgensmeyer and McMahon 1998). During the national reconstruction directly following independence, economic development became a concern of the government. The constitution of 1951 facilitated government involvement in social welfare, and some voluntary organizations were taken over by the state. Businessmen of this era contributed to national development through trusts inspired by a Gandhian theory of trusteeship of wealth (Birla 2009; Sundar 2010), which existed alongside large-scale state-driven development programs.

By the 1960s, the development model initiated by the new government left large segments of the population poor, and although a generation of government servants came into being through the civil service, the failure of government programs led to protest movements. These protest movements were reined in during the Indian Emergency of the mid-1970s when the authoritarian policies of the state weakened voluntary action. In 1976 during the Emergency the Indian Parliament passed the Foreign Contribution Regulation Act (FCRA, Sundar 2010) in an effort to control the voluntary sector. Meanwhile, voluntary organizations continued to register under the Societies Registration Act, and the voluntary sector came to be influenced by global trends. As bilateral and multilateral development organizations began to influence national policy, less-formal forms of voluntary action continued, including individual, community-based, and small-scale welfare provision.

When India opened its markets through economic liberalization in 1991, the market reforms did not mean the end of state-sponsored welfare programs. In fact, new forms of social welfare provision emerged, including government-organized NGOs that sought to mediate empowerment through the government (Gupta and Sharma 2006). In the liberal agenda, NGOs were expected to be more accountable than governments and to perform more efficiently (Sen 1999). Some argue that as the rural hinterlands of India were integrated into global capitalism through the work of NGOs (Kothari 1986; Sen 1999), globalization challenged the power of radical voluntary groups to effect change (see Appadurai 2006 for a contrasting perspective). Still others (INCITE! Women of Color against Violence 2007) argue a more pernicious outcome: through the "nonprofit industrial complex," capitalist interests and the state sought to use nonprofits to monitor, manage, and control social justice movements and social dissent. Philanthropy under this lens is a vehicle for capitalism to assimilate the resistance to its practices.

In contemporary, economically liberalizing India, the emergence of new wealth is associated with arguments for harnessing charitable efforts into instrumentally rational forms. Today, the high-tech boom in India has led to an incredibly wealthy Indian diaspora and created a new economy of Indian philanthropy.[10] Mark Sidel (2004a) argues that Indian diasporic philanthropy from the United States to India has a counterequity focus: it neglects the truly poor and instead promotes giving to those to whom donors are related or for whom donations satisfy immediate needs. Mark Jurgensmeyer and Darrin McMahon (1998) argue that in the history of Indian philanthropy, for Hindu nationalists such as the Bharatiya Janata Party (BJP), temple building became sectarianism. The secularism of the Indian National Congress Party does not exclude religion; on the contrary, it includes it. The BJP's emphasis on Hindu religious philanthropy totters between the broad-based secular giving encouraged by the West and translated into an Indian idea of samaj seva encouraged by Gandhi and older, Indian practices of dān and seva. Although dān and seva may be expressions of generosity and service, they can also be hijacked for political and hegemonic aims.

## Global India Gives: Indian Nationalism and Diaspora Giving

Philanthropy provides a template for the actions of others. Robert Gross (2003) and Lawrence Friedman (2003) outline a historical progression from charity to philanthropy that mirrors the growth of the United States as an industrial nation in the 1920s and attributes some of its success to the formalization (or Weberian rationalization) of charity to philanthropy. In the case of the voluntary sector in the United States, philanthropy has become a mark of civility (Silber 2001: 391), a more "modern," institutionalized, and rationalized form of giving than charity, which is described as impulsive and without long-term effects. Although distinctions between charity and philanthropy may not be useful for understanding contemporary practices of dān, the mark of civility, progress, and "development" manifest in the ability to come to the aid of those in need is a contemporary discourse of Indian national identity.

Philanthropy, as a relational practice, is connected to global identities. Silber notes that "modern philanthropic giving is perhaps best understood as rooted in the urge for the expression of one's personal identity, at the same time as it is also a deeply relational practice, having to do with the imagined interaction between oneself and an often abstract group of others in and through the public sphere" (2001: 393; also see Silber 1998). Instead of detachment from the gift (as in an anonymous gift to a stranger), "a major feature of current philanthropy is precisely the contempt for anonymous, impersonal giving, and the search of many actual or potential philanthropists for enhanced personal involvement or, as is so often called 'partnership' with the cause and the organization sponsored" (2001: 395; cf. Stirrat and Henkel 1997). With this perspective the civility of the gift lies in the relationship. Much giving is done through localized, communal frameworks in which donors and recipients know each other. Silber (2001) writes: "Trends show a decrease in trans-local giving and increased giving to local, communal goals and institutions" (396). In this global, cosmopolitan, world community, identity-related aspects of philanthropy come to the fore. People give in order to be connected to a group or a cause and to forge or change their identities.

Silber rightly points out that the gift need not be governed by one set of motivations. In philanthropy, gifts range from strategic to altruistic. In an era of what Silber calls "loose solidarities" and in which we may consider, for example, a globalized India, philanthropy is potentially a relational and connective process, which causes a tension with the liberating aspect of dān as a form of social renunciation (that one will not be connected to one's gift). As we will see in subsequent chapters, philanthropy in global India does become an aspect of community solidarity, an act of belonging in an imagined community in a globalized world. Although some say philanthropy supports elite interests (see Odendahl 1990), what matters is not whether philanthropy is interested or disinterested but where rewards are anticipated (Silber 1998). For American philanthropists, rewards are subjective, psychological, and expressed in terms of "self-fulfillment" and "self-esteem." Instead of reciprocity versus exchange, or interestedness versus disinterestedness, the tensions I emphasize here are between the impulse of the gift and expectations regarding how the gift will be used and between the act of giving and one's relation to a wider social world.

Philanthropy in India is part of a wider milieu of diasporic Indian giving for Indian development, some of which may be fueled by discourses of nationalism and religious nationalism. Because research for this ethnography was conducted in India, one might not expect diasporic concerns to be considered. Yet, as we will see, contemporary expressions of dān are not bounded by the nation-state; they are situated in a global economy of rapidly moving people and capital. Arvind Rajagopal (2000) makes important distinctions between Hindu nationalism in India and Hindu nationalism in the United States. Although the two are connected through globalization to form a global social movement, participation at either end is motivated by different factors. In India, Hindu nationalism is linked to the independence movement and to secular nationalist politics after the failure of the Congress Party's promise of national economic development. In the Indian context, the Hindu nationalism of the BJP rose further with programs of economic liberalization. In the United States, Hindu nationalism has a different politics geared toward the Indian diaspora. This U.S. diaspora is an immigrant community, and to this group Hindu nationalism enables cultural reproduction (an antidote to racialized politics and threats of assimilation). Hindu nationalists in the United States are the guardians of Hindu values. The globalized movement of the Hindu right embraces these two different constituencies through distinct strategies. In India, Hindu nationalism targets individuals to challenge secularism, while in the United States, it targets families for cultural preservation (though these families may also support Hindu nationalism in India through their donations).[11]

Some evidence supports the claim that funding for economic development in India from the global Indian diaspora may feed the religious nationalism of the Rashtriya Swayamsevak Sangh (RSS), which is registered as a charitable organization. Although I did not encounter this in my ethnographic research, it is worth exploring briefly here. Biju Mathew and Vijay Prashad (2000) have studied the fund-raising efforts of Hindu nationalist organizations in the United States by asking, "What does the militant and ideological Hindu right do to attract Indian Americans?" They find that tensions of diasporic life in the United States facilitate the efforts of the Hindu right in garnering support. When the Hindu right organizes fund-raisers geared toward diasporic Indians in the United States—many of whom express guilt for having left India—it does so under the guise of charity and development. Much of this "charity," unbeknownst to migrants, is collected by agencies of the Hindu right for their activities in India (520). For example, money sent for "education," even supposedly nonpolitical charity work, may contribute to Hindutva hegemony. The mission is twofold: "to offer charity and to provide ideological education amongst those with whom it works" (520). The appeal of Hindu organizations for diasporic Indians who themselves may experience racism and intergenerational anxiety is about the potential loss of cultural authenticity (Kapur, Mehta, and Dutt 2004; Sidel 2004b, 2010).[12]

Because religious trusts are exempt from reporting their finances publicly in India, some Hindu temples in the United States associated with religious extremism may raise money that is tax exempt (Kapur, Mehta, and Dutt 2004: 201). Although charities in the United Kingdom and the United States are not allowed to spend funds on political activities with tax-exempt status, diaspora philanthropy is difficult to track. In addition, different laws and regulations apply to religious organizations in India (Bornstein 2012). The work of Devesh Kapur, Ajay Mehta, and R. Moon Dutt (2004) and Sidel (2004b) both mention the study of one NGO funded by Indian diaspora philanthropy that has been serving the interests of the RSS in India. Sidel notes that most philanthropic giving to India occurs through informal channels such as family and nonorganizational ties directly to India. This may be due to issues of mistrust: "The Indian diaspora has a great mistrust of official institutions and formal organizations. This cynicism is not confined to state institutions but extends to formal civil society organizations as well, unless there are personal links or affiliation" (Kapur, Mehta, and Dutt 2004: 186).[13]

Although some philanthropy may support extremist Hindutva organizations, the informal channels through which much diaspora philanthropy travels have been under increased scrutiny since the terrorist attacks of September 11, 2001. Indian diaspora philanthropy supports religious organizations and developmental work, but the distinction between religious and secular philanthropy for development might not be so easy to distinguish. As Priya Viswanath and Noshir Dadrawala have noted, in India religious trusts and societies are "expanding religious-based work into new secular arenas such as disaster relief, education (often through the establishment of new institutions) and the promotion of renewable sources of energy" (2004: 272). Much of the work done by religious organizations is carried out directly. There are no reliable statistics on the extent of funds used by religious organizations for development. Sectarian political activities in humanitarianism may be less overt since the Congress Party took over the political arena from the BJP in 2004 (my research was conducted during 2004–05, immediately after the Congress Party's victory). Just because the RSS and other Hindutva organizations may be registered as charitable organizations does not mean that all religious organizations are Hindutva. The same could be said for Islamic NGOs as well (see American Civil Liberties Union 2009; Benthall 2010).

The discourse of philanthropy in New Delhi differs from its diasporic counterpart. As already mentioned, after the 2004 Indian Ocean tsunami, India refused to accept aid from other national governments. At the time seeking a place on the U.N. Security Council, India also sought the position of benefactor, rather than of recipient, in the geopolitics of donation (Nagi 2005). In daily newspapers, article after article documented how India was helping its own. A piece in the *Sunday Express* titled "India Giving" (2005) described how an eighty-two-year-old woman had canceled her husband's *shradh*[14] ceremony to donate to tsunami relief; a seven-year-old had emptied her piggybank, and "from slumchildren to corporates, India puts in a never-before effort for tsunami victims. In two weeks, PM's Fund receives 403cr. [more than $90 million], almost matching a year's collection for Gujarat quake." In this moral story of progress, India was imagined as being a developed nation, a benevolent donor, and no longer a needy recipient. The euphoria of "India giving," however, was tempered by the anticipation of long-term effects. Although the urgency of tsunami relief inspired many to give, other journalists questioned whether the giving could be sustained. A headline in the *Sunday Hindustan Times* read "Does Delhi Have a Conscience?" (2005) and asked whether Delhiites would continue to donate funds for the long-term rehabilitation of the tsunami-struck region.[15] These queries echoed other scholarly concerns of whether charity can transform into social change and development (Sundar 1997a). Newspaper reports maintained a certain moralizing tone, lauding India's ability to give but questioning long-term effects.

Giving requires a proper attitude. If a gift is given with a selfish motive or with the expectation of personal benefit, for example, it is seen to be less of a "good" gift. When giving from pity, one can approach contempt, which is, scripturally, not the proper moral state from which to give dān (Heim 2004; gratitude as a social emotion in Appadurai 1985). In both impulsive forms of spontaneous compassion and more calculated forms of donation to formal organizations, the intent of the giver and the worth of the recipient are scrutinized. In fact, widespread suspicion and policing of intention surrounds acts of charity and seva in India (Gold 1988; Laidlaw 1995).

The gift also requires a worthy vessel (Anderson 1997; Heim 2004; Nath 1987; Parry 1994). Jonathan Parry points out that although ideally Brahmin priests should approximate the lifestyle of world renouncers, the funeral priests he studied in Banaras lived a compromised ascetic existence, enmeshed in the material world (1989: 74). Their acceptance of dān, which contained sin, endangered their potential transcendence. To translate this grammar of donation to institutions: when one gives to an NGO and the organization does not spend the donation as intended, the giver is also scandalized (Bornstein 2006; Feldman 2011). In this instance, the aspect of classical giving that dictates the need to give to worthy vessels (Laidlaw 1995; Parry 1989, 1994; Raheja 1988; Raheja and Gold 1994; Snodgrass 2001) is reproduced in interesting ways in more contemporary philanthropic contexts. As with giving dān to priests, where the responsibility of the vessel's worthiness rests with both the recipient and the donor (Parry 1989: 75), one could make the same argument for NGOs. The anxiety over the worthiness of an NGO, and whether or not the donation will reach its intended beneficiary and not be squandered by the NGO, echoes the case of Parry's funeral priests (see Feldman 2011 for secular instance in CARE; Benthall 2011 for zakat; American Civil Liberties Union 2009 for Islamic charities more generally; also see Sidel 2010). It is in this sense that the significance of giving to worthy recipients structures the gift and enters into the equation of whether one gives with immediacy, impulsively, or through more regulated forms.

The impulse of philanthropy—the selfless giving away of wealth that arouses strong emotions and can bring people to tears—contrasts markedly with formalized practices of regulated and legislated giving that track the results of a gift.[16] Of course, one can give impulsively to organized charity, and conversely, impulsive giving can become ritualized. My point, however, is that dynamic aspects of the gift are often overlooked when one focuses exclusively on results and effects. In the three portraits that follow, I situate different forms of donation and dān in New Delhi in the context of different attempts to regulate giving in the Indian voluntary sector. These portraits—of a family who gave dān daily out of their Delhi home, of the wife of an industrialist who pursued development schemes in an attempt to "rehabilitate the poor," and of a businessman who built a temple and school for girls—each exemplify the Derridian "impossibility" of a gift that seeks regulation. The regulated gift is the interested gift. It may not be reciprocal in the Maussian sense, but it does produce relationships of obligation.

## Case 1: Daily Giving

A few blocks from our flat in south Delhi, at 10 a.m. every morning, saffron-clad *sadhus* (world renouncers) and mendicants lined up outside a row of expensive gated houses across the street from a public park. The owner of one of the houses was the founder of a large private hospital with its own charitable sector. Yet he and his family gave dān every day in the form of raw rice or 5 rupees to sadhus, the elderly, and the disabled. Sometimes the man gave dān himself; sometimes his wife did, and sometimes his children. Six brothers and their extended families also lived in the house, and dān was a family practice. It was the ritualized impulse to give, to address social suffering immediately and directly that inspired his daily dān. Some people in the neighborhood spoke of his regular donation as a way to take care of "black money"—or income from activities, which may be illegal, that are not reported for tax purposes. As I show, although his daily dān may have been a form of ritual action inspired by dharma, elements of instrumental rationality also emerged in practice, as he and his family aimed to render the gift accountable.

Dān was not given indiscriminately, and only certain members of society were eligible in this family's independently organized scheme: they gave no dān to young and able-bodied people. At the time of my research, the owner of this large house had been giving daily dān for seventeen years. The dān was anonymous and "free" in the sense that Laidlaw (2000) has discussed for mendicants; if it was regulated, it was regulated by habitus, duty, or dharma but not by the state. Although many of the sadhus had been coming to the house to receive dān for years, none of them claimed to know the name of its owner. The anonymity of dān worked in both directions, at least in its performative aspect. The performance of giving and receiving dān legitimized the gift as dān to appropriate, in this case ascetic, claimants. The sadhus did, however, know that the owner had founded a hospital.

I had noticed the line of sadhus waiting for dān each morning as I passed by on the way to research engagements in Delhi. One morning, my research assistant and I tried to speak with the sadhus as they waited for their daily offering. The men were angered by my assistant, who was Indian, and started yelling at her in Hindi, telling her that she should already know about dān. One of them huffed: "Dān is regarded as a good deed, it's the earning of life; it is for prosperity and to earn merits." After this brief remark, the rest of the men refused to speak with us, moving away and sitting in a line on the edge of the curb to protest our inquiry. The men seemed insulted by our ignorance. Although they had attacked my assistant verbally, I was immune, being a foreigner. I was not supposed to know what anything meant, especially scriptural practice. My ignorance, however, was not met with the pedagogical encouragement I had encountered elsewhere. The male sadhus proceeded to pronounce me nonexistent by their silence and their gesture of moving away.

But as the men distanced themselves, a group of five women gathered around us, eager to tell us their stories. Unlike their male counterparts, they were not wearing saffron. Each had a walking stick in her hand and looked more like a beggar than a sadhu, although the line between the two categories is often visually ambiguous. Parry (1989: 73–77) distinguishes between *biksha* (alms given to sadhus) and dān. With renouncers, no relationship is possible because they stand outside the social world. Dān, in contrast, is threatening because as a gift without a return, it repudiates the moral basis of society that relies on reciprocity. In this instance, the donor described the gifts to the sadhus who came to the door daily as dān, not biksha. Although there seemed to be no ambiguity about whether these people were receiving dān or biksha, there was ambiguity regarding their status as renouncers. In the women's narratives describing how and why they came to the door to receive dān, it became clear that they were not sadhvis at all but instead were destitute and in need of charity. The men standing in line waiting for their daily dān, in contrast, refused to speak with me and may well have been sadhus. Identifying the gift as dān and not biksha conferred a respectability to the gift that biksha did not.[17] Perhaps in this instance, dān was a stand-in for multiple forms of giving.

As the men continued to stay away from us, the women flooded us with stories of poverty and difficulty, or, in philanthropic parlance—need. One showed us her wrist, which had no bangles, and explained that she was a widow. Another woman said she was married and had a son and daughter, but because of poverty she was compelled to leave her house on her own. They did not have any fertile land for agriculture, and landlords did not pay for their services. She had come to collect dān so that her daughter could marry. She said people gave dān for their own good: "People get rid of their troubles and sufferings" through dān. Another woman said she and her family were laborers; her son was a rickshaw puller, but she also had to leave her house to earn money. She started crying while narrating her experience, and said about dān: "A woman who doesn't have a child, when she has one she gives dān, for marriage, to get rid of worries, to build a house. Those who remember their ancestors give dān." Dān came in the form of rice, blankets, saris, clothes, money, shawls, socks, and sweaters. When people gave them a part of their earnings, those people would prosper. Another widow had a twenty-year-old son who was hospitalized because of an accident. She had been coming to this house for the past twelve years to collect dān. Dān fulfilled the economy of need for these women, entering in where the state was unable to provide welfare and answer the problems of increasing inequality.

When the woman giving dān that day came to the gate, the sadhus rushed to stand in a line. She distributed 5 rupees to each sadhu, who touched the rupees to his or her forehead before leaving. I spoke briefly with the donor, Mrs. A, and we set a date for an interview because I was curious about the structure of daily household donations. Each day between sixty and seventy people came to receive dān at the door, she said, sometimes one hundred. "Tomorrow is rice," Mrs. A said as I left. "Less people will come." My research assistant was shocked that the family gave dān daily but did not give medical assistance. One woman was suffering from thigh pain and was unable to walk properly, but her ailment was ignored. Here, dān was open to critique for its lack of immediate empathy toward the pain of others. Compassion was a more regulated space that reflected an internal tension of giving dān between the selection of a worthy recipient and the liberating impulse to give.

One month later, I arrived at the house for an interview with Mrs. A, who was the daughter-in-law of the man who owned the house. On that day, she gave one cup of rice to each sadhu, who received it in his or her shawl or a plastic bag. And as Mrs. A had predicted, far fewer sadhus were lined up this day than had been on the day money was given. After the sadhus left, she led me inside the gates and we sat by a small garden. It was a modest location, abutting the driveway of the large house and close to the noise of the street. I was not led into the interior of the house or the courtyard.

Mrs. A explained that "like in every society, you have to do a little dān, helping the poor people who are in need." Here, the way she began to describe it, her donation was a duty. There were practicalities involved that instrumentally rationalized the giving. When the family first started giving dān seventeen years ago, they gave 2 rupees to each sadhu, but then they increased that to 5 rupees. One day they gave money, and the next tea and biscuits, but that did not work. So they tried bananas, but what to do with the extra bananas? During the mango season, they gave mangoes. They tried apples and *atta* (flour), but these also did not work, so finally the family settled on giving rice and money on alternate days.

Mrs. A's impulse to give was also framed by social directives: "I don't encourage children," she said. "I don't want to encourage begging right from childhood." She made the correlation between children, begging, and narcotics, invoking the prevailing urban rumor at the time that beggar children were drugged. And she said, "I don't like to give to young men; I tell them go out and work." Her father-in-law was a very religious Hindu and was on the board of many temples. A family trust ran the hospital, which offered charitable outpatient services. She declared that their hospital was one of the few that did this. Although they had taxes waived for doing free outpatient services, she exclaimed: "It is not charity. Everything belongs to God. We are just actors. Once you get involved in it, you've had it. You have to give it to everybody. For me everybody is the same." The individuals in the line of sadhus to her were equivalent. She did not make any distinction among them except for the relevant qualification of their being elderly or infirm.

In the case of this daily dān, Mrs. A sidestepped the problem of nefarious and ambiguous usage connected to money by also giving food. In this sense, it was, as far as its usage was concerned, a delimited gift.[18] "It's good to give food," she said:

> They eat it and they remember you. Money gets into the wrong hands; it goes from here to there but at least food, you cook it. When you go to someone's house, you bring food and are given food. Prasad is given to the goddess. If it goes to the right people, it is done well. If it goes to the wrong people, it is your

> luck. But your heart should be clear—you want to do charity. But how they take it and what they do with it, what can you do? It is good to give charity from your own hands so in your next life it will be smoother for you.

While the impulse to give may have been ritualized in practice, and perhaps motivated by religious ideas of blessings and merit, this form of philanthropy was regulated by habitus and not by the state. In the informal economy of dān, one is faced with the immediate need of a stranger and presented with the opportunity to respond. Plenty of wealthy homes in the neighborhood did not open their doors daily, but some did. And I also I interviewed less wealthy families that gave water to laborers or clothes to children or food to people who knocked on their doors. Need presented itself, and it was an acceptable and integrated aspect of being a good human being to respond on impulse. That impulse was at times cultivated and articulated in ritual practice.

## Case 2: Rehabilitating the Poor

Mrs. A and her family gave from their house daily, but other women were involved in the philanthropic sector more formally.[19] For instance, Mrs. B, the wife of a wealthy industrialist who owned the largest sugar factory in India, had started an orphanage in the colony surrounding the factory to—as she said—"rehabilitate" the children. In this case, the impulse to give was inspired, and fettered, by the social responsibility to change society. Mrs. B's mother-in-law had been involved with social work and had created an industrial school for women that included a handicrafts center where women embroidered pieces for sale. The institution was run by a family trust: 150 girls since 1955 had been through the training center and were "rehabilitated." Mrs. B considered the program a model for other NGOs involving women, although she was critical of NGOs and their tendency to be "created as clones of government largess because it's fashionable." She considered NGO funding through government schemes as "individual nongovernmental organizations": a person who retires from the government and sets up an NGO. In contrast to the politics of this sort of nonprofit, the money through which her orphanage was started came from her mother-in-law's family trust and her husband's sugar company.

The name of the orphanage was Suhrid, which means a good heart or goodhearted. Forty to fifty children came to Mrs. B through word of mouth:

> Some of them were found in the bush, some on the rail track. You know, just babies. There was one child—a boy—where the mother was working in homes.

> She got pregnant and her parents said they would kill her, so I took an assurity from them that as soon as the child was delivered I will get that child and they should do nothing, . . . so that child came when that child was not even an hour old. At night at 11 o'clock they brought her.

Although other people besides Mrs. B looked after the children, her philosophy was to bring them up almost like she had brought up her own son, in the same colony. She was not remote from them, as other social workers may have been; she described herself as "totally involved." She said: "If they went to the school, the only thing I asked of these children was to study or participate in school activities. If they tore their bag or their shoes or some books or something, immediately they would be replenished. Because I knew that I would not do that with my son. I would just tell him, Go with a broken bag, you know, and don't keep on doing it." She feared people would say, "Oh, they are orphan children," the implication being that if they are orphans they will be neglected. So to avoid this response, Mrs. B gave the children special attention, and they received "everything on a platter." However, they continued to do poorly in school. "They just wouldn't study," she repeated. This frustrated her because she had hoped to put them through vocational school. She did, however, get the girls married and gave their dowries. At one point she tried to give up some of the children for adoption, but the bureaucracy was so difficult to wade through, she abandoned the effort. Her orphanage became the legal guardian of the children she was caring for.

The orphanage was a saga for Mrs. B, and she was frustrated that she was not able to meet her objectives. Some of the children became urchins once they turned eighteen and lived on the streets, but some of the girls who had married were happy and had children. For one boy, she started a small business of a long-distance phone booth. "I wanted to make something of them," she said. "That is something I could not do, but they all got rehabilitated, though not in the way that one would have really [wanted]." Despite all she offered the orphans, they did not prosper as she had imagined, and she blamed the children for their failure, for "not studying."

The orphanage was no longer running, although two girls remained for whom Mrs. B planned to find husbands when they turned eighteen. As Mrs. B attempted to transform the impulse to give into a more instrumentally rational form, she met with failure—perhaps because her recipients were not capable of being transformed by the gift in the way she had intended, or perhaps because the structural conditions of her gift did not incur as many rights as might be required for long-term change.

In addition to the orphanage, Mrs. B started other social schemes in the colony surrounding the sugar plantation, including a feeding scheme for children at the local school and the creation of a public swimming pool. She tried to cultivate a culture of civic responsibility so that "people [would take] pride in their houses, in their gardens." More recently, she had been involved in family planning and reproductive health with an international NGO of which she was the president. Her next plan was to create homes for elderly people near the sugar factory. She was certain her giving was not religious in nature. She did not believe that her affinity with people in need had to do with acquiring merit or getting to heaven. And she was critical of both organized charity and supporting beggars on the street. She was convinced that the beggars were part of "rackets . . . people are making them do it and so you are encouraging the situation." Instead, in her own way she had either found herself in or created environments in which to support charitable work. She gave funds to other organizations, such as a school for the blind, but it was not as if 10 percent or a tithe of her income went to philanthropy. Instead, she felt she was immersed in it. I was surprised to learn that she had not been able to involve the wives of her husband's friends in her social work. They either made up excuses, or they wanted to start their own NGOs.

What interests me here is the impulse to help those in need that motivated Mrs. B's involvement in various philanthropic schemes. At times, it seemed that in her philanthropy, impulse was framed by the socially instrumental action that rendered it accountable—by rehabilitating the orphans for whom she cared, for example. However, the recipients of her aid were neither claimants nor kin. And when the children turned eighteen, the orphanage ceased to be their legal guardian and they were on their own.

## Case 3: Philanthropy of Epic Proportions

Mr. P was involved with charitable activities, but unlike his wife, who ran welfare homes and technical schools for women, he focused on building a temple. He had been a successful businessman involved with manufacturing air-conditioners and thermal insulation materials. His son had expanded the business into laying cross-country oil pipelines, and Mr. P had since spent 10 crore rupees (more than $2 million) on the temple and an associated school and facilities.

As he began to tell the story of Sita—one of the characters in the Indian epic the *Ramayana* and in whose honor he built the temple—I realized Mr. P's philanthropy was of equally epic proportions. As he told the story, he wept, and at one point during our interview I lost track of the shift between inspiration and actual narrative sequence. This is not uncommon in colloquial Delhi speech, where epic references meld into the details of daily life. Indian epics are used both as points of reference and as commentaries on life. In this case Mr. P used Sita as an exemplar of womanly and wifely virtue. He narrated the story of her arduous life. An orphan discovered in a furrow in a ploughed field, Sita was wed to Rama, prince of Ayodhya, but shortly after their marriage, he was exiled and Sita joined him to live in the forest. There, she was kidnapped by Ravana. In captivity, Sita maintained her chastity until Rama rescued her. However, on their return to Ayodhya where Rama was crowned king, the citizens found it difficult to believe Sita's loyalty while she was held by Ravana. She was banished, pregnant with twins (Luv and Kush), whom she raised alone in a forest ashram. Once the boys were grown and reunited with their father, Sita sought refuge in the earth. The ground opened up, and she went into the earth. The site of this return to the earth was the spot where Mr. P had built the temple. The narrative epic served both as a context for his philanthropy and as its explanation.

Mr. P had known a swami who had walked from Rishikesh in the Himalayas to Banaras along the banks of the river Ganges. After many months he came upon the spot where Sita had returned to the earth, called Sita Madhi and today the name of the temple. He meditated at the spot for five days and then decided to stay there. Noting that a sadhu was sitting at the site, villagers started to bring food, and he remained for many months. Children played where he had leveled a field, and they chatted with him. After two years he came to know that the girls in the area were not educated and instead were married young, becoming, as Mr. P described, "child-producing machines." The swami had two objectives: to build a temple and to build a school for girls, so he began to raise funds. He met Mr. P's mother, who told the story to Mr. P, who then donated 5,000 rupees toward the cause. After three months, Mr. P went to the site and sat and felt powerful vibrations; it was not a normal spot. He was so moved by the experience that he returned to Delhi and arranged for architects to design the temple. Once the temple was constructed, the swami began using two of the rooms as a school. He sent Mr. P a statement every month, and Mr. P reimbursed him for expenses.

Then tragedy struck. The swami and a young teacher from the school were electrocuted by a telephone line that had started a fire under a carpet, and Mr. P found himself taking over the operation of both the temple and the school. He built an ashram guesthouse at the temple site. The school was growing, and he added a higher class every year up to class nine. He arranged for teachers to teach English at the school, but it was difficult to retain them. He traveled every month to the temple and school and realized that although people would pay money for boys to attend, they would not pay for girls. So he made a scheme to sponsor girls and pleaded with his friends to help; he received sponsorship for nearly one hundred girls.

However, very particular conditions were attached to Mr. P's largesse. He explained: "Those [parents] who have more than two kids a family must attach a certificate of family planning of either parent, that is tubectomy or vasectomy. You see that would be the qualifying thing. I mean, I may give education free to three kids, four kids, no problem. But I don't want them to be producing more." This, of course, strongly recalls the notorious history of forced sterilizations during the Indian Emergency (Tarlo 2003). Mr. P continued to explain that although he wanted to give up to one hundred places for children, he received applications for only twenty-six because parents would not attach the certificate of family planning. They were willing to receive free education, but not with such restrictions. Mr. P was adamant on the certificate, however: family limitation as a condition of the provision of education. His religiously inspired impulse to give was regulated by his desire for social accountability. As with Lawrence Cohen's (2004) account of kidney donations and sterilizations, where the worthiness of organ *donors* was significant and made possible through family-planning operations, in this case, it was possible to transform people into worthy *recipients* through family-planning operations. In Cohen's case of the potential for kidney donors to be operated upon (Cohen terms this "operability"), as well as in the attempts by Mrs. B, who sought to "rehabilitate" the poor, and in Mr. P's philanthropy, a foundational basis for giving is an opportunity for social reform. This possibility for reform reins in the impulse of the donor.

In addition to the school, Mr. P started camps where eye cataract surgeries were conducted. Also, at the start of winter, he and his friends gave blankets to the poor, along with 10 rupees and clothes. They organized food for one thousand hungry people on certain days. The level of hunger shocked him: some people would return to the queue three or four times in a day to collect food for the evening and for their families. He told me that once, an elderly woman returned for the third time and fainted. Fortunately, a doctor in the group of donors revived her and instructed her to stop eating. The doctor explained to the woman that if she continued to eat, she would die because her body could not process the food, given her level of hunger and malnutrition. After this, Mr. P decided that it would be better to give people dry rations so they could cook as much as they wanted and store the rest. On two occasions, donations consisted of a packet containing 7 kilograms of rice and half a kilogram of pulses. He and those assisting him packed the food into bags and distributed slips to infirm village residents, telling them when and where to pick up the food. Infirmity or disability was the first criterion for recipients; the second was poverty and then age. Mr. P explained: "First time we distributed to about eight hundred persons, and then next time we distributed to four hundred, and now on this Friday, that means three days hence, we are distributing to two thousand."

I asked Mr. P why he helped the needy, pointing out that there were many people for whom the gods made life easy, and they did not choose to do this kind of work. He attributed his attitude to the teachings of his parents:

> You have to be grateful to the gods, and if they have given you bounty, you must share it with the poor. My parents are very religious and pious people, and they have always told us to look out for the poor, so such like thing is happening and many people feel that they should be grateful to the gods and share their wealth with others by looking after the poor. . . . We have a feeling that if you do the charity, god will take care of you, so it is that basic idea.

Mr. P had been moved to organize charitable activities, but he also felt that to do so was part of his family's teachings on how to exist in the world. He justified his impulse to give—to build a temple and to start a school for girls—in terms of the social responsibility he felt toward society, a concern that manifested itself most clearly in the instrumental rationality of his ideas about family planning, for example. These three portraits are examples of how the impulse to give is embodied in people's lives and tempered by concerns of instrumentally rational action.

## Gifts to NGOs

In professional development, unlike the previous individual cases, what starts out as a disinterested gift may be transformed into an interested one. This process forms the basis of fundamental contradictions that lie at the heart of philanthropy for relief and development. Private donations are part of chains of transactions among NGOs that ultimately end up reinforcing social hierarchies. R. L. Stirrat and Heiko Henkel write about this phenomenon in an article titled "The Development Gift: The Problem of Reciprocity in the NGO

World" (1997). Although development NGOs are funded through private donations, those gifts depend on the distanced relationship between donor and institution. In this relationship, the donor sits on one side and the recipient on the other. Moreover, donations not only provide an important economic basis for the NGOs, they also buttress the institution's moral and ethical purity. As Stirrat and Henkel write, "NGOs present themselves as the standard bearer of civil society: the embodiment of disinterested humanitarianism, a means by which such impulses can be made manifest in an organized form" (69). The authors concur that acts of private giving to NGOs are examples of pure, disinterested gifts. Donations to NGOs are given without expectation of return, in support of a "generalized impoverished other" (72). Donors do not know recipients; there are no direct ties. The obligation is to give, not to maintain social relationships.

Although this gift may be free of ties for the donor, it contains the potential to become poisonous for both recipients and NGOs. At worst, gifts to NGOs provide the means for controlling populations, asserting power, and reinforcing inequality. And despite inhabiting moral high ground, NGOs operate in a humanitarian marketplace within inherent hierarchical relationships. Thus, such gifts also serve to reinforce the inequality and dependency not only among recipients, but also among NGOs themselves. This trend was exacerbated in the 1990s when the development gift shifted from money to advice through the discourse of empowerment, which moved development away from charity. Donors considered empowerment and advice better than funds, though recipients preferred access to material goods and services to self-realization. This trend only increased a model of dependency (Stirrat and Henkel 1997: 73; also INCITE! 2007). But the provision of advice instead of donations only helped increase the hierarchical model of dependency according to which NGOs in the global north and global south operated. Unlike dān's uncontested reproduction of hierarchy, the development gift is given with the hope of inequality being overcome, yet the discourse of equality and empowerment within which it functions makes the development gift an impossible gift. Ironically, gifts to NGOs are "entrapped in a system of rules and regulations that are antithetical to the spirit of the free gift. Rules that govern the use of donations turn these gifts into accountable items" (Stirrat and Henkel 1997: 76). Ultimately, the chain of NGOs involved in development encounters masks the unequal dependence between northern and southern NGOs that supposedly work together as equal "partners."

In the case of post-tsunami relief in Sri Lanka, for example, the competition between NGOs as donors to needy tsunami victims illustrates the exaggerated contradiction at the heart of philanthropic approaches to relief and development: that philanthropy is based on disinterested principles but that in humanitarian work interests are increasingly important (Stirrat 2006; Ramani 2010).[20] The tsunami gift of humanitarian aid is not unconditional; humanitarian assistance garners expectations of worthy recipients and how gifts will be used. These conditions have the potential to culminate in patron/client relationships between beneficiaries and the state. The ethical tangles of giving to NGOs evoke Gloria Raheja's "poison in the gift" (1988) and Parry's "moral perils" (1986, 1994). In Raheja's case the "poison" was the fact that giving in rural north India reaffirmed relations of power and privilege, specifically related to caste. In the jajmani system of Pahansu village, gifts reinforced caste hierarchy. In Parry's case of Banaras funeral priests, the moral peril centered on the spiritual requirement that dān should go to a good end. In both of these cases, prestation was structured and regulated by habitus and not by the state. When the impulsive gift is regulated by the state, it may also lose its freedom and, as Michel Foucault (1991) has pointed out for the welfare state, have the potential to reconstitute subjects in the service of the state (see also Bornstein 2007a).

## Regulating the Gift

Religious gifts are not regulated in India. Most dān, for example, occurs outside the purview of secular law. Dān and zakat are regulated by Personal Law, which integrates religious law but is not tabulated or taxed by the state in the same manner as secular philanthropy.[21] The issue of regulation is a concern for both the GOI and Indian NGOs (Sidel and Zaman 2004; Sundar 2002; Sundar, ed., 2002b; Bornstein 2012). The three ethnographic cases presented in this chapter do not fit entirely into the regulated sector of NGOs in India. Mrs. B's orphanage, Suhrid, was registered with the state. The school associated with Mr. P's temple was registered, but the donations to the temple were religious donations and thus not regulated. The family that gave daily dān sat outside tax-based regulations of donation.[22] Hybrid forms of regulation exist as well: Mrs. B and Mr. P exist between the informal sector of voluntary and uncalculated giving and the formal, regulated sector of NGOs. In these two cases, *parts* of their philanthropic work were registered with the government, and some donors may have received tax advantages for their gifts.

Some of the slippage between accounted-for and unaccounted-for donations may be explained through the religious aspect of dān and the legislative dilemmas that ensue from it. That donations to religious organizations confer no tax advantages to donors makes sense in the religious context of gupt dān where there is intentionally no accounting and no relationship between donor and recipient—a condition that purportedly affords greater merit to the donor.[23] A study on donation in India conducted by the Sampradaan Indian Centre for Philanthropy (2001) concluded that most giving to charity in India is informal and ad hoc, with approximately 77 percent of donations given "to individuals in distress, known to oneself, and to beggars." Only 21 percent of donation goes toward organized, secular charity. Activists in the voluntary sector find it problematic that "informal, ad hoc charity takes precedence over giving for long term change and development or philanthropy" (48).[24]

In the voluntary sector of NGOs, issues of accountability are paramount, and narratives of corruption mirror those of the state (Gupta 1995; Parry 2000). Mistrust of NGOs is one disincentive for giving to organized agencies or institutions (see Chapter 2). In addition to a generalized suspicion toward the organized NGO sector, in South Asia issues of accountability are framed as a matter of obligation to governments and not to the general public (Sidel and Zaman 2004). This may be due to the fact that some NGOs in India receive funds from the government—hence the obligation to government regulators. NGOs are rarely required to provide the public (donors) with annual reports or details of financial transactions. This is in contrast to the United States, for example, where any NGO registered with the state must submit annual, public financial statements. In India, issues of accountability are beginning to overflow into the religious sector as well (Agarwal and Dadrawala 2004; also see Sidel 2010). Alongside donations to individuals, religious donations to temples (which often function as religious charities) constitute a large undocumented economy in which donors and recipients conduct exchanges outside account books. Donors contribute cash or in-kind gifts at religious temples and shrines without claiming tax deductions:

> Donations to religious charities are not eligible for deduction, except a limited purpose deduction for renowned religious places under section 80G(2)(b) of the Income Tax Act. One of the most famous temples in India (Shri Thirupathi Devasthanam Trust) receives Rs 188 crores (approximately US $41 million) annually in cash donations. In addition to this, pilgrims donate gold, jewelry and other valuables. The sale value of hair donated by pilgrims comes to an addi-

> tional Rs 20 crores (approximately US $4.36 million) annually. Mata Vaishno Devi Shrine in Jammu has an annual income of Rs 75 crores (approximately US $16 million), mainly from offerings by devotees. There are thousands of other temples, *gurudwaras* (Sikh temples), *dargahs* (Muslim shrines), churches and other institutions across India that receive significant donations. (Agarwal and Dadrawala 2004: 152–53)

The lack of documentation attributed to this "underground economy" of religious dān combined with the prevalence of "paper charities"—false charities set up in name only to shelter funds and provide tax advantages—perpetuate an environment of suspicion and distrust surrounding the work of the nonprofit sector. This may be a factor in attempts by the GOI to assimilate dān into a system of regulation.

In addition to the lack of charity regulation in India, the legal context for charity is a complicated landscape in transition.[25] Currently, nine laws regulate giving practices in what is, at the time of writing, an extremely decentralized system of legislation. No single body of law covers all of the classes of nonprofit organizations; instead, specific laws and regulations—many of them state-based—exist for each major type. In other words, different legal provisions, a combination of colonial legislation and more current attempts to transform these laws, come into play at national and state levels. The laws governing nonprofits are (1) public trusts acts;[26] (2) the Societies Registration Act of 1860;[27] (3) the Indian Companies Act of 1956; (4) the Income Tax Act of 1961; (5) the Cooperative Societies Act of 1904; (6) the Trade Union Act of 1926; and (7) the Indian Trusts Act of 1882. Within the realm of organized charity, nonprofits can register as (1) a public (charitable) trust (1950s legislation),[28] (2) a society (1860 legislation),[29] (3) a company (1956 legislation), (4) a cooperative (1904 legislation), or (5) a trade union (1926 legislation) (Nabhi 2004; Rajaratnam, Natarajan, and Thagaraj 2004).

Although this legal landscape can be difficult to navigate for NGOs, it also creates space for negotiation. Because many of the laws are state-based, the implementation of NGO registration can mean bureaucratic tangles and potential government corruption. Currently, an intense debate surrounds the regulation of foreign contributions to the voluntary sector (Agarwal and Dadrawala 2004). Key to this debate are the deductibility of tax donations, with a tendency for the GOI to restrict it, and new legislation to restrict money laundering linked to suspicion surrounding the accountability of the voluntary sector. There are also attempts to amend the Foreign Contribution Regulation Act of 1976 (Koshi

2004; Sundar 2010), and to develop a National Policy on the Voluntary Sector, which specifies guidelines for a "partnership between government and the voluntary sector" with an intent to encourage "accountability" and "transparency" in the sector (Government of India, Voluntary Action Cell, Planning Commission 2007: 18). Some of this attention focused on the voluntary sector is related to the increasing globalization of the Indian economy and difficulties identifying whether donations are from foreign sources, particularly regarding diasporic philanthropy from nonresident Indians (Dadrawala 2003b; Government of India, High Level Committee on Indian Diaspora 2002; Shiveshwarkar 2004; Viswanath 2003). In an attempt to limit money laundering, one of the proposed regulatory adjustments was that anonymous donations (gupt dān) to charitable organizations no longer be tax exempt.[30]

Perhaps dān is a Weberian "ideal type" of philanthropy. Yet once secularized and translated into the rational mechanics of capitalism (accountability, governance, credibility, transparency), it becomes—like the Derridian gift—an impossibility.[31] In the context of struggles over control of resources, the Vedic sūkti[32] presented as the epigraph to this chapter reminds us not only of the poetic power of spontaneous and unregulated aspects of giving, but also of the unfettered beauty in the social directive to give away more than one receives.

In philanthropy and dān, recipients make no claims on donors—recipients have no right to demand the gift, although this does not stop beggars from requesting it. This differs from forms of social welfare that structure NGO activities and that operate within state-based regimes of entitlements and rights, often called "humanitarian." Dān evokes the structure of the pure gift by requiring the radical annulment of a relationship between recipient and giver, with no interest and no obligation for the donor or recipient. The work of humanitarianism, in contrast, as a particular type of gift, may focus on social and moral obligations and the rights of recipients (Englund 2008; Wilson and Brown 2009).

Despite these important distinctions, philanthropy, dān, and humanitarianism entail the impulse to give and various forms of regulation. On the side of impulse is the freedom of the gift and of the liberation that occurs from spontaneous giving. The danger of impulsive giving, to strangers and to immediate others, however, is that it perpetuates inequality. Recipients of the impulsive gift have no rights; they can only beg. But when philanthropy focuses on relations of accountability, it becomes instrumentally rational. The danger of fully instrumental giving is the rational overlooking of immediate, and at times viscerally troubling, social experience, often embodied in specific others with urgent needs. Donations to NGOs that provide a buffer zone between givers and those in need are one alternative to giving directly to those in need. Yet, debates surrounding the regulation of NGOs in India speak to the tension between giving away without expectation and the importance of finding a suitable recipient for the gift. Here, contemporary philanthropy, like classic dān, is riddled with ethical dilemmas. In the next chapter, I address these issues through an analysis of trust in humanitarianism.

Because the system of reciprocal accountability that the voluntary sector in India is currently demanding is part of an attempt by the state to regulate civil society and the resources of donation (dān), the effects of this regulation will be governmental. The recipients of donations by NGOs have rights—they are claimants, a status that some might argue represents progress. However, I caution against such an approach. To coerce the impulse to give into rational accountability is to obliterate its freedom; to render giving into pure impulse is to reinforce social inequality. The only solution is to allow both to exist and to create structures to encourage them. Although much of what is written on charity and philanthropy focuses on the effects of the gift, I suggest more attention be paid to the impulse of philanthropy. Specifically, how philanthropy differs from welfare that involves rights and claims. Although rights-based forms of social welfare respond to organized attempts to address social need, rights are not always afforded to those whose circumstances warrant immediate, if fleeting, attention. Philanthropy, as an impulse, addresses the relational, affectual, and dynamic aspects of the gift, which is perhaps its enticement.

## Chapter 2

# Trust

**HUMANITARIAN WORK** is evaluated through moral discourses. I begin this chapter with a site where these discourses are produced. The setting is a nexus of suspicion—an ensemble of mutual distrust at the intersection of rich and poor schools, NGOs, the private sector, the GOI, and concerted efforts of humanitarian relief.[1] Against the grain of my previous experiences with NGOs in southern Africa as harbingers of global civil society (Bornstein 2005; Fisher 1997), in New Delhi I found that NGOs were deeply distrusted in both public and private. The business sector, on the other hand, was considered trustworthy. Was it the overt intent of profits (not service) that gave business a cloak of invincibility against fraud, exempting it from suspicion? Despite the fact that particular accounting forms and audit cultures have emerged to address issues of mistrust (Power 1997; Strathern 1996/7, 2000), they have not mollified suspicion. In the case of India, at least in its capital city New Delhi, the practice of auditing itself is distrusted. This chapter explores how the culture of suspicion functions as an audit.

Accountability is a topic of concern for practitioners within NGOs and theorists of global civil society. Book titles abound in NGO circles on how to be more accountable, for example, *NGO Accountability: Politics, Principles, and Innovations* (Jordan and van Tuijl 2006) and *Global Accountabilities: Participation, Pluralism, and Public Ethics* (Ebrahim and Weisband 2007). An international humanitarian organization called Sphere emerged to address issues of accountability in practice (Oxfam 2007: *Impact Measurement and Accountability in Emergencies: The Good Enough Guide*). Questions regarding accountability within NGOs ask the following: If the audit is a way to manage NGO obligation and responsibility, to whom should NGOs be accountable? (Stein 2008; Sooryamoorthy and Gangrade 2001: 99–112). As nonelected institutions in a democratic context of political engagement and social welfare, are NGOs accountable to their donors, the communities they serve, or the nation-states with which they collaborate, or are they morally accountable to an ethical public? In humanitarian and development work, the environments in which NGOs operate, these ethical principles are paramount. NGOs are part of a global civil society whose very presence embodies the auditing principle on a global scale. If states are corrupt, then NGOs are often called upon to come to the moral, financial, and ethical rescue. Moreover, in globally liberalizing markets that encourage the reduction of state welfare programs, NGOs provide social welfare under the name of development (Bornstein 2005; Feher 2007). Social welfare, in general, is highly political and morally laden territory. Transnationally, issues of corruption, coercion, and mismanagement take on a more sinister shade when the topic is saving lives or rescuing victims (de Waal 1997; Hancock 1989; Marren 1997; Rieff 2002; Terry 2002), often in times of war (Goodhand 2006; Pandolfi 2003). Organizations such as Médecins sans Frontières, for example, operate according to what Didier Fassin (2007) has called a "politics of life" (also see Redfield 2005, 2011). They are under great scrutiny to be moral barometers of social welfare.

In India close to one million voluntary organizations (VOs) are registered as trusts, societies, trade unions, or Section 25 charitable companies. India has the largest number of VOs in Asia (see CAF India 2000, as well as for the statistics that follow). In 2000 (when the Charities Aid Foundation [CAF] report was conducted) foreign funding constituted 80 percent of organized funding to VOs. The report stated that as a result, some NGOs and VOs would "be held culturally and politically suspect" because they were not accountable to authorities in India (2). The total foreign funding for VOs in India is in the region of 4,000 crore rupees (roughly $1 billion). Out of the estimated one million VOs in India, only eighteen thousand are registered under the Foreign Contribution Regulation Act (FCRA) of 1976.[2] The GOI also contributes substantially to NGOs and VOs largely through its ministries. The trend for the GOI to fund NGOs increased with the Seventh Five-Year Plan in 1985. In 2000 the estimated state funding for VOs was in the region of 5,000 crore rupees (more than $1 billion). Yet these are only the documented and formal figures. Undocumented support for NGOs is even greater, particularly regarding religious charities, to which people donate without any benefit of tax deductions, as we have seen.

## After the Disaster Comes the Accounting

Soon after the December 2004 tsunami hit the shores bordering the Indian Ocean, a wave of relief was rallied alongside a flood of social critique. Amidst pleas for public donations, which permeated the press, was documentation of scandalous abuse. Newspapers were filled with reports of corruption by the GOI and NGOs. More than mere sensationalism, the discourse of corruption was an ethical commentary on the actions of the GOI and NGOs regarding social welfare (cf. Parry 2000; Gupta 1995). One could say that the feverish media coverage offered its own rituals of verification to the reading public. The outrage voiced by the media at corrupt practices in humanitarian work provided an ethical critique of how such work "should" progress. By outlining what was not right, the articles alluded to what should be.

In the first week of January 2005, the *Indian Express* ran a series of articles on corruption in tsunami relief. On January 1 an article titled "Tsunami Donors Should Be Wary, Say Charity Groups" advised donors to be suspicious of con artists posing as charities. It suggested that donors avoid "intermediaries" and give as directly as possible for tsunami relief. Although the article was not specifically about the GOI or NGOs, it defined a particular culture of suspicion regarding humanitarian relief:

> Some fear that it's only a matter of time before con artists take advantage of the disaster and falsely claim to be collecting money for relief efforts. Others fret that new charities will spring up, with little experience in directing aid to help victims in a crisis thousands of miles away. . . . Watchdogs advised donors to avoid giving cash or through intermediaries whenever possible. Instead, donors can usually donate directly to charities online or send them a check through the mail.

Another article on January 4, "As Relief Pours In, Vultures Start to Gather," described how "thieves, rapists, kidnappers, and hoaxers" preyed on tsunami survivors and the families of victims. The next day, a third article titled "Relief Arrives Then Touts Take Over" told the tale of how relief supplies to Nagapattinam were being met with "touts," who posed as victims and hijacked the aid. For instance, a truck of relief supplies was "intercepted and driven away to the outskirts by those who claimed to be government officials." The victims then had to pay for the aid. A fisherman explained that a man "told us that if we paid him Rs [rupees] 50 per head, he would ensure that a truck came our way at least twice a day." Other reports, such as one titled "Net Fraud in Tsunami Aid" in the *Hindustan Times* on January 15, documented corruption in cyberspace, where "cyber-crooks" sent unsolicited emails and set up "bogus websites to siphon off relief money meant for tsunami victims."

These particular cases of misappropriation of aid fed into a larger critique featured in newspaper editorial pages. An editorial in the *Hindustan Times* on January 7 titled "In a Ready State" railed against the government's relief efforts in the context of general social welfare provision: "The Government of India is being projected to deliver relief and facilitate rehabilitation of those affected by the tsunami. But how effective has it been in dealing with 'crises' in normal times?" The editorial continued with the provocative statement, "After the disaster comes the accounting." It was an opportunity for a larger social critique:

> Virtually every kind of relief operation mounted by the government in India has suffered from delays and is often tainted by corruption. It is impossible for the private sector to match that level of perversity. . . . Apart from the chaos and delays in providing relief, there is a more fundamental problem in government-dominated relief operations. The government operates on the basis of coercive taxation; citizens don't have a choice in the matter. By contrast, private relief operates on the basis of voluntary donation. The resultant problem of "moral hazard" isn't an abstract speculation.

In India, many lived in permanent tsunami conditions. A January 9 article in the *Indian Express* titled "The Lull after the Storm" documented that "nearly 30 percent of the population lives on less than Rs 10 a day in living conditions so degraded that they could be described as being permanently tsunami affected. . . . After every disaster, manmade or natural, there is a fuss for a while and then we all forget and this includes the media. If we did not there is no way our governments could have got away with decades of criminal negligence in the social sector."

The tsunami was a portal into a larger moral critique of the government, of NGOs, and of social welfare practices. The critique was like anthropological analyses of witchcraft in Africa that treat accusations of malevolence as a social commentary on wider political and economic issues such as the radical inequality of globalization and the difficulty of survival for many in the new world order.[3] These press accounts targeting abuses and scandals by the GOI and NGOs in tsunami relief were a discourse of corruption that provided indirect commentary on the ideal responsibilities of the state and NGOs regarding social welfare.[4]

The suspicion meted out to the GOI extended to NGOs, which people accused of "doing nothing" or "helping their families and friends" instead of those they were intended to serve. Before supporting an NGO, donors asked questions such as, "Where does my money go?" and "Are the recipients worthy?" NGOs in Delhi, situated as they were in a nexus that contrasted suspicions of government corruption to a corporate sector model of accountability, embodied both the potential for corruption (self-interest) and the model of accountability (to ensure general good). As Parry (2000) has noted, if there is an increase of perceived corruption in India, it is actually an acknowledgment of the public domain as a site where the state is supposed to be a guardian and where the appropriation of the public domain for private interest is morally unacceptable. That bribes are sometimes spoken about in terms of a donation (dān) is more than a euphemism. There is *always* a suspicion in donation practices that the gift will be misused. In his discussion of givers and receivers of bribes taken for public sector positions, Parry writes that because "givers declare themselves but receivers in general do not" (43), the moral onus is on the receiver of a bribe. With charitable activity as well, the moral onus of the gift lies with the recipient—to be "worthy" and to "use the money well." In the Indian context, particularly in religious giving, the giver has the obligation to make sure that the gift is offered at an appropriate time and to a worthy recipient. The sin of a gift that is misused or misdirected reflects back upon the giver (Parry 1994). Generally, however, one could surmise that in both religious and secular contexts, whether referring to a conduit such as an NGO or a group accepting a donation directly, receivers are responsible for justifying the moral worthiness of a donation and for demonstrating how funds are used. Perhaps to address and resolve issues of suspicion oriented toward recipients, many people I interviewed in the NGO sector said that in New Delhi, and in India more broadly, people wanted to help someone or some group with which they had a relationship. In other words, they wanted to see their assistance going to a specific site, geographical or conceptual, with which they were associated—whether this was a region they came from or a special interest with which they had personal experience (such as the needs of the elderly or children in a neighboring slum). This giving was relational and not anonymous; it was also direct. One could say it was the opposite of the more generalized efforts of humanitarian relief as exemplified by the tsunami disaster. It was also the opposite of scriptural accounts of dān. In direct philanthropy, social networks functioned as the guarantor. People funded NGOs that they knew. Perhaps someone they knew worked for it, or started it, or was on its governing board.[5]

At the time of my research, to inspire more generalized giving in the frame of "civil society," foundations were supporting programs that met the standards of disinterested social welfare (as opposed to welfare programs that were relational). The Ford Foundation's program on philanthropy in New Delhi, for example, was part of its Governance and Civil Society Program. It supported NGO infrastructure, or, in other words, NGOs that oversaw the accountability of other NGOs. Through a language of self-help and a discourse of need, this program defined itself against the term "charity." While two of the issues that concerned this type of philanthropy were accountability and credibility (as in Power 1997; Strathern 1996/7, 2000), there was also an expectation of transformative results. If this form of giving was a crusade against corruption, it was—as another foundation officer explained—an audit for the sake of change.

In Delhi, the field of NGO oversight was dense and organized; to me, it seemed strikingly so. A website providing resources for Indian NGOs held a cyber forum on "credibility" in which NGO experts gave advice on NGO good-governance. I met with directors and employees of organizations in Delhi that were set up to help NGOs be more "accountable" and provide guidelines for governance. Of course, this superstructure of institutions existed in dialogue with NGO work on the ground and provided a moral conscience for the welfare sector in the absence of state regulation. Yet I was unsure why suspicion was so pervasive and why there was such an institutional urgency to this sector's existence. Why was the NGO sector under such scrutiny when other realms of life were also permeated by corruption? Was this a case of attacking the messenger? An officer at the Ford Foundation considered the criticisms of transparency and advocacy in the NGO sector to be criticisms of advocacy in general, because, she explained, "oftentimes the messenger gets attacked, not the message. You know, like if they're saying 'We promote human rights for women,' well, what better to do than just say 'Hey, you're not accountable; your funds, where are your funds coming from? How much does the director get paid?'" Because NGOs challenged the status quo and advocated for change, some felt threatened; it was easier to attack the NGOs for corruption than their aim of social transformation. Moreover, unlike government officials, who were elected by the public (corrupt or not) and accountable to the public, the issue of accountability was ambiguous for NGOs. The foundation officer surmised: "People feel threatened, they're like, 'Wait a minute, I didn't—a government is . . . I was elected, who elected you?'" Accusations of corruption in the NGO sector also may have stemmed from the historic allegiance NGOs have had with the GOI.

Many NGOs emerged in partnership with the state after independence (CAF India 2000; Sharma 2006; Sooryamoorthy and Grangrade 2001; Tandon 2003). During my research, the term "mushrooming" was frequently used to describe the growth of the NGO sector as something that was uncontrollable. As much as the state had a reputation for corruption, like the dust on the wings of a butterfly, some of it rubbed off on its NGO collaborators, damaging the way a scrutinizing public perceived them.

Over and over I heard people say that although some NGOs were doing good work, most were not to be trusted. The comment "oh, anybody can start an NGO" and the rumors that NGOs were being set up for people to pocket money instead of to serve a constituency circulated as frequently as stories of a master beggar who broke the limbs of poor children and then sent them off to beg. Whether or not these stories were true—and I did not have the opportunity to verify any of them—they were often repeated with a sort of certainty that defies explanation. It was the same "everybody knows" certainty that I also heard in my research in Zimbabwe when people spoke about witchcraft. "Have you seen it?" I would ask—about malpracticing NGOs in India or witches in Zimbabwe—and hear the same responses: "Oh, I haven't seen it myself, but I know it's true." What do these stories keep in check? They have a dual moral function: they circulate suspicion in attempts to keep corruption at bay, and they express (more indirectly) suspicion of contemporary institutions.

If the support of foundations such as the Ford Foundation and other NGO-auditing organizations worked against corruption, theirs was a fight against the inevitable. One must assume that *chai-pani* or *bakshish* (both euphemisms for a political bribe) occur. The film *Chai Pani* (2005), for example, has a scene in which a governmental permissions officer asks for a "donation" to his daughter's school. Here the bribe is a "donation," and, as the young and naive journalist who is the protagonist of the film soon learns, corruption in government is a "way of life." Everybody does it (demands bribes). In the last scene of the film we hear the mentor of the protagonist explain that one must work *within* the system to change it. Naiveté and idealism do not bring about change. It is in precisely this context that the two sectors, NGOs and the government, are moral mirrors of each other. The NGO sector is accused of corruption—the term "paper NGOs," for example, refers to those that exist only to receive funds but do no social welfare work—but NGOs also accuse the GOI of requesting bribes for grants. I was frequently told that the going rate was 20 percent of a grant in bakshish for an NGO to receive money from the government. The concept that the GOI, and by proxy NGOs, was to be distrusted was met with the alternate idea that the corporate sector was comparatively clean. Perhaps it was the overt nature of self-interest in the corporate sector that garnered trust, while perceived altruism to strangers was considered less trustworthy.

A final component in this puzzle is that NGO work, like employment in the government sector, is relatively low-paying. In a liberalizing economy, elitism in the middle and upper-middle classes may encourage people to work for multinational corporations instead of the government. Working for the civil service in India used to be one of the most prestigious professions, offering unlimited social capital and power; but in contemporary urban India, NGO and government salaries have been much lower than those in the corporate sector. In some cases it may be financially more lucrative for a person to work for a call center than to work for either the GOI or an NGO.

## Case 1: A Nexus of Suspicion

In the welfare sector in New Delhi, at the confluence of NGOs, the state, and donors, lies the nexus of suspicion. There are many such sites in Delhi. By "nexus," I refer to "an affinity or attachment in which a civil institution is deformed by an underlying relation to criminalized interest" (Cohen 2007: 106). I entered the nexus at the posh playschool where I sent my son in central New Delhi. This school had a bad reputation among expatriates, who preferred the American school or the British school, because this school, some said, was just "too Indian." Shortly after the December 2004 tsunami, the school put out a call for donations. These were not solicitations of choice, however; it was mandatory for the parents of each child to donate 500 rupees. Like the pundit who accosts devotees as they enter a temple to give dān, my son's teacher accosted me in the hallway one day as I dropped him off. "Where is your donation? You have to give," she said. But some parents were concerned, asking: "Where is the money going? What if I want to give money to another NGO instead of this one?" The NGO to which we gave funds was located near the school, and I soon learned that it was a literacy organization and a vocational school that provided free education to slum children and destitute women.

The donation request reverberated in the national context. In addition to media reports of corruption in tsunami relief, Delhi newspapers were filled with lists of donors and headlines on the editorial pages questioning whether the local philanthropic response to the disaster was a marker of Maussian social solidarity. Within this evaluative frame were questions of trust. The NGO to which parents donated through the posh school took donations directly to a tsunami-stricken area because it did not trust the relief efforts of other NGOs or the GOI. Meanwhile, the director of the posh school was furious because the local NGO (which I will call the slum school) had not provided any reports on how the money had been spent. Several plane tickets were purchased, but otherwise, the question "Where is the money going?" was not being answered.

Charity was part of the posh school's identity. Just a few days before the tsunami struck, I attended a Christmas celebration at the posh school. Parents sat on the school's front lawn watching their children perform onstage, drivers stood outside the gate, and maids watched from inside the school building. The Christmas celebration was a ritual of class and status. The schoolchildren performed first, and then special guests performed—poor children from Kanpur brought by a famous NGO called Child Relief and You (CRY). The poor children sang songs about Jesus, although most of the audience members were Hindu, as were the directors of the posh school. Celebrating Christmas did not signify any particular religious identification; instead, it celebrated membership in a global elite. The director of one of the most prestigious secondary and high schools in Delhi attended as an invited guest overseeing the performance of charitable relations. There was a certain instrumentality to her presence as well, for many of the children from the posh school would eventually apply to her intensely competitive institution. Here, social networks mattered. The media was present, and cameras documented the special guest performers and interviewed the director of CRY. That the posh school had included poor children in its Christmas celebration was symbolic of its good social citizenship. Of course it was staged; it was a performance. Nonetheless, the charitable inclusion of poor children from Kanpur reinforced the position of the wealthy parents who sent their children to the posh school.

A few days later, on December 27, *The Hindu* ran a story about the event titled "A Time to Share." The section about the school event was subtitled "Gifting Smiles":

> In a season when many of us have been busy buying ourselves expensive gifts for the festive season, some organisations have made an effort to bring joy to those for whom life's rough edges are generally reserved. A little school called [name of the school] is starting off the New Year well by its initiation of sponsoring education and health care for a group of children from CRY—Child Relief and You—for one year. Some days ago, in true Yuletide spirit, the children of the Jorbagh-based school shared their Christmas celebrations with underprivileged

> children from CRY. Children of the school welcomed children from CRY with Christmas gifts and exuberant smiles. A range of cultural programmes including skits and Christmas carols performed by the children followed the effusive welcome. "The basic aim behind this programme was to make these children feel special and let them enjoy things that privileged children of their age do. At the same time, we also want children studying in our school to interact with these children, understand their plight and become sensitive towards them. The whole idea is to create awareness and a link between people," said [the director of the school]. . . . The event was resplendent with playfulness and empathy as the children interacted without hesitation. The celebrations concluded with Santa Claus distributing toys and sweets. An endeavour to wipe the tears of millions of underprivileged children, the sympathetic gesture brought together two entirely different worlds under one roof.

It was the type of article one might find in the *New York Times* or any local newspaper in the United States at the end of the calendar year, where the selfishness of an elite institution contrasts with, and is absolved by, its relation to charity. It was through contact with the poor that students of the posh school were taught to be good citizens of the world.

I learned later that the posh school, through CRY, had offered twenty children from a local slum the cost of preschool education in Delhi. I asked, naively, whether the children from the slum would attend the posh school. "Not [our school]," the director replied. "The parents will flee. You can't have them come here. People will flee. Instead, we have hired two teachers to go into the slums to teach: all in Hindi, nothing in English." They had donated the same materials that the children at the posh school had access to—the same blocks, the same curriculum—"what [my son] does in circle time, these kids do too," the director said. He then pulled me aside to explain in a muted tone that there was a lot of corruption in the Third World: "Lots of police, electricity people wanting money. Lots of NGOs, the fishy ones, where we don't know where it goes." He had structured his support for the slum children in this context of suspicion: "I hire the teacher. I want to know where the money goes. It's the same curriculum. The money is coming out of my payroll. Whatever I bring in terms of arts and crafts, the menu in school, it's the same for them. I feel the only way I'll be satisfied is if I micro-manage the whole process. No matter how well managed it is, I don't trust where the money goes." In contrast to the public performance of charitable relations at the Christmas celebration, his support for the slum children was a secret, and he told me, "I don't want you to tell anyone about this." If he advertised his charity, the director said, he would open the floodgates of request: "We will have all these people asking for bakshish."

At the director's encouragement, I visited the slum school to which we had donated for tsunami relief and spent three months (January to March 2005) interviewing its director, whom I'll call Mr. J, about the school's work. At the time of our discussions, the school had been working with approximately one hundred children on issues of literacy; it was primarily self-funded. In interviews, Mr. J repeatedly exclaimed, at times in exasperation, that the school operated without any GOI support. Members of the NGO contributed their own money every month. In 2002–03 (according to the school's brochure) the NGO had 150 children in a literacy program, 100 people in a computer program, 100 adults in a shorthand/typing program, and 100 women in a beautician program.[6] In addition to educational and vocational training courses, the organization was also involved in "rehabilitating street children" and sponsored medical camps for the urban poor. The children for the school came from a nearby slum area, which was about half a kilometer from the school and office. A vehicle picked up the children and took them to the school. The organization, like many of the organizations I encountered and studied in India, aimed to serve those ignored by official channels of aid.

When he first began his work, Mr. J conducted a household survey of the slum areas abutting the Lodhi colony near Jor Bagh (the plush area surrounding Lodhi Gardens in Central Delhi). In the household survey, the director asked for the following information: (1) name, (2) husband's name, (3) age, (4) marriage condition, (5) number of children, (6) education, (7) profession, (8) income of parents, (9) house number and address, (10) whether parents were providing education or not. In 2004 Mr. J and volunteers covered more than four hundred households in three days. He considered the primary social problems in the slum colonies to be "population, hygiene, pick-pocketing, inadequate manners/education, and children who had dropped out [of school] and worked in shops." He added, "People are not cooperating with each other." The GOI had given water pumps to the slum areas, but Mr. J wondered how long they would work because of the "uneducated peoples." He was critical of the recipient community with regards to his own efforts: "No use giving money directly to these people. They will buy the wine. They will buy the alcohol from the market, and they will not give the money to their family. That is the basic problem."

Ten staff members of the slum school worked in the building they rented for 10,000 rupees a month. "These people like to help running the NGO,"

Mr. J said. He criticized both the GOI and NGOs, saying that 80 percent of NGOs were not operating properly. Many, he claimed, paid politicians before getting government grants. "Money doesn't go to where it should," he said; "money goes to politicians." In this context, neither NGOs nor the GOI was worthy of trust; both were complicit and worthy only of suspicion. It was difficult to start an NGO as a "society" organization in India, according to Mr. J.[7] At the time of my interviews, the NGO that ran the slum school was operating schools in three states: Uttaranchal (now Uttarakhand), Uttar Pradesh, and Delhi. Mr. J was running this school primarily out of his own pocket, which caused tension in his family. As a result of his commitment to his charitable work running the NGO, his wife was barely speaking to him. Without children of his own, he had, in a manner of speaking, renounced his family in favor of his NGO work.

Although the slum school did not receive government grants, it had government employees in its membership. There were two hundred members at the time of my interviews, and of those, fifteen were working in the organization. Some of the teachers were volunteers; some were paid (2,000–2,500 rupees per month). But the slum school was in dire straits. When I spoke to some of the teachers, they complained that their salaries had not been paid for the past few months and that the tone in the organization was one of financial desperation. Mr. J said he had asked the director of the posh school whether he was ready to support the slum school but wondered, "When will he support it?"

Immediately after the tsunami, Mr. J took it upon himself to collect donations for victims of the disaster in the Nagapattinam district of Tamil Nadu, which was made up of fishing villages. This area was one of the hardest hit on the Indian subcontinent. He went door-to-door, collecting utensils (pots and pans), silverware, rice, clothes, books and stationery, and medicine. One day as I left the slum school, Mr. J asked me to find someone to pay for the airplane tickets to transport the tsunami relief packages, which were stacked up and tied in boxes filling the office. He aimed to take them to a particular village. I suggested he find an NGO that had people going there and mentioned that airlines may donate baggage space for tsunami relief. "No," he said, "all the things being donated are just lying there. Someone must go and make sure they are distributed properly."[8]

As Mr. J described his tsunami efforts on one cold Delhi day, he begged me to solicit donations for his organization in a manner that emphasized my elite status as an American woman. The NGO was not doing well, financially.

As he solicited my support, sweet incense wafted from a shrine in the office. The NGO needed resources, he said: "Wherever.you go in the future, you can ask people. Some organizations are there; you can help. We never ask you to donate the money, to donate the computers. No, we ask you to ask the people—if you go in your country, to help this organization." It was an awkward conversation. I had visited the organization partly out of my own curiosity and partly at the encouragement of the director of the posh school to check on its accountability (in other words, was it doing what it said it was doing?). One reason there was no trust was because there *was* corruption. Mr. J explained: "A lot of NGOs are run like a business. Money comes in and goes out in the pocket. A lot of NGOs are working like this. . . . If some foundation, they want to donate one hundred rupees, so what they will try to do—they will ask: 'We will give you one hundred rupees,' but they want to take eighty rupees back. Thus the foundation can declare that they gave one hundred rupees, but they only gave twenty rupees." The suspicion of money laundering pervaded the world of "official" donation in Delhi.

One day, I arrived at the posh school to talk to the director about the work of the slum school and the concerns that I had. A man sat in the director's office. When the director saw me through the glass door, he seemed irritated and came out to tell me that he couldn't meet me at that moment. He complained about the reporter sitting in his office who wanted something from him. "A reporter?" I asked. "He was starting some program for kids in Rajasthan—a whole community. He heard I did this and that, and now he wants my support," he said, exasperated.

I mentioned that I had just come from the slum school, where Mr. J wanted me to ask the director of the posh school about an event that was being planned at a five-star hotel. My comment enraged him, and I soon saw the web of obligation into which I was woven. "I don't want to do that event!" the posh school director said. "I've told him a million times. What part doesn't he understand? What did you tell him?" He was angry with me as well. I asked the director about his sponsorship of the slum school kids. "No!" he exclaimed, returning to my earlier query. "Did I say that I would do the event?" He was defensive. "We've given them so much money. Where has it gone? I want to see something from the government for taxes." I mentioned the receipts that parents had been given for their donations. "No, I want to see how they've used the [tsunami] money. Our parents need to know where their money went!" He was exasperated. I mentioned that that day they were feeding the children in a special event that was being videotaped. "That's my camera!" he said. "I gave it to them. How much do they want from us? I said let's do something at [the posh school], not at some five-star hotel. It's getting too materialistic. Let's have his kids make some cards or wrapping paper and we can sell them to parents. I'm not doing that event. Or, I said I'd sponsor some kids at [the posh school]—separate from the regular classes—but here, why not?"

I was troubled by how quickly I had become a pawn in the rally between the two school directors. My research into the rich and the poor school and their relationship, which had previously seemed so exciting and metaphorically beautiful—quickly became a social nightmare. I mentioned that the teachers at the slum school were not getting paid. "Those teachers all apply to teach here," he said, "but their English isn't good enough." English was a marker of class status in Delhi. Then he continued his rampage. "Where has all the money gone? He used to have three hundred kids, now he has eighty. Where did they go? What is happening?" He seethed with distrust. The posh school accused the slum school of not being responsible; the slum school accused the slum-dwellers for not being responsible and for not sending their children to school. These were issues of credibility. Things were neither what they seemed nor what was expected. And in such a context, giving was dangerous because it could quickly multiply to unlimited requests. The posh school wanted to keep its charity private and quiet. It did not want to hold an event at a five-star hotel. Simultaneously, it wanted to collaborate with the slum school when the audience was the parents of students enrolled at the posh school. When philanthropy becomes a performance, a ritual of verification, one must ask: Who is the audience? Where is the stage? Who is on the stage? The nexus of the posh school and the slum school may have been a microcosm for relationships of poverty and need in Delhi, but it was not a binary relationship between donors and recipients. The slum school was also a benefactor, providing education for the poor.

One must remember that suspicion was aimed in every direction. The GOI was also suspicious of NGOs and conducted inspections before giving grants. Mr. J recounted such an inspection with great frustration. Where was the money? Was it forthcoming? As much as grantors desired to follow their funds, potential grantees also questioned the money trail. One Friday the GOI inspected the slum school. Mr. J thought the inspection had been successful because fifty-six children were in attendance that day. The four GOI inspectors who came to the NGO had "even inquired [about] each and every thing." It was a surprise inspection without notice orchestrated by the Education Ministry from the Delhi government; it took more than two hours. The inspectors were very curious to know about Mr. J's life—who was the founder? they inquired; where is he getting funds?

NGOs have other rituals of verification besides audits and inspections. Specific performances that validate the institution are geared to an audience of "the public." For example, on Valentine's Day 2004, the slum school held a public event, which one could say was analogous in form to the Christmas event at the posh school. It was a charitable performance at the Samarat Hotel in Delhi—the same event in which the director of the posh school refused to participate. Mr. J invited five government ministers, but only one attended: the honorable chief minister of Delhi. The event started with cultural programs and culminated in the release of a ten-minute video featuring the slum school's tsunami relief efforts in Nagapattinam district. This ritual of verification between the slum school NGO, the slum children, and a representative of the government was a plea for funding and a manifestation of intent. The attendance of the honorable chief minister—a witness to the work as a distinguished audience member—was another form of social accountability and validation.

Because of the apparent success of the event at the hotel, Mr. J continued to request my help, asking me to go with him to governmental ministries to talk about his program. My presence was, in his eyes, the embodiment of a ritual of verification; he said I would lend credibility to his organization. I doubted the capacity of my presence to provide validation, but he was adamant. The financial situation in the organization was worsening. The three teachers still had not been paid, and Mr. J had used up all of his personal savings to run the school. He borrowed some money from a friend and promised to pay him back. The slum school was a labor of love for him. "I have sacrificed everything," he said—his family and his finances. In this way, he seemed a madman to me. His charisma and drive appealed to me until I got too close; then it seemed unstable, a bright light that threatened to burn up in a bottomless pit of desire for helping others. His unbridled need and the urgency of the services he provided were the passions that kept him going and also kept me, as an outsider, at bay. I, too, was developing my own suspicion.

The next time I visited the slum school, Mr. J told me that things were not going well. The organization had had seven inspections by the GOI but had not yet received a grant. Apparently, the funds were not coming through even though the school had received "approval." So Mr. J decided to embark on desperate measures: he was going to take legal action against the government and was writing a letter to the president of India when I arrived. “I think it is because of corruption [that we have not gotten the money],” he said. “If I pay 20 percent, my grant-in-aid will be cleared. People have said if you give me something, I can get your proposal signed.” He arranged for a local newspaper to publish an article about his situation, and he asked again whether I would go with him the next day to the government office to discuss his proposal. “Eighty percent of the problem will be solved with your presence,” he said. “If I go [without you], they will just say ‘we will see.’ I know the Government of India. Your presence is most important for us. If you come with the reporter . . . they will not do this.” The press and the foreigner were embodiments of the audit, and I was embedded in the institutional context as a responsible yet slightly disinterested researcher. He continued to urge me to visit the secretary of education with him, but I had my own family obligations and could not help him. “Only one hour I ask for your help,” he pleaded. “They will listen to you. Only one hour.” In Delhi such a request was reasonable. Presence was a resource to be tapped, one that was often more reliable than plans or appointments. But he seemed a desperate man with an organization on the verge of collapse. At a table behind us a board member composed a handwritten letter to the president of India.

## Case 2: An American Doctor Follows Through

The landscape of suspicion also created concern for foreign donors who expected their funds to go to “those most in need.” To counteract distrust, donors often went to unusual lengths to give directly and to track their funds—often bypassing both NGOs and the GOI. I met with an American doctor, Dr. S, who knew India well. He had been sending money to purchase HIV medicines for four people through a doctor in India. Dr. S traveled to India to present a paper at a medical conference and to volunteer his time in an AIDS ward, and he took the opportunity to meet with the Indian doctor to whom he had been sending money. He told the Indian doctor he wanted to meet the patients who were helped by his donations. He agreed to give these patients, through the Indian doctor, HIV medicines annually for as long as they needed them. When Dr. S arrived in Delhi, he was surprised to find that two of the four people being supported by his donations lived far away—one in Sri Lanka and one in Nagaland. “I was puzzled why he was treating patients so far off when there were so many people needing care in Delhi,” he said. He could not understand how the Indian doctor selected the recipients for his medications. Dr. S met a couple for whom he was funding HIV medications, but they were from the same geographic region as his friend, the Indian doctor. I suggested that perhaps the selection logic lay in a practice called "direct philanthropy," which a foundation officer in Delhi had explained to me. In India, the officer had said, people practice direct philanthropy that is relational and not utilitarian (the good for the greatest number). People seek to give to someone they know with a specific outcome, instead of to a general cause.

Dr. S commented that he had a dual purpose for his gifts. He was motivated by personal satisfaction, which he received through volunteering his time and donating the HIV medicines, but he was also driven to make sure his gifts went where they were intended to go:

> When you do this kind of [voluntary] work, it's for yourself. . . . Even though you're helping people there [in India] directly or indirectly, it's the personal satisfaction you get that is the real motivator to do this work. But second, it is to see where is the money going; is it being used appropriately? Sadly, I think when they know you're coming, they'll be a little bit more motivated to make sure it's going to the right place.

He used an unusual method to raise and transfer funds to pay for the medicines for the Indian HIV patients. As a doctor, he received surveys from drug companies to see how doctors were prescribing their medicines—and was offered between $100 and $150 a month to complete the surveys. Rather than rejecting the surveys and payment, Dr. S completed them and deposited the money in a U.S. bank account. The doctor in India, who was associated with an international medical charity (an NGO), had an ATM card that he used to withdraw those funds in India.

Dr. S considered this method of giving a kind of experiment, and he did it this way because it was *direct*. "If I go through the organization, they take 20 percent off the top," he told me. (Coincidentally, as already mentioned, this was the same percentage that Delhiites recounted as the amount requested for bribes.) Dr. S realized that if he organized his donation through the NGO, he could use the donations as a deduction on his taxes, but he felt that if he gave the money directly to the HIV patients in need through the Indian doctor, it would be more efficient. If the Indian doctor received the funds directly, he would have to go through an organization. At the same time, Dr. S had entered into an experiment that he could not easily end, for he had made a lifetime commitment to the patients in India. "Once you cover someone with HIV medicines, to say 'no' to them, would be pretty harsh," Dr. S said. He compared this lifetime commitment of providing HIV medications with his previous experience of sponsoring a child to point out the difference. With child sponsorship there was a clear endpoint to the gift—when the sponsored child grows up and the obligation of support ceases. He had sponsored several children until they graduated from their sponsorship programs and then he lost touch with them. In the past, when sponsoring children, Dr. S had also visited one of them to see "if this money was actually going to where it should be." When giving to a child sponsorship program, one's gift had lasting effects in a person's life, even after a child graduated from sponsorship. Providing HIV medicines for people afflicted with AIDS, in contrast, presented a challenge of ambiguity. Giving to AIDS patients was existentially finite—as patients would eventually die—and temporally indeterminate in terms of when the commitment would end.

Like visiting the children he had sponsored, Dr. S traveled to Delhi partly to meet with (and check up on) the Indian doctor to whom he gave money and the patients to whom the Indian doctor provided HIV medicines. After I interviewed Dr. S, he was scheduled to meet two of the patients. He was a bit ambivalent about the meeting: "Initially, I didn't want to do that, but then when he [the Indian doctor] had mentioned it as a possibility, I thought maybe it is best that I talk to the patients saying, 'Are you actually getting the meds?' . . . I'm not there to get a 'Thank you, oh thank you, doctor.' I don't want that, I just want to see, 'Are you getting your meds, are you getting them on time?' because that's essential for HIV." If there was a lapse in the medications, the patients would acquire resistance and the medicines would no longer be effective. Dr. S did not know how the Indian doctor selected the patients to support, and he was skeptical of the Indian doctor's selection criteria: "I thought they'd be treating, you know, what I would have picked myself was a widow who has children." He had his own criteria of need that did not match that of the Indian doctor; nevertheless, he trusted the Indian doctor enough to keep sending funds for the medicines.

Along with funding HIV medicines for life for these four patients, Dr. S was involved with a clinic in Ahmedabad in northern India that was treating thousands of HIV patients, each of whom paid a small fee. For Dr. S, this payment was also a type of accountability:

> It's a private clinic and you think, "Oh, they're charging money," you know, but they're doing a wonderful job charging the minimal amount. And also when people are paying, I think this is controversial, but I think they're more apt to really comply, they're more apt to listen [to] what the doctor's saying, they're

> more motivated [than] when they get everything for free. It may be a little bit, you know, sloppy with getting their medicines and stuff, but they're paying for them, they realize the value. And that's a highly controversial topic of this debate—whether we charge people or give [medicines] for free.

The clinic charged 2 or 3 rupees. As Dr. S stated, the clinic felt that the patients were more "motivated to comply with the therapy" if payment was involved. This attitude was similar to other development strategies in which those being "developed" were required to contribute some form of investment, whether labor or materials, to the development project.

Dr. S saw his work sponsoring the four patients as more efficient than NGO work. He was able to bypass the marketing costs of a large institution and give the funds internationally and directly. His primary concern was, as he said, "getting the biggest bang for my buck," that is, making his donations go the farthest. He was critical of organizations in the United States that used a lot of money for marketing, and he was proud that he had managed to bypass this by sending money directly to his friend. And this direct relationship made the direct funding possible.

On his trip to India, Dr. S also spent time in Delhi volunteering in a hospital. He arranged for a U.S. drug company to donate sixty textbooks and distribute them in the hospital. He also persuaded his medical partners in the United States to donate their old PDAs to the Indian doctors in Ahmedabad and arranged a medical software company to donate more than $1,000 of software for them. He was his own personal donor organization. He also brought over thousands of dollars worth of HIV medicines. I found this ironic, as many of these medicines were produced at a much lower cost in India. When I asked Dr. S about this, he explained that it as a form of recycling. Rather than throw out unused and unexpired medicines in the United States, he brought them to India. But this created an ethical dilemma for Dr. S; Indians were critical of this scheme because the medicines were a temporary supply. He explained:

> If I could add one year to the life of my nine-year-old daughter, I'd want it [the year of life]. If someone's offering that to me, I'd take it. . . . maybe I have enough money to pay for three years of medicine, that makes it four. I know these things are ethical dilemmas.. . . . I'm quoting one who I respect fully, he says, "I won't start a patient on any retrovirals if it's a relative that's sponsoring them because I feel that's not going to continue. Unless they can pay for it themselves, I don't start it." That's one end of the spectrum. Another is I bring over these medicines

> which may give a person even enough for three months. You know, it's up to the doctor's discretion. You know, [*he pauses*] but for instance, one of the meds I brought over, a woman had become resistant to the Indian medication. The next step up was out of her reach financially so I said, "Hey, I've got enough for a year of this newer medicine that covers this resistant virus," and so that's what we did.

Beyond the technicalities of providing medicines, for Dr. S, these relationships of accountability had the potential to transform people's ideas and to create momentum for change:

> It's something. It may be there'll be some momentum that starts from this somehow. . . . Plus, the other thing is our country is bombing Iraq and killing people right now. So here's an American face that's not doing that. Maybe there's some benefit on that. But you know, the other physicians are—I don't claim to be some messiah over here or anything. Don't get me wrong . . . I'm just wondering if maybe, maybe I'm justifying again this plane ticket. . . . but I think the more we're in contact with each other, Indians and Americans, through this means of helping, there's going to be some benefit.

The context of Dr. S's suspicion did not deter him from his hopeful outlook on international relations. He saw his actions in a wider frame, of mending bad associations.

## Performance-Based Funding and Credibility

A discussion with Mr. D, a local officer for a transnational foundation in Delhi, confirmed my hunch that in post-tsunami Delhi, mistrust of NGOs had increased. People were concerned with the questions of who to give their money to and how they would know where their money would go. In Mr. D's line of work supporting NGOs in programs of economic development through the foundation, he was suspicious: "We are permanently on guard that we are not being ripped off." The foundation did not trust the Indian financial audit system and instead arranged for an annual international audit. Mr. D's mandate was to check each NGO the foundation supported: "Are they transparent on their governing board? Do they have a gender policy? A sex harassment policy? Do governing boards meet regularly? . . . We fund organizations to help them run better and develop their capacity to be more efficient." The overarching sense of mistrust was fed by the very process of monitoring and evaluation that his foundation encouraged. For example, he said, "We have NGOs thumping on the desk, saying 'Mr. [X], you don't trust us!' But the foundation wanted to know at the end of the grant what was being achieved." He had worked with NGOs before taking up his position with the foundation, and he was familiar with monitoring and evaluation in the NGO sphere, but monitoring had moved into philanthropic practice as well. "The foundation is not happy to rest with the feeling of giving away $250 million to the world. It wants to say, with $250 million what has changed." It was focused on results. In this case, social obligation was tied to effecting change. This is key: it was not audit for the sake of audit, but audit for the sake of *change*.

Things had changed in the philanthropic community. "Board rooms have changed," Mr. D said. "There are no longer family members on boards; they have to report differently as a result." Giving was no longer kin-based, and credibility involved giving to strangers. Relief, as in post-tsunami work, had become the function of the state. In such instances, he explained, "We have to work upstream. It is an opportunity for development. We are not dealing with the wreckage—part of our money [donations] is for counseling and education, long-term support. The drive to get results is pushing us: we are saying what works and what doesn't. We [foundations] are shaping NGOs. But NGOs are smart enough to negotiate with us." At the time of our interview, the foundation gave $4 million to international NGOs with offices in India. Mr. D wanted to support Indian NGOs, because, "One million dollars goes much farther with an Indian NGO than an international NGO." This tension in the Indian NGO community was embedded in the intricacies of international politics. For example, he said, "If I give a grant to someone named Mohammed, there is so much paperwork I have to fill out to give the grant. The U.S. partners have security issues." The tentacles of the audit were everywhere—extending to the recipients of the foundation's grant, to the reasons why the foundation gave it, and to how the grant was used. The audit was embedded in the grant itself.

Mistrust was common in Mr. D's work, and it was transnationally expressed. "A parish in Amsterdam is doing local fund-raising for rural health care in India," he explained.

> The parish is giving money away for reproductive health and doesn't ask for anything in return. If I were an NGO I would operate in this first model. No. 1 says, "We give you money, I trust you." No. 2 says, "I give you money, I trust you, but I want to know what you are doing with it." We are thinking like No. 2 when working with an NGO in a remote area of Bihar. The NGO's annual budget is not more than 10 lakh rupees [approximately $20,000], but members are also members of the International Association for the Rights of Women, the Interna-

> tional Association for Tribal Rights. NGOs are not isolated; they are connected to global civil society.

These rural NGOs were as isolated as the transnational foundation that funded them, and this network of association formed a component of the audit (or, at least of accountable practice). Rural political leaders saw NGOs as *samaj sevas* (giving service to society or social service), a morally superior force in relation to villages. But the language of NGOs was changing from samaj seva to *samaj karya karta* (social activists, or literally, one who does the work). The discourse was not an abstract notion of belonging as to strangers, but a direct and engaged one built on relationships. "By working in a particular community, I claim my relationship to the larger world," Mr. D said. "People work with NGOs; through working with the tribal community, they are not building a relation to the community, but people volunteer to be in relation to a wider world."

Some NGOs resisted the foundation's quest for measurable results. The director of one NGO in particular had been refusing measurement models, and the foundation was unlikely to continue funding it. "He never gives a narrative of what he has achieved," Mr. D explained. "I understand, but I can't bring that into my boardroom. I need to give a narrative of what has changed." Without indicators of success, the foundation was compelled to measure the impossible. Measurement was an essential component of evaluating change, and of the audit itself:

> If I were in his shoes, it is exactly what I'd do [challenge the foundation], but he will not get his grant renewed. What programs like this do—including the World Bank—they use a proxy indicator and it is a proxy. They imagine it for the real. The retention of girls in school is only a proxy for the change in age of marriage. This is where philanthropy creates its myths. It uses the proxy in place of the real. The question is, is it possible to use core indicators that are transparent and are only proxies? For example, the number of condoms selling in Bihar, because money is attached. In order to obtain incentive, the condom seller has to earn revenue [buying condoms from the foundation]. Economic models say that which is measurable will create change. There is a difference between the report of condom use versus "have you bought condoms?" The purchase requires an active choice. Or, "have you bought textbooks for your daughters?" as an indicator of changing child marriage. Under the guise of economics—people think when people pay they use more, but really when people pay we can measure use better.

Monitoring and evaluation extended to the NGO and back to the donors as well. "Reporting back to the donors," Mr. D explained, "this is where you see the core of philanthropy. What kind of reporting philanthropy asks for will unpack what kind of relationship the donor has with the gift it is giving. Or, do they see it as gift giving anymore at all?" In the donor world, "performance-based funding" was a relatively new trend.

An NGO working with street children, for example, could create alternative livelihoods. For a ten-year project, the foundation might give $5 million. It would ask, "What will you achieve in year one?" After year one, the NGO would submit a report for benchmarks. If these were not achieved, then the foundation would continue with a one-year grant. If the benchmarks were achieved, then the NGO would receive a second year of funding. Mr. D explained: "We enter into a contract about this: both satisfied with what we have achieved, charting a course from point A to B. There is no possibility of there being an A that is different from the A planned. The relationship between the promise and the future is already planned." Grant proposals were also supposed to include a theory of change. How would the NGO go from point A to B? Good proposals aimed at change. With empowerment of women, for example, how does forming microcredit groups enable women to be empowered? The proposal built linkages with the market for the women to sell their goods; this was performance-based funding. It made people speculative, but at the same time it required results and was driven by the idea of indicators. What could be done was what could be measured. Mr. D struggled with these models. "What makes me decide that the grant will work is my social interaction with the individual," he said. "I see if there is a fire in their belly. Technical capacity can be trained." This will resonate with another auditor who used a formula that included gut feeling in his calculation of risk.

Many of my interviews with NGO directors took place in offices located in residential areas. I met Mr. A in a small office in one of the cement multistory apartment buildings. The Hindu mark of sandalwood paste on his forehead, or *tilak,* showed him to be a religious man, and for some reason this surprised me. Mr. A was a researcher and had been studying Indian scripture on the topic of donation and accountability. He had prepared diligently for our interview with photocopies from the newspaper, copies of his monthly organizational newsletter (called *AccountAble*), and quotes from ancient scripture. At one point during our interview, Mr. A brought a colleague, a social worker, to join our discussion.

Mr. A's organization, mentioned in Chapter 1, was a private consulting firm set up to provide accounting, financial management, and regulation compliance services for NGOs. It charged fees from donor agencies for its services. It also published *AccountAble*, which included in-depth analysis of accounting issues, and helped to organize workshops for NGOs on topics such as accounting, regulation, budgeting, reporting, and the state regulation of foreign donations. It was started in 1990 after providing consulting services for Oxfam America.

For Mr. A, the term "accountable" was insufficient in the Indian context. He sought an appropriate translation, considering *uttar dai*, which means "answerable," but then realized he was still working in what he thought to be a Western framework—when someone gives money, you are accountable to that person. Instead, he decided to use the term *lekha yog*, which is part of *yog* (which roughly translates as a combination of practice, discipline, devotion, and union; an online Hindi dictionary includes twenty-four definitions for yog). Lekha yog is not enforced by an external agency but, rather, is brought about from inside. It is a spiritual answer—being answerable from within. By spirituality, Mr. A explained, "We do not mean religion." Instead, he meant "responsibility, purity, clarity." Instead of religion, which he considered to be a particular way of worship, he considered lekha yog as *dharm*, a sense of duty or righteous path.

Following the logic of Hindu cosmology, Mr. A considered the Western world to be dependent on external regulatory logic, whereas the Eastern world was more self-regulatory. *Karm phal*—the fruit of one's action (or, as known in English, karma)—was the effect of this alternative regulatory potential. "Karm phal will find you after millions of years as a heifer will find its mother in a big herd of cows," Mr. A said. "When you do something in this life, you remain accountable for it. You will get rewards in this lifetime or the next or one hundred lifetimes later." This accountability was not restricted to this lifetime. Philanthropic action, in the Indian context (and according to Mr. A), was not philanthropic in terms of love of humankind. People gave philanthropically—in terms of dān. "Dān is your dharm," he said. Giving is a duty. This concept of dharm or duty was an action-oriented code of conduct, a spiritual duty that translated into prescriptions for daily life.

When one donates according to duty, the ideal form is secret and anonymous, or gupt dān. "When we talk about it [donation], it loses power," Mr. A said. "When we want eternal benefit we should not tell people about it." Religious ritual and prayer (*puja*) are done in private. Mr. A translated this kind of secrecy to the NGO sector in India, which discouraged announcing donations. For instance, he was critical of Microsoft founder Bill Gates, who had recently given a corporate donation of millions of dollars to help combat AIDS in India. "He was doing it because of XYZ," Mr. A said. "Corporate social responsibility is a mocking of social responsibility. When [an NGO] is working on its public image, it is not corporate social responsibility." He saw rudiments of this concept in Indian giving. "Indians won't tell you where and how they are giving. There is privacy about disclosing donations. They will not tell you."

In India an enormous number of donations take place according to religious conceptions of dān—for example, when astrological conjunctions dictate auspicious times for giving. Giving donations in secret directly conflicted with Western assumptions of transparency and accountability in the NGO sector—also known as "ethical practices." NGOs were modeled on a Western ideal. "In India, people do charity directly and locally," Mr. A said. "Organized charity is not the way. You do it and forget it." NGOs in India are structured around the Western model to take advantage of money flowing into the country, but many local NGOs are not able to tap these funds. As Mr. A said, somewhat ironically, Western agencies considered Hindu organizations as "untouchable."

When Indians donate to religious organizations, they do not get a tax break—and in this way, from the perspective of transparency and accountability, religious charity is underground and noninstrumental. The language of the external audit was not translatable to the language of Hindu donation, of inner regulation.[9] Religious giving was a self-regulating social process. In religious doctrine, Mr. A pointed out, "the money donated should be earned legitimately and should be earned after thinking of the region (or place), time, character [*patra*]. Don't give to a person who is not suitable." Meanwhile, many in the NGO world considered the funds used for religious gifts as "black money."

Mr. A had a hypothesis. He felt that charity in India was not working correctly, at the time of our interview in 2005. "In India everyone goes his own way," Mr. A said. "Charity naturally has to follow the same course," so there was not much organized charity. Mentioning in passing V. S. Naipaul's 1992 book *India: A Million Mutinies Now*, he saw charitable activity in India as vibrant and unconstrained by institutional forms and discourses of accountability. Charitable giving in India was direct and not aggregated:

> Each person has to find his own truth. There are a bewildering variety of sects and religious practices [in India]. When you have so much individualism and say charity should be organized, it does not relate with the ground reality of tradi-

> tional India. Only for people who think in English and who have been educated in a modern way, accountability arises because of the distance between the donor and the donee. In India, businesses are not on a corporate model. They are a family model. Corporations are a Western thing. We feel the problem of accountability, but in the long run India will not need money from the West. India will become a giver rather than a receiver. Two streams of work may continue: first, the Western model, which is corporate and involves accountability and distance, and second, the Indian model. We don't know what the Indian model will look like. We are not looking at a model for charity. The way Indian charity works is direct—like the corner shopkeeper. Indians do charity and do it in various ways that are not aggregated.

For Mr. A, the expenses of external auditing practice were scandalous: "The bulk of money is being wasted because of the inherent wastage of the corporate charity model; wasted on overheads. The corporate model promises efficiency, which is precisely what you don't get with the corporate model." Despite his critique, his organization was in the business of regulation and compliance. Donors paid the organization to monitor their grantees.

Mr. A was part of the dense environment of organizations in India that monitored NGOs. On an online NGO credibility forum, Mr. A discussed the task of measuring risk, which included gut feeling:

> We have been advocating that each grant carries a financial risk, just as it carries a program risk. Once we recognize that financial risk is an inseparable part of grant-making, we can look at the next step: managing the financial risk. We work with donor agencies in Risk Management of their grants, so that level of financial risk is optimised. [My organization has] designed an arithmetic model for identifying which grants are at higher relative risk. Relative risk is calculated by measuring the following three factors: the state of internal controls and accounting systems; the financial environment, which includes the environment of the state, NGO and sociocultural factors; and the gut-feel of the people monitoring the programmes (this provides cover for intuition and other subconscious factors that cannot be identified or expressed numerically). The weights to each of the three factors are adjusted from time to time. Then we look at the size of the grant. An ABCD grid is built with relative risk on one axis and relative size of the grant on the other. The projects that are at higher relative risk float up to the top. These projects are prioritized for additional inputs, financial monitoring and capacity building.[10]

Mr. A's arithmetic model integrated and calculated intuition. His organization also conducted grant-management skills with donor agencies. The critical gaze of fiscal credibility was cast upon both donors and NGOs. For Mr. A's organization, credibility involved making realistic plans—for both donors and NGOs. "To us, credibility is not about accounting standards and vouchers," Mr. A told me. "It is about doing what you say, and saying only what you can actually do. The key credibility indicator is your results against plans. The truth is that 'plans' are also susceptible to influences in the external environment, which provides another spin to the issue of credibility." Two of the external forces he mentioned were the quest for funds and media pressure. In other words, donors and the media fed a certain inflation of possibility that cultivated an environment of suspicion.

"The audit" can take many forms, not all of them bureaucratic. In a tight-knit social group there may be social pressure for ethical practice, but discourses such as media accounts of corruption by the GOI and NGOs offer a similar refrain. Such accounts paint a moral backdrop for the densely populated landscape of actors engaged in social welfare in New Delhi. I am not arguing that Delhi is more corrupt than other places, but rather that in Delhi mistrust is a more public event than giving. One trusts family and known others, but one does not automatically trust strangers. Thus forming an NGO with strangers (to avoid nepotism) and giving services to strangers (again, the neutral other) are somewhat antithetical to Indian concepts of service to society. Seva may be described as that which is carried out toward a known other, traditionally to a guru or an elder family member. One does seva for specific others as a sign of respect. There are other types of seva, to the nation for example, and voluntarism with NGOs is often discussed in these terms (also see Watt 2005).

The nexus of suspicion formed between the posh school, the slum school, the GOI, and individual patrons and donors is one example of a context for the audit. Another example is Dr. S, the American doctor who bypassed an NGO structure in order to give directly to those in need. The gift that does not require a return (dān) is one form of philanthropic practice. The gift that demands a return is another. Whether called coercion or social obligation, this form of giving also serves society, but it is not silent. It is the gift that is offered in the form of development and social services by NGOs that requires rituals of verification. Whether in the form of an internal regulatory process (lekha yog), external audits and site visits, or the demand for a receipt to track "where the money goes," the efforts of NGOs are defined by rituals of regulation. In New Delhi, this regulation is not colonized by the state, although this process is also in transition as the state attempts to gain more control over NGOs' fields of engagement and the funds that support them.

In India, one could argue, suspicion is a reaction to the liberalizing frame in which greater disparities between the rich and poor are marked by opacity as to why and how those conditions arose. I do not think this is a useful analysis. Just as witchcraft in Africa is not new—although it seemed a particularly salient discourse to anthropologists in the 1990s, including myself—perhaps it has achieved a more intense valence because of global capitalism and increasing economic and spiritual insecurity. In India, suspicion is also not new, and it is commonplace. The wealthy and the poor alike use it as an evaluative frame, to mark those whom one knows (and hence can trust) and those whom one does not. Why is the audit—rational, bureaucratic, economic—associated with truth? Why are other forms that are less verifiable, with observation being the primary vehicle for ethnographic understanding, considered alternative or occult? Both witchcraft in the African context and suspicion in the Indian context are moral languages of evaluation, of social obligation and responsibility.

Chapter 3

# Orphans

IN 2008, in the United States, a UNICEF donation campaign solicitation arrived at my doorstep. An arrow pointed to a bulge in the envelope and explained, "The enclosed nickel could save a child's life!" The plea for funds, addressed to "Dear Friend of Children," pointed to specific categories of donation, ranging from $25 up to $500, or "other," under a banner stating, "I want to do whatever it takes to save children's lives." Also included were free labels with my name and address. Like many Americans bombarded with similar requests, I usually dismiss such pleas as emotionally manipulative. And this time, after reading the brochure's concluding line—"Even if you can't make a donation today, please return the enclosed nickel as a sign of your support for children in desperate need around the world"—I could not shake the feeling that there was something distinctly uncomfortable about receiving money from a charitable organization. Realistically, I thought, if I took the time to send back the nickel, I would donate additional funds. If I did not respond to this plea, I risked becoming a moral spectator. My lack of donation made me complicit in the plight of needy children; my apathy was against humanitarianism. Yet my discomfort at the urge of engagement was itself a predicament in which inaction implicated me in a child's suffering. The power of the UNICEF appeal, and others like it, lies in the potential for evoking an emotional response. If the appeal were to inspire a donation, it would rely on the possibility of impulsive philanthropy described in Chapter 1, like the immediate response to a beggar in need. As I have shown elsewhere (Bornstein 2001), even programs of child sponsorship that rely on these emotional appeals to enlist donors support long-term development programs that aid villages and districts, not single children. The desire to assist on impulse and the desire for long-term solutions to poverty and need are both valid approaches to humanitarian aid that are often integrated in such appeals.

The children pictured in the UNICEF brochure are alone, without parents, without an explanation of their circumstances and without context. Orphaned from kin, they are in need of support. Where are their guardians, one might ask? Why are they in need? What potential economic factors have led to their situations? That these questions are neither asked nor required is a particular aspect of humanitarian appeals that focus on children and build on the humanitarian value of orphans. With this framework as my entry, I examine the relationship of orphans to the gift. We have seen that the gift is a form of ethical engagement, a part of humanitarianism, but only if the gift is free from self-interest. The call to assist an orphan builds on this assumption and engenders a specific response. Adoption of an orphan is one possible solution to the plight of abandoned children; in this alternative an orphan is transformed into kin. Provision of care by child-welfare NGOs and the state in an orphanage is a second possible solution, and child sponsorship is a third. Of these three alternatives, the second two are sites for giving dān in India. Between these avenues of possible assistance lies a contentious moral terrain where the secular Indian state, as guardian of its citizens, acts as a mediating force to limit adoption, protect orphans, and encourage donation as a form of ethical engagement. While anthropological definitions of orphans may draw upon the notion of being bereft of kin, children are also orphaned by poverty—when conditions make parents unable to care for their children. The fact that parents see abandonment as a viable alternative when faced with extreme poverty is an important part of this picture.

India, when envisaged as a nation of poverty and need, is a fertile site for philanthropic activity toward children; a short search on the Internet yields myriad websites that encourage and facilitate donation to orphans. One such site maintained by the Hindu reform movement Arya Samaj offers a "Charity for Children" page with pictures and profiles of children.[1] Through the website one can choose a child and—with no more information than a picture, a date of birth, a name of a village, and maybe a sentence or two of comment—sponsor that child with online donations. The website for GiveIndia, under the category "Child Welfare," offers a list of "Donation Options" that include providing for such things as education, living expenses, clothes, food, and medical expenses. Each donation option is correlated with a particular NGO and an amount—between 750 and 14,800 rupees.[2] One can click on "add to cart" and "purchase" the donation.[3]

Understanding the Hindu aspects of dān given to orphans and Hindu laws surrounding adoption are essential for understanding how the gift to an orphan becomes a viable form of humanitarianism in India. The notion of dān, like all cultural forms, is vibrant and changing. In my research, I found that people preferred to give dān to organizations such as orphanages where they could "see the results over time" and "make spontaneous visits" instead of giving dān to a pundit or priest at a temple. In this way, the orphanage, through dān, becomes a sacred social space. As we will see, some donors also considered their donations to schools for the education of impoverished children to be a form of dān. Here, we can see that dān is more than a scriptural reference; it is lived practice. It is also a form of donation, like responses to the funding plea marked by the nickel from UNICEF. In New Delhi, orphanages have recently emerged as ideal places for people to give dān as donation without any expectation of return. Recall that dān is to be given to strangers, not to kin, and orphanages provide ideal sites for this. New Delhiites gave service (seva) at orphanages in the form of volunteering, they donated used clothing, and they made monthly payments to sponsor children. Some Indians sponsored the weddings of orphans through a particularly sacred form of dān called *kanyā dān*, which means the gift of a virgin and involves the ritual of marrying off one's daughter.

## The Value of Orphans

Orphans play a significant part in the discourse of humanitarianism, meriting analysis of the category itself. While the UNICEF plea does not specifically refer to orphans, it refers to children who need to be cared for, of which the orphan is the most extreme case. As a humanitarian social category, orphans are valued—particularly in the "humanitarianism as a politics of life" that seeks to assist victims of humanity (Fassin 2007). For UNICEF, orphans fall under a combined category of "orphans and vulnerable children," or OVC. The number of children orphaned globally is astounding. According to UNICEF's "State of the World's Children 2006," "at the end of 2003, there were an estimated 143 million orphans under the age of 18 in 93 developing countries. More than 16 million children were orphaned in 2003 alone" (UNICEF 2006). Some argue that the category of the orphan in humanitarian assistance has been overemphasized because of the powerful reaction it inspires from donors

(Henderson 2007; Meintjes and Giese 2007). In Africa, for example, children orphaned by HIV and AIDS live in contexts of historically fluid guardianship due to rural-urban circulatory labor migration. This condition has led to a statistical overemphasis on orphans and is an injustice to the complex experiences and survival strategies of destitute children. Scholars such as Patricia Henderson (2007), Helen Meintjes and Sonja Giese (2007), and Didier Fassin (2008) convincingly argue that an orphan's socioeconomic status may not be worse than the status of other children who live under social deprivation and exclusion caused by conditions of extreme poverty.[4]

An orphan's status has historically said more about poverty and need than about abandonment. In line with work that explores changing conceptions of children and childhood (Stephens 1995; Zelizer 1985), Lydia Murdoch's (2006) book *Imagined Orphans* explores attitudes toward orphans in Victorian England. She points out, as with the case of orphans in India and other well-documented cases of orphans in southern Africa, that most Victorian orphans were not "full" orphans; that is, their parents had placed the children in institutions for periods of time because of life circumstances such as illness, the death of one parent, injury, and poverty. In other words, they were not necessarily given up entirely. Although most of the children in Victorian state and charitable institutions were not orphaned or deserted, social reformers represented them to the public as either parentless or victims of parental abuse. Photography was an important medium for engaging the public in Victorian programs of social welfare, with "before" and "after" pictures documenting melodramatic transformations of savage waifs into reformed and civilized British citizens. What is salient about this example from Victorian England is the disjunction between the popular representation of Victorian poor children as orphans and the ways that families strategically used state and private philanthropic welfare services. While reformers represented poor children as orphaned and endangered by abusive and "demonic" parents, the adult poor were the ones being excluded from the national community. Thus, in the political economy of orphans and humanitarianism, when one thinks about orphans, one must also consider the parents who are economically excluded through their poverty.

## Children of the Nation

An estimated forty-four million destitute children live in India, more than twelve million of them orphans. These statistics might imply a booming national adoption program, but the number of annual official adoptions in India is estimated to be very low—one NGO estimates only five thousand.[5] Herein lies a puzzle. Why are so few children being adopted in India when so many are in "need" of adoption? Reflecting the potential "need" for children to be adopted, a case study by Catalysts for Social Action documents that approximately three hundred NGOs are working on the issue of adoption in India. Adoption in this case becomes a cause for NGO activism. Members of India's NGO community advocate for the rights of children and for the care of abandoned children as a right in relation to the state. In this dynamic context, NGOs become a voice for abandoned children and speak on their behalf. In 2005, the NGO Child Relief and You (CRY) initiated a national advocacy program on quality institutional care and alternatives, the premise of which was that the ideal environment for children is the family, not institutions.[6] CRY advocated for standards of quality care, for the deinstitutionalization of children, and for efforts to prevent institutionalization. If parents and children must be separated, the separation should be as brief as possible, with the ultimate goals being either to restore children to their families or to rehabilitate them into communities (CRY 2005: 3).[7]

Historically, joint families and caste groups in India provided a community of care for children without parents. However, a CRY study documented how, with the disintegration of the joint family system, the crumbling of caste groups, urbanization, and the consolidation of industrial capitalism, "the extension of the state interventions in the community process as well as on the lives of individuals, saw the withering away of the cushion space for such children" (CRY 2005: 4). The state, which was strengthened as a sociopolitical institution in the nineteenth century, built secular and temporary "homes for children" in a process connected to the growth and emergence of reform schools and prisons. Residence in these state-sponsored institutions for abandoned children, with the state as guardian, was seen as a temporary solution for care. Since the emergence of these institutions, new legislation, such as the Juvenile Justice Act (2000), has introduced noninstitutional alternatives such as adoption and foster care.

Although child-rights NGOs such as CRY advocate for unprotected and abandoned children, not everyone agrees that adoption is an ultimate humanitarian cause. When I met with the director of the Central Adoption Resource Agency (CARA; a department of the Ministry of Social Justice and Empowerment), the national agency responsible for coordinating adoptions in India,[8] I tried to describe my research interests on charity in India. "What does charity have to do with adoption?" the director asked. Our interview was notably brief.

I asked why there were so many difficulties for foreign parents who wanted to adopt children from India, and she replied, "They are our children, so we give the preference to our people first." I interviewed her with a friend of mine, an American who was trying to adopt an Indian child. The government officer seemed irritated by our presence and referred us to the CARA website for instructions on adoption. International adoption was not something one could address in that particular office in New Delhi; foreigners who wanted to adopt had to go through an adoption agency in their country of national origin.

In the spectrum of care that is possible for abandoned children, adoption is one possible outcome, and it is contested terrain in India. As already mentioned, the orphan, as a social category, represents the destitute, the abandoned, the excluded, and the unwanted. With no one to care for them, orphans are assumed to be free of kin ties, and in this manner, they inspire everyone in the social body to care for them through humanitarian action..

While some anthropologists no longer consider kinship a useful analytical category, especially after David Schneider's critique (1980, 1984), others have reinvigorated the study of kinship as a social process through an analysis of "cultures of relatedness" (Carsten 2000) and alternative families (Weston 1991). Some have used the social relationships that emerge through new reproductive technologies (Franklin and Ragone 1998; Franklin and McKinnon 2001; Konrad 2005; Ragone 1994; Ragone and Twine 2000) or international adoption (Modell 1994, 2002; Bowie 2004; Volkman 2005; Yngvesson 2002, 2004) to rethink the social categories of kinship. John Terrell and Judith Modell (1994) argue that studying adoption as a category of meaning has the potential to shed light on ideas of family, ethnicity, belonging, and citizenship. Adoption is about who belongs and how; it is a social transaction, a "social fiction," as Jack Goody so aptly wrote in 1969, that involves fundamental beliefs about persons. This social fiction, legislated by states, articulates the value of particular human beings in an international context and speaks to issues of kinship in humanitarian assistance. Notably, discourses of humanitarianism that highlight children fail to represent both the social conditions of poverty that compel parents to abandon their children and existing kin relations.

Although the word "orphan" may imply an unparented and therefore unprotected child, in India, the government- and NGO-run orphanages have officially taken over the role of guardian so that orphans become children of the nation, with certain rights and responsibilities. Children occupy a symbolic position with regards to the state, which orients itself as a modern entity and a protector of children's rights. Writing about the history of the Turkish state, Kathryn Libal (2001) notes that children are living, symbolic indices of "modernity" and that support for child rights by the state is the "symbolic pronouncement of sovereignty and legitimacy of the nation state" (38). For the state, the issue of children's welfare in nationalist discourse can also be used to highlight social injustice in society more broadly. Children become "seers of truth" and ambassadors of peace, visionaries of a common humanity (Malkki 2010).

Related issues are those of child labor and compulsory education. In 2009, India passed the Right of Children to Free and Compulsory Education Act. Through the care of children, with education as a right and a legally enforced (compulsory) duty, the state solidified its role as guardian of its citizens and legislated education as a form of development. Before this legislation, children were considered economic assets for poor families (Weiner 1991). It was argued that the poor needed the income of the children's labor to survive. We see here how a modernizing state does not mean a less active state. As India grows in the global economy, the state has not relinquished control of all areas of social life. Orphanages, as schools, are temporary sites for the care of children for parents who lack the means or ability to educate their children. Before the 2009 legislation, the orphanage schools were a welcome alternative to compulsory, national education policy.

The status of Indian orphans as children of the nation has made India a less likely country from which one can adopt. This may be part of a larger trend. At the time of this writing, a global movement against international adoption was growing: in 2006, for example, China added more stringent guidelines in terms of age and income for prospective adoptive parents. Skepticism has also grown in places such as Guatemala because of the influx of foreign parents wanting to adopt and the incentive of rural poor to sell their children to adoption brokers (Lacey 2006). In India's contemporary secular state, different legal procedures must be followed according to adoptive parents' nationality and religious identity before an orphan can be adopted. The Hindu Adoptions and Maintenance Act of 1956 (Diwan 2000) governs Indians who identify as Hindu, Buddhist, Jain, Sikh, or atheist.[9] The Guardians and Wards Act of 1890 governs the guardianship of orphans for Muslims, Christians, Parsis, and Jews as well as governs foreign adoptions. An orphan's religious identity, however, is not always clear. As subjects of secular legislation, orphans embody a more generic humanity that must be translated for adoption purposes into particular legal identities. In 2005, when I asked the administrator of an Arya Samaj/Hindu orphanage in an upscale neighborhood of south New Delhi whether any of the children were Muslim, he replied: "I don't think any Muslim child ever came here, but you never know. An orphan is an orphan." Orphans in the humanitarian imagination code as "pure humanity" unmarked by kin relations.

There is an affective dimension to an orphan's exclusion. Orphans give rise to a politics of pity (Boltanski 1999; Cartwright 2005). Once abandoned, they contrast with the bonds of belonging characterized by kin. Orphans have no one, and in this status, they inspire humanitarian assistance. When a child is adopted, that child is uprooted from biological kin ties and transplanted into a new social family. Like the refugee in the family of nations (Malkki 1995), the orphan is assumed to be exiled from kin. Neither here nor there, the orphan reenters society as a "member" only after rites of passage, rituals, and ceremonies, such as adoption, have been performed. Both refugees and orphans allude to the temporality of their status: that is, refugees will be repatriated, for example, and become citizens again, and orphans will be adopted and become kin again. However, like refugees in permanent refugee camps, some orphans remain in orphanages, which, as boarding schools, are a far better alternative than destitution.

In order to understand why and how the Indian state mediates the care and adoption of orphans, it is helpful to know how legislation regarding adoption and the care of orphans in India has changed historically from a focus on the needs of adoptive parents to the needs of adopted children. Before 1956, when the Hindu Adoptions and Maintenance Act was passed, adoption was governed by Hindu scripture and colonial legislation. Adoptions in India were of sons and took place between close relations. The 1956 act allowed for adoption outside of families and the adoption of girls and of orphans. In order to distinguish this postindependence legal context from its historical antecedent, I elaborate here upon scriptural practice—especially the ways in which it both informs contemporary legislation and differs from it.

In Hinduism, having a son is spiritually and materially important and has historically been an impetus for child adoption. In her study of sixteen adoption agencies in India, Shalini Bharat (1993) writes:

> According to the Hindu scriptures, a man is born with three debts—debt to *rishis* [sages or saints], debt to gods, and debt to one's ancestors. The debt to *rishis* is paid by studying the *Vedas*, the debt to gods by offering sacrifices and the debt to one's *pitra* or ancestors, by the birth of a male child. The son is required for conducting the last rights of the parent(s) without which it is believed, the soul

> would not attain *moksha* [liberation]. The son is also valued for continuing the family line and ensuring perpetuation of the name of one's ancestors. Thus, in the Hindu religion, it is the supreme duty of the son to solemnize the final rites of the parents and ensure continuity of family lineage. Besides this "spiritual" requirement of a male child, there is a secular or social desire to inherit and manage the family property. (5)

Bharat documents how the scriptural bias for sons continues in current practice. This may be due to the fact that in northern India, female children are bigger burdens on poor parents because of the need for dowries.[10] One of the largest contemporary orphanages in New Delhi is called Palna (the cradle). Outside the tall gates of the orphanage is a cradle where babies can be placed in the middle of the night. Giving and taking a child, adoption in the case of orphans, occurs on sacred territory. This is especially true in Hinduism, where sons are necessary for the spiritual merit of a person; if one does not have a legitimate son, one must adopt one.[11] In my fieldwork, sons were adopted first: most of the older children waiting for adoption at Mother Teresa's Missionaries of Charity orphanage and at Palna were girls, adding a gendered dimension to adoption practice in India.

Historically, in ancient Hindu law (see Manu 1991, cited in Diwan 2000: 87), adoption occurred within families through a ceremony of "giving and taking." The filial relation of an adopted son was created by proper ceremonies of adoption (*dattaka mimansa*), which included the acceptance of the child and the performance of a ritual called *dattak-homa*.[12] The filial relation of the adopted son occurred only by performance of the proper ceremonies, of gift, acceptance, and homa. The courts viewed the ceremony of giving and taking as mandatory and enough to validate an adoption. For filial relation, it was necessary that after the adoption the child was treated as a son (as the law was for males). The mere placing of the registered deed of adoption was not sufficient; the child placed under adoption had to be given and taken.[13] During the British Raj these practices continued. Since only fathers and mothers could give children for adoption, orphans could not be adopted; the adopter had to be Hindu (either male or female); and the adoptive parent could not adopt more than one son and one daughter.

In 1956, the Hindu Adoptions and Maintenance Act was passed in a post-war international context marked by an increase of displaced, abandoned, and orphaned children and a correlative new humanitarian concern for these children. Only at this point was adoption seen in India as a humanitarian solution

(Bharat 1993). The social reforms initiated after Indian independence included a shift in the language of care of destitute children from "charity" to "welfare" and led to an increase in welfare services for children. This may have been related to the growth of welfare programs for children in the West and their influence on Indians returning to India after working abroad. The Hindu Adoptions and Maintenance Act made it possible for a couple to adopt a female child, for single females to adopt an orphan, and for adoption to take place outside a family-caste group.

Most importantly for the purposes of my argument regarding humanitarianism and orphans, the Hindu Adoptions and Maintenance Act transformed adoption from a practice within a related group to a welfare practice among strangers. From the act's inception, foreigners adopted the majority of children. This was attributed to cultural factors, primarily the social stigma of adoption in India, which marked couples as infertile (Bharadwaj 2003) and inspired anxiety about the child's past and his or her potential undesirable traits (Bharat 1993).[14] The stipulations regarding people who may be adopted by the Hindu Adoptions and Maintenance Act is simply that they be Hindu, have not been adopted already, have not been married, and are not yet fifteen years of age.[15] Although in ancient Hindu law, caste was a determinant category in adoption (see the *Dharmashastra*), in the 1956 act caste and subcaste were no bar to adoption. Caste was not discussed in my fieldwork although some people I interviewed mentioned that families would try to find a child that phenotypically resembled the adoptive parents—further building a narrative of potential kin and belonging. I observed one Indian family returning to Mother Teresa's Missionaries of Charity orphanage with the child they had adopted, visiting the nuns who had arranged the adoption. The mother, a bit overweight and visibly content, continually kissed the adopted daughter during the visit. When the family left, the sisters excitedly remarked how the child looked just like her adoptive parents and joked that even her skin had become darker to match theirs. The fact that these people resembled a biological family was a compliment in an ultimate kinship narrative of success.

The 1956 act originally stated that a guardian could give a child for adoption only if the parents were dead or had "completely and finally renounced the world" or had been "declared by a Court of competent jurisdiction to be of unsound mind" (Diwan 2000: 74). In 1962, this legislation was amended to include abandoned children or those with unknown parentage. This amendment enlarged both the category of possible children to be adopted and possible guardians to include those appointed by courts, such as managers, secretaries, or others in charge of an orphanage. An attempt was made to impose uniform adoption law in India with the Adoption of Children Bill of 1972, which was opposed by minority communities (particularly Muslims; see Bharadwaj 2003; Bharat 1993). The bill was allowed to lapse in 1976. In 1984, the Supreme Court of India further codified processes for adopting children by creating specific government agencies tasked with oversight of all adoptions. A new requirement was implemented for orphans to be certified abandoned by the state before adoption could be considered an option. A marked increase in Indian adoptions took place between 1977 and 1987, which corresponded to a decrease in international adoptions. In 1977, 80 percent of adoptions were by foreigners and fewer than 20 percent were by Indians; one decade later, adoptions by Indians had increased to 50 percent, and adoptions by foreigners decreased to 50 percent (Bharat 1993: 119).

In this landscape, transnational or domestic adoption is not the only possible outcome. Some orphans are kept in orphanages, and, as already mentioned, the state becomes their legal guardian. Another method of care for orphans is social adoption, in which the state remains the legal guardian and an individual or family unrelated to the orphan economically supports the child's education and care. This practice is in line with other forms of sponsorship found in programs of economic development and humanitarianism, such as those in which a donor sponsors a child or a village.

However, as we have already mentioned, what is often not considered, but is extremely important in understanding the figure of the orphan in humanitarian aid, is the relation of orphans to poverty. Many children who are defined as orphans have not lost both parents. In Delhi, as elsewhere in India and perhaps throughout the world, parents place their children in institutions because of poverty. Although not the extreme form of abandonment caused by parental death, poverty has the potential to strain ties between people and create social exclusion. When one looks closely at the orphan as a figure in humanitarian discourse, one begins to see a symbol of "the excluded," which is an important part of the pathos that orphans engender. Sometimes these placements are temporary because of the loss of one parent or because the child's family is weathering difficult economic circumstances.[16] As a stopgap welfare strategy, an orphan's status may not be a permanent phenomenon (see Fassin 2008b). Orphans who cannot be adopted—which is the case for many who live in Delhi's orphanages—are children whose parents are destitute but who have not abandoned them. A study by Noor Jahan Siddiqui on adolescent girls in four orphanages in Delhi indicated that 52 percent of the residents were "partially orphaned" girls, meaning that one parent was deceased (1997: 43–45). In the case of the remaining girls, the reasons listed for entrance into an orphanage were either that both parents were dead (36 percent), lost, or unknown or that the parents were extremely poor (26 percent). In 53 percent of the cases, mothers brought the girls to the orphanages; in 25 percent, distant relatives; and in almost 13 percent, the police brought in children they found abandoned. In India, orphanages are also often boarding schools. Fatherless girls are sent to these schools, which also arrange for their marriages. Relatives may visit on weekends during certain visiting hours.[17] As Siddiqui's study attests, poverty also orphans children.

## The Orphanage as a Sacred Site for Giving

While researching giving practices in Delhi, I soon made orphanages my locus for study, although I did not initially set out to investigate them. As a participant observer, I made repeat visits to three orphanages and interviewed people who came to donate goods and time, as well as those who managed, directed, and facilitated the daily operations of the institutions. At first I was dismayed that I did not get to know the orphans at all. This was partly due to my interest in humanitarianism and giving and partly due to the fact that I did not live at the orphanages and did not confine my research to one particular institution. With my ethnographic attention more diffuse, my presence was always novel and I never became "part of the group." I was perhaps seen to be a foreign donor, certainly a foreign researcher. Sometimes I visited with a research assistant, sometimes I visited alone. In all cases, when I spoke with children living in the orphanages about their lives, they were reluctant to talk about the past. In one case, one of the wardens of the orphanage told me not to ask questions about the pasts of either the orphans or the women who worked there because my questions might upset them. Many women who worked in the orphanages were themselves destitute or had been abandoned by their families. When I asked the children about their lives, they gave me simple answers in both English and Hindi. Sentences like "everything is fine here" or "we like it here very much" raised methodological challenges regarding the difficulty of studying recipients of humanitarian aid ethnographically. Because of the danger of "looking a gift horse in the mouth" or "biting the hand that feeds you," it was difficult for me to obtain information about humanitarian aid from those who may have been critical of it but at the same time depended on it and did not want to jeopardize its continuation. In addition, the institutional nature of the orphanages—some were gated, all were highly monitored—did not allow for objectification. I was not permitted to take pictures, for example. This is an important part of the ethnography of humanitarianism that may require anthropologists to rethink what it means to study a group partially, as part of a larger group more fully, over time.

One institution in which I spent a great deal of time in south Delhi was an Arya Samaj orphanage for girls aged eleven to twenty-one. The compound was a calm oasis that had tall gates sheltering its residents from the hustle and bustle of the busy urban streets; it was well maintained, with a manicured lawn and a guard who restricted visitors. Built in 1967, it contained a residential girls' hostel (the boys' hostel was located in north Delhi), a school, and a naturopathic health clinic and hospital. One part of the compound housed a stall for cows, where veterinarians from an organization called "Love for Cow Trust" came daily to take care of them. Girls received cow milk every day, and a wealthy woman fed the cows regularly.

Private donations provided most of the funding for the orphanage, which was registered as a charitable trust; approximately fifteen hundred members gave to it, many of them through regular monthly dān of 10 to 10,000 rupees or more. In the orphanage, girls learned skills such as sewing and tailoring alongside their academic lessons. A director of the orphanage described it as "a house for all those children who don't have anybody in this world." At the entrance, a blackboard listed donation requests under the heading "Hostel's Requirements," which included various food items, tea, dishwashing and bathing soap, cloth, shoes, stationery, and bags. Donations were often given in-kind (for which, like religious donation, there is no tax benefit in India). One day, as I sat in the office chatting with the staff, I noticed a pile of bags filled with donated clothes. On a subsequent visit three men rifled through another pile of used clothes that had been given to the staff for distribution. When I inquired about taking a picture, I was reprimanded by a warden and told no, that this aspect of donation was private: "This is our internal matter. It all comes through dān and they [recipients] collect it." Dān, as we have seen, is best when anonymous.

Out of approximately three hundred girls in residence, only fifty to sixty were "full orphans" without any surviving parents; these children had all been socially adopted by Indians who paid for their care and visited them at specific times. Those who socially adopted the children (as a form of dān) bore the girls' monthly expenses. They met the girls whom they sponsored once a month, or at the time of festivals to give them gifts, although there was no obligation for them to do so and it was up to sponsors to initiate such visits. The warden explained that social adoption aimed to provide "emotional security for the child." The orphanage decided which of the resident girls were most eligible for social adoption, and the warden described them as "intelligent" and girls who "don't have anybody." An NGO I visited had socially adopted eighteen of the girls at this orphanage, and one elite school in Delhi required each of the teachers to socially adopt one child. Through schemes of social adoption or sponsorship, the state in partnership with the NGO became the guardian of its excluded. I asked the warden of the NGO (which was called a *vidyalaya,* or school, not an orphanage) why the institution did not allow formal adoptions. She explained, "People used to adopt children from here, but they didn't care for them and brought them back when they had their own [children]." Other staff members told me of children running away from their adoptive parents back to the school. At the time of my research and for the previous thirty-five years, the school permitted only social adoption.

For those girls who were not full orphans and who still had a living parent, their local guardians visited them on the first Sunday of each month. Others who did not socially adopt girls also donated in the form of dān at the time of religious festivals or on special occasions such as birthdays or on the anniversary of a death of a family member. Certain festivals required giving gifts to children, and in the absence of one's own children, some gave to the children in the orphanage. The logic of dān applied here as well: people gave for *punya* (merit); as one woman explained, "whatever is given in this birth will be returned in the next birth."

Volunteers also donated their labor and time at the orphanage (also see Chapter 4). One woman, who visited with her daughter and brought an elderly resident woman a white sari as a gift, told me: "I try to come a minimum of four to five times a year. I try to do a little bit. I'm not giving to them; God is giving to all of us." She added that she visited the orphanage without informing anyone. "Some people call up and ring and ask what do you need? I am not of the business class. I am of the service class; I'm not working. I love this place. I don't know, I find it very genuine." She had collected donations from her friends and was distributing them. She came to serve the girls "with my own hands," she said. "It was a beautiful experience."

The orphanage also served as a site for kanyā dān—the form of dān that occurs when one marries off a daughter. Those who did not have daughters to marry sponsored the marriage of an orphan, and the orphanage organized these marriages. The institution paid for a matrimonial advertisement, the staff interviewed potential grooms, and girls could voice their preference before matches were made. Once a groom agreed to marry a resident, the orphanage required him to deposit 5,000 rupees in a bank account in her name and then sought donors to sponsor the wedding, which included paying for bridal jewelry and a marriage feast. When I asked whether it was difficult to find husbands for the girls, the warden exclaimed:

> They [donors] always volunteer themselves for this kind of service as kanyā dān, which is considered the biggest dān in one's life. The arrangement cost goes up to one lakh [100,000 rupees], which is paid for by the person who sponsors the marriage. Sponsors also ask about the well-being of the girl from time to time to see if she is happy or not. It is a kind of sponsorship where they try to fund as much as they can.

Boys outside the orphanage considered the girls in the orphanage as marriageable partners because of their good moral character. The warden said, "Boys from rich families also come here because they don't find girls of good character outside." The girls who married were well educated and had finished their studies before they were allowed to marry.

I also met women who worked in the orphanage, and even some who had been raised there. One woman was married but returned to live and work at the orphanage with her two children. Many of the destitute women who worked there lived with their biological children, who were also residents. Mataji, the sari-clad woman in white from the introduction who had been living at the orphanage for thirty-five years since her husband had died, lived with her grandchild there. Other women who lived in the institutional setting were not able to care for their children, and some of those children were given up for adoption. For some of the resident children, family-type relations emerged in the institutional setting. I asked one woman who grew up in the orphanage and had returned to visit whether she missed her mother when she lived there. She pointed to Mataji and said: "She is my mother. She is very good, and she has given her life here."

The orphanage was a socially sacred space. Certain themes emerged both in a brochure for the orphanage and in comments left in a visitor's book, reinforcing the protected nature of the orphanage as an ideal site for donation. A doctor commented on the importance of the orphanage to the nation: "This is a very concrete example of nation building and development. This institution's selfless and dedicated service deserves praise. I am confident that this organisation's whole hearted services and devotion will produce people to build up our nation. I give my warm wishes to the management here. These kinds of institutions are really required." Other visitors wrote similarly positive comments:

> After having a look at this institution of Arya Samaj, their management, cheerful faces of children, I feel that this is the heaven on earth. This is an inspiration and an example for human society.
>
> This organization is really helping the needy children and thus it is equivalent to god.
>
> I have felt really nice after coming and looking through the work of the people here, where human morals are being worshiped, this place is really sacred.
>
> To manage god's creation is in itself a great work but turning something ugly into a beautiful thing, making an orphan to feel un-orphaned is a great work.
>
> This is not a school, it's a temple.

One visitor stressed the "moral character of the students," which this person considered the "best example of serving humanity." Another called the site a "moral shelter." Visitors lauded the task of running the orphanage, done with "selfless service" and "living for others." We see here how the orphanage, as a humanitarian space, is also a sacred space, where helping others is a form of worshiping god: "Here education is imparted to make people great. Poor orphaned helpless children are being helped here which is to be praised. This is a great worship of god." But it was a modest and quiet form of help without fanfare, and this is why those who came to give appreciated it: "Here the services are done secretively without any publicity to be praised," as one visitor remarked. Although the orphanage was neither a temple nor a religious site, it was a site for dan.

## Orphans in a Global Frame: Adoption Scandals

In the Indian context, where Hindu ideas of dān make orphanages good sites for giving, the global political economy of orphan care reinforces this protected social space. However, when financial transactions enter the assistance of orphans across national borders, the adoption of orphans intersects the terrain of human trafficking (see Jamal 2005). A celebrity media context frequently sets the backdrop for scandals relating to adoption. On 1 January 2008, the *Times of India* ran a short piece about the singer Madonna vacationing in India. Titled "Madonna in Jodhpur to Ring in the New Year," the five-paragraph article began with a description of Madonna, her family, and five family friends celebrating the New Year at a "private heritage resort" in Rajasthan. The third paragraph was short and abrupt: "Sources in London have revealed that the 49-year-old singer and her husband Guy Ritchie have sent aides to hunt the Asian country for a new daughter." One can imagine agents scouring India for the predatory and wealthy humanitarian music star. The article continued with a comparison of Madonna and Angelina Jolie (another "mother without borders"), who adopted a son from "the poor country" of Cambodia in 2002 and wanted to adopt from Malawi but had "changed her decision because of the difficult adoption procedures there." The last paragraph described how Madonna also had adopted a child from Malawi but added that the adoption had not yet been formalized. Madonna's adoption of her Malawian son had gained notoriety and become a scandal when the boy's biological father announced to the press that he had not realized the adoption would take his son away forever and that it meant "giving up his son for good."[18]

Nor is Angelina Jolie a stranger to adoption scandal. With children adopted from Cambodia, Ethiopia, and Vietnam, and three biological children of her own, Jolie appears to live the humanitarian ideal she promotes as a UNHCR (UN Refugee Agency) Goodwill Ambassador. A cover story for the magazine *In Touch Weekly* (26 November 2007) titled "Zahara's Family Wants Her Back" featured pictures of Jolie, her adopted Ethiopian daughter Zahara, and "the woman who claims to be her birth mother." The story narrated the tragic tale of how Zahara's biological mother was raped by a stranger who broke into her home. Unable to care for the child while working as a laborer, she ran away from her home and left the child with her mother, who could not afford to keep her and took her to an orphanage. Government papers used in the adoption identified the child as being orphaned because of AIDS in the family. If one looks carefully at the narrative of abandonment, one sees that it is not only the Ethiopian child who was abandoned. The state of desperate poverty that led Zahara's mother to abandon her child is an instance of society's abandonment of the mother. That a foreign, wealthy movie star could claim the abandoned child as her own is a critical factor in the political economy of orphans and humanitarianism.

In India, one condition of legal adoption is that there can be no payment. The transformation of an orphan as a member of the family of humanity into a member of a particular family cannot involve a financial transaction. This speaks to the ritual purity of the process of adoption and the transformative potential inherent in the change of status from orphan to kin. In India, the court may attach conditions to an adoption order, such as the payment of the upkeep of the child, the actual cost that a guardian has spent from his or her own pocket. The 1956 Hindu Adoptions and Maintenance Act stipulates that in adoptions, "the applicant seeking permission has not received or agreed to receive, and that no person has made or given or agreed to make or give to the applicant any payment or reward in consideration of the adoption" (Section 9[5], cited in Diwan 2000: 75). This requirement provides a clear categorical distinction between adoption and human trafficking or organ trafficking, which are illegal. A 2004 law limiting organ donation and transplantation in India to blood relatives and close family friends marks the distinction between giving to strangers and giving to kin: no money may exchange hands. Thus, like the organ-donor market that distinguishes the loving act of helping a family member in need from the sale of body parts, the sacred category of the orphan in Hindu law stands in profane contrast to the "adoption market."

Two adoption scandals—one broadcast on National Public Radio in 2007 for a U.S. audience and the other a cover story in a weekly news magazine in India in 2005—are exemplars of the profane equation of money and adoption. The first example details the experience of the Smolin family, who adopted two adolescent girls from India in 1998.[19] When the girls arrived at the Atlanta airport from India, Mrs. Smolin noted that "they were clearly very upset. They were avoidant of us and then eventually they became very emotionally disturbed. . . . I've never seen anyone—and I hope to never, ever see anyone again—as upset as those girls were in the first nine months that they were in our home." Although the girls had been described by the adoption agency as children who had been waiting for a long time for a home, the girls themselves insisted that they had been stolen from their mother. The girls' story was true: their impoverished mother had placed the children temporarily in an orphanage, which then had sold them. The orphanage told the girls' biological mother that they had been sent temporarily to a boarding school. When she returned to see them, however, she was told the girls were not permitted to see her. The orphanage director was later jailed on charges of selling babies. Years later, the Smolins contacted a social activist in India who tracked the girls' mother down with information from the adopted girls about their Indian mother's name and village. The Smolins arranged a reunion of the girls with their biological mother, although by that time the two girls were in their mid to late teens. Mr. Smolin told of the reunion:

> It was really one of the most moving things that I've seen. When Manjula [one of the girls] returned and met her mom, the mom took her in her arms and she wept. And then she started to chant in her own language the whole story of her life. She said that I bore you, I nursed you, I carried you, I raised you, and I lost you. And now, you've been reborn to me. And she said this in this kind of chanting, weeping way as she held her child.

The girls, however, chose not to return to India permanently. When her biological mother asked Manjula to come live with her, Manjula told her, "No, I can't do that. I want to get a job." Mrs. Smolin continued, "And Manjula's trying to explain to her mom why she just doesn't feel comfortable anymore in her own village with her own mother, in her own culture with her own language." The story of loss and reunion is also the story of the permanent transformation of the girls' citizenship from Indian to American. The girls had been orphaned from their history.

The second example is from a May 2005 cover story in India's national magazine *Frontline* that presented a series of eight articles exposing the underbelly of international adoption. The details of this exposé include some moral assumptions about the value of humanity, which the Indian adoption laws are set up to protect. The cover story investigated "a multi-billion-dollar, countrywide racket in inter-country adoption of children." It was not focused on adoption within India, but rather on international adoption, which is significant not because adoption within India does not exist, but because international adoption practices expose a particular ethical political economy of adoption. The *Frontline* articles mention the arrest of kidnappers who "sold over 350 children" and document how "trade in inter-country adoptions . . . appears to be a roaring business for some unscrupulous agencies." The buying and selling of babies, "the commodification of children," contrasts with the sacred value of attachments, which is symbolically elucidated via orphans unattached to kin.

One article titled "The Adoption Market" detailed how

> some unscrupulous agencies made India an international baby shopping centre. . . . Papers are forged and guidelines violated as babies are matched rapidly with

> foreign parents. Touts of private adoption agencies hunt for vulnerable families. Often, the mother has little negotiating power. For as little as Rs. 150–500, a newborn is handed over to touts who are paid about Rs. 6000 a baby by the agencies. Mothers who go to reclaim their babies are turned away. Some agencies look the other way from the trafficking, stealing, and buying of babies.

The "adoption market" structured a moral accounting of purpose that juxtaposed parents from developed nations against those from developing nations. As one article explained, demand grew for children in developed nations due to "fertility declines, the greater availability of contraceptive aids, the legalization of abortion, higher participation of women in the workforce, the rise in the age of marriage, the postponement of childbirth and state support for single mothers." In developing nations like India, supply rose due to "an increasing number of orphaned and abandoned children because of poor and worsening socioeconomic conditions"—namely, increasing poverty. This socioeconomic inequality between nations rears its head at the convergence of demand and supply: "To cut the going global rate of $22,000–$25,000 per child, international adopters come to India to shop for babies, available at a fourth of this price." One nation's prosperity is linked to another's decline.

Abuses of corrupt adoption agencies abounded in the *Frontline* story and included abducting and kidnapping babies for adoption, identifying vulnerable mothers from poor families and enticing them to give up their babies, falsely informing a mother that her baby was stillborn, buying children from poor families, accepting financial or material rewards for the adoption agency in exchange for children, and offering women financial incentives to conceive a child specifically for adoption abroad, further exaggerating the profanity of trying to calculate the value of a child. Moreover, adoption agencies—since they are forbidden by law from charging fees for adoption greater than a specified amount of "maintenance"[20]—asked for "donations." These donations were, in reality, crass demands and were considered unethical when juxtaposed with the sacred basis of giving and receiving a child and the symbolic purity of orphans. One foreign parent explained: "The agency's staff constantly kept harassing us during the time we were in India asking us if we can pay them more. The director even asked us to get him a particular brand of whisky."[21] Another parent wrote of an agency director asking for bottles of whisky for his son's and daughter's weddings. Some parents decided to stop dealing with specific agencies because "their dealing was very business oriented," focusing on profit and not people. In this political economy, adoption became the "privilege of the elite." "In the existing set-up," the article pointed out, "no ordinary childless working class family can afford to adopt."

In the wake of the December 2004 tsunami, the "risks" for orphaned children and affected communities came to the attention of Indian media. Sixty child rights organizations called for a yearlong ban on the adoption of children affected by the tsunami. The media claimed that wealthy and greedy foreign adoptive parents threatened poor, vulnerable Indian children and families. To counteract the potential for clear injustices, the postcolonial Indian state instituted laws that protect orphans, the poor, and their particular histories. A "hierarchy of humanity" emerges in the ethical political economy of orphan adoption, managed by the nation-state (cf. Fassin 2007). As already mentioned, in 1984 the Indian Supreme Court laid out principles that adoption agencies must follow when giving a child to foreign parents for adoption.[22] The judgment was the effect of a petition by a lawyer to the Supreme Court "to restrain private Indian agencies from carrying out further activity of routing children for adoption abroad." Although adoptions by foreign parents are governed by the Guardians and Wards Act of 1890, particular components of the Hindu Adoptions and Maintenance Act of 1956 pertain to the regulation of foreign adoptions—primarily, that a first effort is made to find adoptive parents from within India (Diwan 2000: 143). Reasons given for this include issues of establishing membership in a group and safeguarding the adopted children's future sense of belonging:

> . . . because such adoption would steer clear of any problems of assimilation of the child in the family of the adoptive parents which might arise on account of cultural, racial, or linguistic differences in case of adoption by foreign parents. If it is not possible to find suitable adoptive parents for the child within the country, it may become necessary to give the child in adoption to foreign parents rather than allow the child to grow up in an orphanage or an institution where it will have no family life and no love and affection of parents." (143)

Most cases of intercountry adoption are of "orphans, destitute, or abandoned children, or those children whose parents have been lured into giving them in adoption" (144).

Like dān, the giving and taking of children through adoption cannot have a return; it must be unfettered. Pure humanitarianism, as with pure philanthropy, can have no ulterior motives. Distinct bodies, including the Indian Council of Child Welfare, which conducts home visits and submits child study reports before children are placed, scrutinize and evaluate applications by foreign parents for guardianship. Clearly, adoption cannot be purely humanitarian because of the necessary self-interested motive of building a family. Adoption agencies and NGOs caring for orphaned children, on the other hand, are humanitarian in their concerns.

The hierarchy of humanity that emerges in adoption discourse about care for orphans is based on the legislation of placement and consists of two intersecting components: (1) the hierarchy of desired children based on sex, age, and health, and (2) the hierarchy of adoptive parents based on religion and nationality (Lobo and Vasudevan 2002). The most preferred children for adoption are young, male, and healthy. Next come female children, then older children, and, finally, those with mental or physical problems. In the hierarchy of prospective parents, the first priority for adoption goes to Indian parents who live in India, next are Indians with nonresident Indian citizenship, then mixed couples consisting of one Indian parent, and finally, foreigners (Apparao 1997). This priority list challenges the egalitarian face of generic humanity that humanitarianism often promotes. To protect the orphan as a legal category, history of religious identity (Hindu) and of national origin (Indian) is mapped onto the child. Foreigners receive (or take) the less desired specimens of humanity: older babies, unwanted babies, and children with mental or physical impairments. The most extreme cases, of course, are not adopted at all and remain wards of the state.

## Orphans and Humanitarianism

Excluded from kin, orphans are simultaneously the responsibility of no one in particular and everyone in general. "The orphan," as a social category, is structurally analogous to the sadhu in Indian society: both exist outside systems of kin-based structures of social responsibility and are, ideally, cared for by society. When confronted by a sadhu or an orphan—although the first has renounced the world and the second has been renounced by it—the humanitarian is tested and perhaps compelled toward action to give. With so many children in orphanages who are not adoptable, a growing market in international and Indian humanitarian efforts is focused on children. In Delhi alone thirty-six "children institutions" were registered with the Department of Child Welfare in 2005. A few of these were homes for abandoned children, whereas others were homes for children whose parents had not abandoned them but could no longer provide care. When boundaries of kin are severed by poverty or tragedy, the state steps in to protect its citizens. Orphans considered for adoption in India speak to other categories of destitution and abandonment. Because the state must certify potential adoptees as abandoned and without family before they are adopted, photographs and advertisements of abandoned and missing children are placed in both English- and Hindi-language newspapers. After a waiting period, the state may declare them abandoned and wards of the state, children of the nation, with rights and responsibilities.[23]

Prospective adoptive Indian parents who request a child with a particular shade of skin color and desire their adopted children to phenotypically match their own physical attributes may reaffirm the stigma associated with adoption in India; however, these parents also affirm the possibility of transforming a destitute child into a member of a family. In Delhi, I was told a story about an unwed mother who, immediately after giving birth to her baby, gave the baby to another woman who was perhaps a friend, a relative, or an acquaintance. The adopting mother's name was entered on the birth certificate as if the child were her own. This "systematic misrecognition" of biological kinship (Bharadwaj 2003: 1879; cf. Das 1995) does not announce itself. The stigma associated with gifts and self-interest in Hinduism (as noted already, one of the most sacred forms of dān is the anonymous gupt dān) contrasts with the potential self-interest of building a family, which may be why the director of CARA whom I interviewed was reluctant to identify adoption with charity. As with other sectors of the Indian economy, there is no reason to expect adoption and humanitarianism to exist in purely formal realms. Some adoption, such as that carried out within families, is informal and undocumented, and as such it is difficult to "prove" statistically but evident ethnographically in narratives and lives. In my small circle of family and friends in north India I stumbled upon several cases of women who had "adopted" a relative's son because they could not have their own children. This practice was so commonplace that it was neither something to speak about nor to register as a legal issue.

Yet when one embraces strangers and turns them into one's kin, adoption of an orphan has the potential to become either a humanitarian act or an act of predatory geopolitics of desire in which wealthy families from foreign nations consume poor children in India. Despite the small number of foreign adoptions in India, the most dramatic stories of social transformation occurred in the context of foreign adoptions. And this, I believe, accentuates the value of orphans in humanitarian discourse more broadly as symbols of how the excluded can be embraced. Stories of abandonment that turn into miracles are, of course, prime marketing material for NGOs involved in child welfare. Although such stories can be considered a form of "disaster pornography" (see Benthall 1993), they are nonetheless haunting. For instance, I was told of a girl found abandoned on the side of the road in a suburb of Delhi who was encased in a polythene bag, with her face half-eaten by rats and dogs. A donor provided four plastic surgeries, and then she was adopted by a family in Spain. One may assume that the girl's life continues happily in Spain, as does her transformed status from a painfully and tragically excluded individual into a family member. This is an uneasy, yet powerful, conclusion that the figure of the orphan in humanitarian discourse has to offer: orphans can be cared for, but exclusions of poverty are much more difficult problems to solve.

I was told another story of a boy taken to a government hospital and abandoned by his impoverished mother; he was sick and near death. His mother left him there under a false name and address after she discovered he had a heart condition and needed emergency surgery that she could not afford. He was subsequently given to a child placement orphanage, where the director heroically scrambled to arrange payment for the immediate heart surgery so the boy would not die. As the director told the story, she seemed exhausted by it and said she did not know how she managed to raise the money—a feat she accomplished by persuading a cardiologist friend to do the surgery at a reduced rate. At the time I was hearing this story, the boy was about to be adopted by a family in Europe. The director showed me a book of photos pasted on graph paper with a narrative of the boy's recovery. His sickly beginnings and subsequent transformation were painful to look at, but I knew that the adoptive family would probably treasure the book—and perhaps the boy would too, one day. Stories such as these have an emotional appeal and are disturbing. It is challenging to write about them without becoming either a moral spectator (Boltanski 1999; Cartwright 2005) or, worse, complicit in the suffering they relate (Sontag 2003).

There are other humanitarian alternatives to adoption. In India, orphans are good recipients of gifts because they require no return, no relation, and no self-interest. When a gift has the expectation of a return, in the form of interest or social debt, for example, it is no longer a gift. Instead, it becomes an exchange, commerce, or a right. As already mentioned, Derrida (1992) has criticized Mauss's classic work for mistaking exchange for the gift: when law regulates a gift, it is bound by obligation and becomes part of economy or exchange (rather than gift). Pure gifts are gracious; the donor does not expect a return.

To translate this definition to orphans in India, giving to orphans through dān is a sacred gift. Donating time by volunteering at an orphanage also requires no expectation of a return. Yet adoption, which enters into an economy and involves self-interest, is not a gift. Although humanitarianism seeks adoption for orphans, to relieve them of their social exclusion, they must exist outside any economic transaction. Once orphans enter a market, humanitarianism becomes part of an economy. They lose their sacred standing, and the act of adoption becomes "corrupted" by interests. In order to circumvent the dangerous terrain of the "adoption market" in which orphans are potentially bought and sold, volunteers give their time and presence at orphanages. These efforts and the experiences they engender, the subject of the next chapter, also circumvent the fraught moral terrain of humanitarianism in the contemporary political economy of poverty and the excluded in India.

Chapter 4

# Experience

THE EXPERIENCE OF VOLUNTEERING brings a giver closer to the afflicted, the poor, the suffering, and the needy, if only for a short time. It differs from other humanitarian forms of practice, such as financial donation and professional aid work, in that it is undertaken as an activity outside the productive realm of wage work. A particularly powerful phenomenon that is gaining global currency, volunteering has an affective dimension. Some people seek out this dramatic experience and then try to encourage others to do the same. Volunteering, which exceeds the realm of routine everyday requirements, enters into a realm of free action that is uncoerced and selfless. When constituted in this sense, it can lead to an "experience."

By "experience," I refer to Victor Turner's reassertion of Wilhelm Dilthey's view that "experience urges toward expression, or communication with others" (1986: 37). Emerging from Turner's concept of "social drama," narratives of experience mark rites of passage. Thus they refer to situations that are formative—not simply "experience," but "an experience" that stands out (again referring to Wilhelm). Turner notes that such experiences "erupt from or disrupt routinized, repetitive behavior" and "begin with shocks of pain or pleasure." He notes: "The Greek peraō relates experience to 'I pass through.' In Greek and Latin, experience is linked with peril and experiment" (35).[1]

This chapter features four groups attempting to organize volunteers: a pilot program recruiting students from Delhi's top universities to volunteer over the summer with NGOs in rural India; a group of young urban Indians volunteering their time at an orphanage; expatriates volunteering at Mother Teresa's Missionaries of Charity welfare home for children; and foreign and Indian volunteers who have abandoned their professional lives and careers in a quest for a transformative experience, which they find at a school for disabled children. These groups differ in their experience of volunteering, but the role and value of an "experience" is central to them all.

Bypassing strictly psychological analyses, I favor one that integrates a political economy of sensibilities. The feelings encountered in volunteering are structured and not solely "personal" and "private," hence my theoretical distancing from psychology and its more atomized understanding of emotion. William James (1982 [1902]), for example, wrote about experience, particularly religious experience, as individual, inner, and personal. Émile Durkheim (1995 [1912]) subsequently built upon and revised James's pragmatic conception of religious experience, articulating it as eminently social and mediated by institutions. While James emphasized religious feelings and impulses and their practical use in daily life, Durkheim focused on how social representation made experience possible by linking it to group membership.[2] Only through social institutions could experience be articulated to others. As an anthropologist, I am drawn to Durkheim rather than James, particularly his emphasis on the collective and how social institutions facilitate and mediate experience. All experience, for Durkheim, is mediated by social groups. In the case of voluntarism, the experience is mediated by particular NGOs that facilitate its activity as a social form. By focusing on the social and institutional forms of experience, we can see how volunteering has the potential both to enhance distinctions between groups and to surpass them. Through volunteering, binary categories encompassing "the other"—such as foreigner/Indian, wealthy/poor, internationalist/nationalist, able-bodied/disabled—are recognized, articulated, reified, and possibly overcome. Volunteering simultaneously asserts distinction—"I am not this"—as it strives to efface divisions through the potential of empathic experience.[3]

## Case 1: A Volunteer Revolution—Humanity on the World Stage

Volunteering as organized philanthropic practice is relatively new to India, in contrast to service to society (samaj seva)[4] and donation (dān), which, along with the work of charitable organizations, have long histories (Sen 1992, 1999; Tandon 2002, 2003). As mentioned in Chapter 1, some scholars have traced the history of NGOs and their service to society (as samaj seva) to the Gandhian period of nation-building directly following independence. At that time, many NGOs emerged in partnership with the state in a nationalist project of institutionalized service that emerged in a historically internationalist moment marked by independence from colonial rule (Gupta and Sharma 2006; Sen 1992, 1999; Tandon 2002, 2003). Despite this historical precedent for voluntarism in India, the civic discourse of voluntarism was notably absent in the Indian press, especially when compared with similar efforts in the United States (see Wuthnow [1991] and Allahyari [2000] for voluntarism in the United States; see Mathers [2010] for U.S. volunteers in Africa, and Hutnyk [1996] for "charity tourism," which I will discuss in greater detail later in this chapter, in Kolkata).

After I returned from India, I received a letter from the director of the organization Volunteer Now requesting money to support a National Fellow.[5] I had been involved with the program in Delhi and had supported the director's fund-raising marathon, but this annual plea was to "Sponsor a Fellow" in the model of sponsoring a child. I found this an interesting strategy. It was something we had discussed when I was in Delhi as a possible way of supporting the program. Attached to his request was a description of the National Fellow "experience." Volunteer Now was trying to start a "volunteer revolution," and one of its vehicles was this pilot program, supported by the Sir Ratan Tata Trust, which aimed to give urban, educated youth the "experience" of rural India (70 percent of India is rural). The hope was that if and when these youth entered positions of power in the nation, they would remember the six-week internship in rural development, and the experience would carry into national development policy. Many of the urban college students in Delhi, for example, had never been to a rural area—and this was the experience that the National Fellow program aimed to provide. The first year, the program was run out of the Delhi office exclusively, with the aim of branching out into a national program and the volunteer revolution.

The brochure for the program in 2005 began with the provocative slogan "[Volunteer Now], If you mean it, Do it!" and continued with a narrative that linked development with civic responsibility, voluntarism, and revolution. It began with the impulse to help: "The desire to change lives of the less privileged around us lies at the back of most [of] our minds. Often we make donations of money, medicines, food or clothing. We at times sponsor a child's education or just adopt an animal." The brochure suggested that although these are commendable acts, it would be more beneficial to help those in need "to help themselves" and "share our skills to prepare them to face life more courageously." It followed with the statement that the best way to get actively involved with those in need was by volunteering to spend "some valuable time helping them and in return experience an enriching adventure that would leave its impact all through your life."

The next paragraph took a historical approach, placing young Indians in a global context:

> History has proven that any major change in society has always been made possible by youths only. The indomitable spirit of the young people had always propelled the revolutions, be it French or Russian. Students' determinations to make a drastic change in the community is what we at [Volunteer Now] are aspiring. To curb the rampant insensitivity of the masses towards the development sector, today India is looking at You—the YOUTH of India. Be a leader of the movement called social evolution, be the pioneers of this adventurous journey to the rural India—the real India. Reach out to the millions who are not as fortunate as you are. Many have never seen a school or are those who are braving cancer, AIDS. Or someone just looking for a buddy in you. Come get involved to spread the spirit of comradeship. Join the cadre of [National Fellows]!

The brochure explained how, "to promote the spirit of volunteerism," Volunteer Now, in partnership with the Sir Ratan Tata Trust, had introduced a new internship program called National Fellows. The idea of the program was to create a "cadre" of volunteers like the Peace Corps in the United States and Millennium Volunteers in the United Kingdom in order to serve the country "for a cause" by living and working in a rural community. The brochure suggested that volunteering had national objectives. It would create a sense of national pride among Indian youth and "sensitise them" about problems that rural communities and NGOs faced in their daily operations. It proclaimed that when volunteers returned from their six-week internship, they would have "imbibed the notion of social responsibility" and would use this newfound responsibility in their future careers as CEOs or doctors. The National Fellow program was structured on the model of exchange—the volunteer gave time in exchange for experience and exposure. The question "what do you hope to learn?" was juxtaposed with "what can you give?" The program coordinator had also scouted, interviewed, and selected the NGOs with which the volunteers would work from a list of those funded by the Sir Ratan Tata Trust. It was a matchmaking endeavor for the coordinator, based on the needs and desires of the NGOs and the volunteers.

Originally, I hoped to volunteer as an ethnographic exercise, but I soon found myself interested in understanding the process of organizing volunteers in Delhi. When I encountered Volunteer Now through GiveIndia (a Web portal for philanthropy in India), it was just starting the National Fellow program and I was quickly involved with the venture. After meeting with the National Fellow coordinator, I became enmeshed in the selection process. The challenge of placing National Fellows with NGOs involved very practical problems. For example, one NGO wanted a female Muslim to do interviews and collect data with self-help groups for young girls in the Muslim community. But Volunteer Now had only one female Muslim who would venture into a rural village, and she specified that she would not live in a village. The project coordinator mentioned that despite volunteers' fears of the potential for sexual harassment, the possibility of such harassment was slim because "people in villages are so scared—they are so remote and so scared." Another NGO was charging too much for food (4,500 rupees, and the entire National Fellow stipend was 3,500 rupees). The NGO was in the state of Himachal Pradesh and was used to hosting foreign volunteers; it said the rate of 4,500 rupees was the concession rate for an Indian student, but it was too high for Volunteer Now. Two of the other NGOs specified that they wanted only male volunteers.

The funder, the Sir Ratan Tata Trust, was trying to encourage Indian youth to work in the NGO sector. The trust found that bright students were not going into the development sector—hence its desire for a national program on the scale of the Peace Corps or Millennium Volunteers. The immediate goal of the program was to keep the volunteer at the center of its programs and to focus on his or her experiences, but the long-term goal of the program was to create a cadre of volunteers, to recruit one thousand students from one hundred universities in India. However, volunteering, for young Indians, was not a common social form; it had to be encouraged and taught.

The application for the National Fellow program asked two questions: why applicants were interested in the program, and how they felt it would benefit them.[6] The applicant responses to the first question fell into six categories: (1) 39 percent responded "to help others"; (2) 38 percent wanted "a new experience"; (3) 30 percent were seeking to prepare for a career in social work or development; (4) 29 percent wanted to work for society (which included "to serve country/be a responsible citizen of India"); (5) 26 percent responded "for personal growth"; and (6) 6 percent wanted to do something worthwhile during their summer vacation. The ideal National Fellow had never been to a rural area; those with extensive experience in rural areas were disqualified. The selection process contained the following logic: give an experience to someone who does not have it already—someone with an open mind who has little experience.

Volunteer Now applicants had to be between the ages of sixteen and twenty-five. Those who answered the narrative questions on the application form with stereotypical answers were disqualified. Answers that "came from the heart" or gave an insight into the person's mind or heart were considered good answers. People without any functional skills, such as cooking, were also not interviewed. One question asked, "Have you been to a rural area?" Those who said yes were considered to have already made up their minds, and this was considered negative. The program sought people with open minds, who had not had too much experience. Since the idea of the program was to "sensitize urban youth to rural issues," it was thought best to give the opportunity to candidates without much experience.

I worked with the team of National Fellow interviewers and participated in the selection process. A tremendous effort had been expended to initiate this volunteer revolution: 650 forms had been distributed at universities in the recruitment effort for the twenty volunteer positions. The applicants were told that "real India still lives in villages; you can contribute to the development of India." In a warm-up session, applicants were asked to describe themselves, where they came from, and two things about that place. The candidates were shown pictures and asked to write a paragraph or two about one of them in fifteen minutes. One photo showed the weathered and wrinkled face of an old man, smiling, with one tooth. Another photo featured a dilapidated boat, another a group hiking on a mountain peak; in another a young boy walked barefoot on railroad tracks. Each picture was provocative in its own way, with stories yet to be told. Then the candidates were given a narrative to read of a village social drama and were asked to discuss it. It was a story filled with moral questions that lacked "correct" answers. I filmed the discussions, which generated heated arguments. The candidates forgot the selection process and lost themselves in the drama.[7]

The candidates were subsequently interviewed by two members of Volunteer Now (one interviewing, one observing and taking notes), during which their expectations of the program were revealed. One young woman said about being a National Fellow, "It will help me—it will make me a more responsible citizen." When asked what she expected to get out of the program, she replied: "I'll learn from them [rural people]. I'll try to understand their life. I've never seen a rural person—I've never been in contact with such a person. I'll extract things out of them." "What will you give back?" we asked, and she answered, "Whatever I have—happiness, maybe a feeling of strength." Another candidate said he would bring back "fond memories and new friendships" from the experience. "I will also have acquired a greater respect for life and to not take for granted what I have—for example, electricity and lights." The candidates were asked about how they show concern for others and to give an example of a difficult situation they had faced. We were searching for compassionate, creative, thoughtful young people. One of the staff members interviewing with me explained to a candidate: "We at [Volunteer Now] are trying to create a revolution in terms of volunteering. You will be our ambassadors." What were the qualities of a good ambassador? "Flexibility and adaptability, sensitivity to the needs of others, practical problem-solving ability, and a commitment to learning." Most of all, we were looking for a certain spark that was hard to describe.

Those who were selected as National Fellows underwent an extensive two-day orientation workshop, which I attended and filmed for the NGO. The turnout for the orientation was disappointing to the coordinator and the director of Volunteer Now. She expected thirty-four volunteers to attend the orientation, but at the last minute, people backed out so that only eighteen attended. Some dropped out when they saw where they were placed. "It is hard to get commitments from people," she explained. "Some are saying if they don't get posted in Uttaranchal, they won't go!" Uttaranchal (now called Uttarakhand) is a hill state, whereas rural Rajasthan is a desert region that gets very hot and thus did not appear to be an appealing adventure for many potential volunteers. The coordinator just that morning had fought with the father of a volunteer who had been selected; he demanded that his daughter go to Uttaranchal instead of Rajasthan. Another young woman's parents decided they would not let her volunteer, but she attended the second day of the orientation so the coordinator could save face. One problem was that it was dangerous and not socially appropriate for young women to be placed alone, so volunteers were paired.

The day after the volunteer workshop there was an orientation for the NGOs, and thirteen were scheduled to attend. The coordinator was concerned that there were not enough volunteers to match with the NGOs in pairs. "We'll see who actually goes," she said, "who gets on a bus and goes. A lot can still happen, and people can back out." Another staff member was trying to find some foreign volunteers to go in the place of the National Fellows if they fell short. There was a group of six from the United Kingdom, but they wanted to be posted together: another matching challenge. Whereas Indian volunteers had to be persuaded and encouraged to take up a post in rural India, foreign volunteers paid £200 for the opportunity. Volunteer Now boasted that the organization provided the lowest fee and the most services compared with competitors. Some people were willing to pay for this experience even though it was volunteer work.

Many of the students at the orientation were frightened of the prospect of living in a rural area for six weeks, and the anticipation of the cultural adventure required institutional translation. Along with the student fear, some parents were resistant, and the orientation was meant to allay fears and concerns. For instance, there was a session on health led by a doctor, and another on safety for women led by a women's activist. But the search for experience and adventure held within it a threat: that the very difference which attracted candidates in the first place had the potential to become a danger. There were inspirational and informational speakers, as well as participatory exercises for the Fellows. One speaker asked the volunteers why their world of materialism and air-conditioning was more "real" than the world of the rural villagers they would soon come to know. The volunteers expressed their excitement and nervousness in the conversations that ensued.

Despite the orientation, preparation, and signing of a contract, one volunteer returned to Delhi before the end of the program. I sat with him and the program coordinator and listened to his complaints. He was frustrated and a bit defensive—his experience had not been good in rural Rajasthan. He said the NGO he was placed with had not been prepared for a volunteer and did not know what to do with him. There was no place for him to sleep for three days and no work for him. This was despite the fact that the program coordinator had visited the NGO earlier and made sure they were prepared to accept a National Fellow. The student repeatedly mentioned that his parents said he should not have gone. He waited an entire week, doing nothing from 9 in the morning to 6 or 7 in the evening but reading three novels. He wondered, "Why am I here? I can read novels at home." His health was in jeopardy and he lost weight because he didn't like the food and didn't eat much. "You don't know how to handle the situation," he said. "When you see they themselves are doing it [the rural work] and you see you have come as a volunteer to help them and not be a burden. It was very hard for me." He was used to respecting elders, so he felt he could not rebel; for instance, it was hard for him to refuse the food. He could not say no to the food, but he could not eat it. When asked why, he explained that "the chapatis were four times as thick" as he was used to. The culture shock included the reality of his independence. Wealthy and middle-class students in urban India are sheltered from the world by their families, which is exactly why the National Fellow program was initiated: to give urban, educated students exposure to and experience in rural India. But this experience was not always a positive one, and sometimes came as a shock.

The project coordinator was frustrated. She later told me there was a discrepancy between the "NGO version" and the "student version" of the story of why the student left his assignment. For instance, during her visit to the NGO, she had been shown the room where the student was to stay, although the student said he was not given a room. The student had said that the NGO director told him, "I don't know what to do with you." Since Volunteer Now had asked NGOs funded by the Sir Ratan Tata Trust to host a volunteer, perhaps NGOs felt they could not refuse volunteers because the request came from one of their financial sponsors. Another problem was that most of the students were placed with another student, but this volunteer had been placed alone. There was a discussion about how Volunteer Now should not "have sent a person alone to an NGO where there is no one from the city." There was too much difference for the volunteer to handle alone. The project coordinator expressed surprise that the female volunteers generally were not the ones who had problems with their placements; the young men needed more handholding than the women. Urban Indian children are protected from the world, and when they are suddenly thrust into a situation without guidance, they can be at sea. While used to their studies, these volunteers were less adept without directions to follow.

There was a tension in the volunteering endeavor of the National Fellow program between the families of the volunteers and the open vista of voluntarism that revolved around the question of independence. In college, middle-class Indian youth are not considered independent. It is not until a young man or young woman is married (for a woman) or starts a career (for men and women) that they receive a mark of independence. There was no reason why parents should trust a rural NGO to care for their child. The goal of "experience," while novel for building a nation of civic-minded leaders, was not foremost on the minds of potential volunteers and their parents. In fact, parental consent was such an important factor in the program that the application process included signed consent forms for both of the applicant's parents as well as a question during the interview process about how the parents viewed the program.

Not all the responses to the program were negative. Far from it. The post-experience narratives sent to Volunteer Now (self-reports, or testimonials) were filled with stories of transformation—of surviving trials and experiencing a classic rite of passage. One National Fellow wrote about his apprehension before going to rural Maharashtra to help children in a village. It was his "first tryst with rural India," and he was anxious about the "searing heat in this village." He wrote: "I couldn't shake the one question that continually haunted me all through the signing of the contract at the Orientation and on the day I left: Was six weeks too much?" He arrived in the village after a "grueling fifteen hour journey" and was surprised by what he encountered:

> We got to work soon after and with my first few interactions with students, both dropouts and school going, I was amazed at their humility. Every house that I entered with the lady social worker, they offered us *nimbu pani* [lemon water] and snacks. They earned the most meager wages and yet, they would offer us so much. I wondered why. In the end, I was a total alien, looked at with my yet-to-be-tanned-to-an-appropriate-village-tone skin. Drinking water with Chloriwat [a water purifier] wouldn't really champion my cause either. The weather was stifling though. The temperatures were touching 45c [113°F]. The highest I had encountered in Mumbai was a paltry 40c [104°F]. Add 50% of humidity and I thought I would die. I suddenly wanted out. In three days. So much for will power. I would try to sleep under a fan and my bed sheet would be soaked with sweat in twenty minutes flat. But when the good Lord decides to hurt you, he doesn't stop there. Just when I thought it was cooling off in the night, two words would come back to haunt me: load shedding [electricity outages]. For six hours every day. Life didn't have to be this tough I thought to myself. But then, I've always believed in signs. And I found mine. . . . It was past six in the evening. I had gone to his house. It began to rain. The first real respite from the heat. And then he stood in front of me. Less than three feet tall, a twisted foot, and an asthma patient. I could hear the wheezing every time he breathed in and out. Just then the lights went out. My conscience hit me. Hit me hard. I cried. I felt so utterly shallow, it was ridiculous. To return home now seemed like a farce and if I weaseled out, I wouldn't be able to forgive myself for a WHILE. That much I was sure of. So I stayed. The next day was 45c again. My bedsheet was soaked again in my sweat, the lights went out again, but it was a small price to pay, I swear. I took a new interest in my work and blocked Mumbai out for the

> time being. Before I knew it, I had survived ten days in the wilderness. We took a timely few days off and went to Hyderabad to reward ourselves. The time spent in Hyderabad was good but in the matter of two days, I yearned to get back to Sagroli and continue work. Quite the transformation if I may say so myself. After we returned, I enjoyed my work a lot more and there was a sense of purpose to what I was doing.

The volunteer's exposure to (or, experience of) poverty included doing things he never thought he would do, such as traveling in a crowed auto packed with twelve other people and sleeping on a *khatiya* (string bed) for the first time in his life.

Another National Fellow described her motivation for volunteering as "yearning to be a part of something new, different and challenging from the routine of my normal, mundane life. Something that would really compel me to step out of my comfort zone, of my perfectly organized and structured world." Also placed in Maharashtra for the summer, she described the experience as one of empathy: "The time spent with the people in the various villages also brought in a fresh perspective to life. I tried to see the world from their perspective, tried to analyze their problems and worries. . . . There are so many things I suddenly became aware of and began to feel for, I was sensitized to so many issues I initially used to turn a blind eye on." She described the experience as enlightenment, as being "a complete one" in which she tested herself and grew: "the experience really shaped my thinking and outlook towards life a great deal. The leap I took in the dark at the beginning brought a whole new light in my perception and attitude."

Other fellows wrote narratives that followed the same structure: moving from apprehension and anxiety before the adventure, to a loss of self and transformation in the rural environment, and to a return to their former lives with a new perspective and appreciation for their structural position in the world. Volunteers were encouraged and instructed to keep a diary of their experiences, and many of the self-reports contained excerpts or summaries of their writing in the field. One National Fellow who had been placed in Uttaranchal in 2006 wrote: "Where the people are all about generosity and modesty . . . and where the nature is all about peace and tranquility . . . a heaven where one can experience eternal happiness . . . just by diving deep into its realm . . . what we term as 'the other' or the rural . . . is actually a home away from home . . . another world . . . not as alien as it seems . . . but familiar and intimate . . . welcoming, forthcoming and friendly . . . an accommodating territory."

## Case 2: Fissures of Class—Project Hope

While Volunteer Now was giving Indian youth a chance to experience the "other" India, some urban Indians were seeking this experience on their own. I met Seema and encountered her efforts to organize volunteers at an orphanage in New Delhi through Nate, one of the volunteers she recruited. Seema was in her mid-twenties and was organizing volunteer efforts among her friends. I met Nate, a married British expatriate and engineer in Delhi with two sons, through our sons' class at school. We would meet outside the school in the afternoon, or in the morning when we dropped off our children, and talk about our work, Delhi, and charity. When he learned I was studying charity and orphanages, he told me about Project Hope, which he had joined and which encouraged visiting an orphanage in a slum outside of Delhi. Seema was advocating a different kind of charity—the gift of time—and it was an experiment I was interested in witnessing. She had a very specific vision of what her organization could contribute to the children at the orphanage, which I will call Children's Garden.[8] I asked Seema why she was going to the orphanage and why she was trying to persuade others to go. "They [the orphans] want to see interest," she said. "It's like someone cares for them." She aimed to offer human presence to the children. I accompanied Nate to the orphanage, and in the car, he mentioned how after going regularly to the orphanage, he was getting attached to the children. This was one difference between giving money for charity and giving time.

As we drove up to Children's Garden with Nate's driver, we were overwhelmed by a stench: the orphanage was located next to an open sewer. We stepped over the trickle of sewage to enter the cement block building where we were greeted by a few of the older orphans who were taking a sewing course alongside a baby and one of the caretakers (the rest of the children were in school). A two-year-old girl hung onto the kurta of one of the three wardens, who explained how the girl had "adopted" her. Social adoption works in two directions. The girl, wide-eyed with close-cropped hair, peeked out at us from behind her adopted parent. We must have looked very strange to her; I felt the urge to adopt her myself and wondered about it—the desire to save, to own, to rescue a stray, to love.

The warden directed us to the ninety-three-year-old founder of Children's Garden, who sat in a small room with a hotplate and a bed under posters of Jesus and the Indian guru Sai Baba that hung on the wall side-by-side. He sat on his bed, cross-legged, wearing a brown wool cap and a dirty gray robe, holding court. We removed our shoes, sat down, and spoke with him. He was tall and thin, with a flowing white beard and long white hair; he described himself as a world renouncer and an orphan. He made it clear that he did not get any money from the GOI.[9] Groups such as Project Hope volunteered time to Children's Garden, but dozens of donations helped the orphanage to function in other ways as well. The founder talked to us with the anticipation of garnering resources. He tried to encourage us to donate funds by mentioning how much another NGO had given. Yet another NGO was giving 20,000 rupees (it was not clear whether this was a recurring gift). An elite school in Delhi, similar to "private" schools in the United States, donated regularly in the form of soap, rice, and food; he said this provided about half of what was needed for a month.

As we toured Children's Garden, the children giggled and stared at us. "All of us are foreigners to those children," Seema said. "When we went there, they said, 'How come you speak Hindi?' The first time I went I really felt like I've dropped from Mars." It was true; the class divide was so extreme between Seema and these children—some of whom were not much younger than she—that she might as well have come from another world. The children loved to talk about Hindi movies; this was something they could all do together. Nate and I each had children of our own, and visiting the orphanage made us look at our own lives differently. "Sometimes I feel like I don't give enough time to my own children," Nate thought out loud. It was this gift of time that was salient to this experience, to this exposure to foreignness and difference on all sides. It was not only the orphans who were being exposed to difference—to us—to the experience of difference; the shock of poverty was something we had sought out ourselves—perhaps as a reminder of our own place in the world, perhaps as an effort to change it, or both.

That day, we spent one hour at Children's Garden. On the way back from the visit, we discussed our experience. Nate surprised me by asking whether I would take my son to Children's Garden on one of my volunteer visits. I thought about it and realized that I would not, but Nate eventually took his boys there. He was thoughtful about what it meant to volunteer time, for him, and since he was paid hourly for his work, he calculated that he would donate the equivalent of one half day's work. He was also planning what he could do for the orphans—perhaps bring a video in English with his children, show it to them, and then discuss it. I thought about bringing art supplies for the children. It was interesting to me that both of us thought of bringing tools to structure our "experience." Seema had said: "The place has no structure. You can do whatever you want. You can stay as long as you want." Nate was convinced that it was good that Project Hope was staying away from the fund-raising aspect of assistance, that it was best "to keep it at arm's length" and to focus on giving time instead of money. Another NGO had organized a capital campaign to raise money for a new facility for the orphanage, and Nate pointed out, "Even if they move, the need of Project Hope to provide time will still be there."

When we visited another day, most of the children were away at school again. As Seema said, "We could really see the living conditions." Ten girls between the ages of fifteen and sixteen learned sewing in a small room. They studied for school in the evenings. Some were shy; some were curious about Nate and me. There was a language barrier, and even though Seema translated, communication was awkward and stilted and the visit felt voyeuristic, although I was not sure who was viewing whom. It felt like "charity tourism," a term that has been used to describe how Western volunteers travel to India to encounter the "other" as a form of postmodern pilgrimage (Hutnyk 1996; Mathers 2010; Mustonen 2005). As foreigners, Nate and I stood out visually: he was tall and blond and I was much shorter, with short hair; together we were exotic birds. If Project Hope's mission was to provide company, time, and exposure, then we were exposing the children to difference.

It was difficult and inconvenient to get to the orphanage, which was near Dwarka, close to the domestic airport. One had to drive forty-five minutes each way through small and crowded streets—a time-consuming task. Thus, the commitment of time to the orphanage included the time it took to travel there. Seema warned me that Children's Garden was in a slum area, but the neighborhood did not look much different from where I was living in south Delhi—until we took the final turn at the open sewer. When we were offered coffee in the orphanage, it was impossible to forget the drainage, and Nate, Seema, and I declined. This was the shock of difference compared with the middle-class India where I was living, with its water purifiers and immaculately clean homes. It was also a very different environment from the area where Nate lived in central Delhi, which is inhabited by foreigners, U.N. workers, and wealthy Indians in extraordinarily expensive flats. His wife was an executive for the World Health Organization. They lived a semi-subsidized life, as did the other expats in positions similar to that of Nate's wife. Despite the inconvenience of traveling to Children's Garden, Seema tried to go there twice a month. She was also starting a high-end mail-order lingerie business that concentrated on lingerie that retailed for 5,000 to 8,000 rupees an item, roughly between $100 and $200. I wondered about the meaning of luxury in the context of a place like Children's Garden. The experience of volunteering brought these contrasts to the fore.

One day when Seema, Nate, and I were on the way to the orphanage, the car was surrounded by beggars as we stopped at an intersection. They knocked on the car windows, asking for donations. "Do you give money to them?" Nate asked me, and I said that I did, when I could, impulsively. Nate and Seema seemed taken aback. They gave me the "you shouldn't do that" argument in tandem, as if "it only supports that activity." Nate said he would rather buy his children balloons from the beggars even if they broke in ten minutes. That way, at least he was helping the beggars do some work. Seema agreed and said that beggars were part of gangs and rackets and they should not be supported. I decided to try out on them a challenge that I had been working on in my head for some weeks, although I knew they would disagree. I told them that I would rather give something directly, such as money or food, instead of supporting a supposed business. The illusion of supporting a business instead of a human being begging makes the giver feel better because an object is exchanged for the money (in this case, the balloons). It is a form of commodity fetishism, in which the thing given (in this case, balloons) takes up and absorbs the emotion of the moment; it neutralizes social relations and makes disparity easier to comprehend or make sense of. When someone supports a business venture, the donation becomes an exchange—things for cost—instead of philanthropy given on impulse. Visiting the orphanage made me acutely aware of the inequality in India, and the world. As we drove through the crowded streets, Nate asked Seema, "Have you ever been on a bus?" "No!" Seema exclaimed, "You couldn't pay me enough to get on a bus." Social divisions and class divides remained clearly delimited.

About a month after our initial visit to Children's Garden, I went for a walk with Nate in Lodhi Gardens. We talked about Project Hope and Nate's involvement with the organization. He said he had been thinking about the best thing he could do to help the children at the orphanage; he had been sorting it out for a while yet remained unresolved. The previous week, two Swedish friends had visited him and his wife, and he took them to Children's Garden. They also had pondered how they could help. They decided they could easily tap into their social networks and raise money for the orphanage and discussed the issue of how difficult it was to give money from so far away and thereby be unable to "be sure where the money is going." They realized it would be a lot easier to do this with someone like Nate there who could take photographs regularly and report to them on the orphanage. But Nate, too, was not sure about his commitment and was in the midst of deciding what best to do.

The previous week, Nate sat with the children at Children's Garden for an hour, reading to them from English vocabulary books. They enjoyed it, and he thought it was useful for them to hear an English speaker pronounce the words. He had enjoyed it too; it was not that different from the kinds of things he did with his own two small children. He could go every two weeks for a day, but he thought he would rather find an organization closer to where he lived. Nate realized that if he gave his time, it made him feel better about himself and the world, and perhaps it made him happier and a better person with his own children; hence, it was worth the effort. But he had to give without expecting anything back. That was what was different about giving time. When he gave money, he wanted to know where it went. But, he said, "It is a hell of a lot easier to give money, to write a check and be done with it." Nate and his wife discussed this and agreed that it would be different to volunteer at an orphanage from which they were considering adopting a child. In such a circumstance, with a kind of investment in the organization, one would see and treat the children differently. Nate was unusual. As a husband who had followed his wife's career to India with their two children, he reminded me of women I met at Delhi Network, an organization for expats, and its American Women's Association who had time on their hands and wanted to be purposeful through volunteering. Charity required time and resources, preferably both.

Seema, Project Hope's organizer, was unusual as well. She had grown up in India and had sponsored a child with her family when she was a child herself. She "just gave money," she said—write a check and it's gone. But her undergraduate education in the United States at Cornell University changed her perspective. There, she volunteered for the Special Olympics and was part of the Big Brothers Big Sisters program. She conceived of Project Hope in the United States at a time when she was planning to return to India before applying for business schools, and she wanted to get involved in a different way. She imagined Project Hope as giving one's presence and company at an orphanage, spending time there. Sponsorship was not the primary goal, and she was not concerned with the funding aspects of Children's Garden. She was critical of the financial decisions that were being made but kept her distance. For example, someone had donated one hundred leather shoes for the children, but they were stored away unused for so long that a fungus destroyed them. The children received the shoes only after they had been destroyed. Also, there was not enough bedding for the children; however, later Seema learned that there was plenty of bedding, but it was being saved for the move to the new building in two years.

Seema was very conscious of differences in class and how they played out in volunteer efforts in the United States as compared with Delhi. "In India the classes don't mix," she said. "It's oil and water." In India, people knew where they fit in the scheme of things. Social mobility was not assumed, and hierarchies were relational. In the United States, on the other hand, the discourse of meritocracy perpetuated an illusion of mobility and fluid status. "Here [in India] I'm somebody," Seema said. "In the U.S. I'm a nobody. In the U.S. I've done this social service and I wanted to see if I could do it in India." It was a challenge. The first five volunteers she took to Children's Garden were conscious of the dirt of the orphanage. Two of them wouldn't drink the tea that was offered, and no one would touch the water. All felt unclean afterward.

After several visits to the Children's Garden, I met Seema at the hotel that her parents owned in New Friends Colony, Delhi, where she grew up. The hotel was a sprawling estate, a palace on a cloudy Delhi winter day. International jazz music played in the hotel lobby. The hotel's brochure promoted its luxurious surroundings: "Built in the '50s in the leafy Friends Colony district of New Delhi, The Hotel offers an intimate, ten-suite retreat set in one acre of landscaped gardens, removed from the hustle and bustle of the city but within easy access of its sights. The residence features Italian marble floors, warm wood paneling and silk furnishings. Upstairs, the open-air Roof Terrace is fitted with cushions for lounging, snacks, or pre-dinner cocktails." She discussed how it was easier to give money than to volunteer, and what it was like to visit the orphanage, spend time there, and then return. It was not about bringing something that the children "needed":

> It's not that I say, they need English classes, so you've got to teach them English when, you know, they'd rather just do some painting. So I'm giving people the option to do whatever they want, because these kids need everything. . . . So I'm trying to make it as flexible as possible, and I want both parties to enjoy it as well. So if you have a passion that you want to share with the kids, by all means, please do so. So that's what I want them [the volunteers] to do the first time. And then the second time, third time, they're coming back to me and saying, Oh, this is what I want to do, and then I'm making the arrangements for that.

The first time Seema took volunteers to the orphanage, she took her friends, who were, as she recounted, "really surprised that the kids were so happy. I don't know what they were expecting, but the kids were happy and they loved seeing people." She elaborated on the children's eagerness and experiences with the volunteers:

> They're used to seeing new people come, and they remember. If you come a second, third, fourth time, like when I came back, I promised them I'd come, and it took me a month to go back the second time. And they said, "Well, you promised you'd come," you know, and I said, "Yes, I know my promise. It's taking me a little bit longer than I anticipated, but I'm back, I promise I'm going to come back. . . . I might come back next week, I might come back in two weeks. But come I will." So they remember you. . . . you don't even have to do anything with them. You just sit with them, or they'll tell you what they want to be, or they'll ask you to help them with words in English, or they'll sit, play a game with us. Or anything . . . they're just really happy to have you there. It's companionship. So even if you don't want to do anything but just hang out with the kids, we'll spend the day, that's completely fine, because it's companionship. And you still teach kids. But it's just by looking, you're so different from everybody else . . . that they learn by just talking to you. And I think that's great too. Because you get exposure. Because otherwise, they don't have an opportunity to step out of the orphanage and go to school.

Seema's goal of giving the orphanage children exposure and experience was separate from the life of relative affluence she led. In addition to applying to MBA programs and starting her luxury lingerie business, she was working on creating a business plan for a spa at the hotel. I asked Seema what would happen if she brought a group of children from Children's Garden to the spa. It was a hypothetical question, but one that embodied some of the extremes I saw in her life and the contradictions she inhabited. She did not see them as contradictions. Rich and poor in Delhi lived side by side and did not mix. They coexisted. To bring them together, to soak in the same water was, I knew, a trick anthropological question of pollution (as in Douglas 1994 [1966]). She responded, "Oh, my God I would lose a lot of my [customers] . . . because the kind of spa that we are planning to have here, it's really high end." I suggested, "You could have a special day." She said:

> Well, yeah. We'd have to have a special day. We'd have to get in special products. Because the products themselves also cost a lot of money. So, you know, if I

> began to smear them all [the children] with La Prairie crème, I'd be losing a lot of money [she laughs]. I don't know if I want to bring them to a spa, but what we're trying to do is to create outings for them to take them on a tour of Delhi and show them historical monuments, teaching them about their culture. You know, things like that. But there's a spa, fine, I'll bring them one day, but then so what? I can't bring them once a week. Right? But if I take them on a tour of Delhi, for instance, what they're studying in school. . . . I wanted to bring these kids to a school, but no school will want to have these kids there, because they're like, wait. . . . Parents will call up and be like, "Why are you having these kind of people in school where our kids go?"

I mentioned that I had heard this before in other charitable contexts in New Delhi, and she replied, "So that's a challenge. . . . So, the classes don't mix. Seema was conscious of the issue of social pollution and her own participation it its perpetuation:

> There are bars—like when I go to the orphanage, I'll wear closed-toe shoes; I'll put on a full slip. I'm not a big fan of, you know . . . I'm just generally not a touchy-feely type of person. But even at the slum, when I come back, I will have a bath, wash my hair and everything. So there is a part of me that's like, oh, my God, you know, they're not so clean, they haven't had a bath; they're all touching me and everything. . . . So even I have a fair bit of . . . hmm. I'm not that open. But I'm still willing to give it a shot.

I asked her whether she felt the same way when doing volunteer work in the United States, and she said she did not. There, she could befriend the people with whom she volunteered. For instance, in her work with Special Olympics—although she said "it's tough to look at some of these people; you know, they can't speak properly, or they can't walk"—still, for her, "there was no problem at all. There were perfectly normal people that I could be friends with and hang out with." But in Delhi she said: "We can't be friends. You know, it's clearly [a] I'm-coming-to-help-you relationship. None of these people I can be friends with. We just don't come from the same worlds." It was easier to overcome differences due to physical disability than those symbolizing class-based pollution. Volunteering in India both exaggerated the fissures of class, and culture, and allowed people to coexist. In the United States, perhaps, one does not see the poverty and despair, or, one can have the luxury of avoiding it with the buffer of wealth. When expatriates from the States, however, came to Delhi, many were shocked by poverty and felt compelled to try to address it.

## Case 3: Fissures of Culture—the Circle of Care

An informal organization of expatriates, which I will call the Circle of Care, volunteered at three orphanages in New Delhi, including Nirmal Hriday, which was run by Mother Teresa's Sisters of Charity. I encountered this group through a membership organization for expats called Delhi Network consisting mostly of wives of businessmen and embassy workers stationed in India's capital, and its smaller American Women's Association. Notably, the Circle of Care was composed of women. It was not a registered NGO and therefore did not keep receipts or confer tax advantages to its members. One of its foci was to provide medical care for orphans at the orphanages—often arranging it at no cost or well below cost. The Circle of Care took children who were unadoptable in the Indian context—particularly those with physical disabilities such as cleft palate, clubfoot, or heart defects—and made them desirable for potential adoptive parents abroad for whom physical disabilities, especially when corrected, were less stigmatized. For instance, one boy had open-heart surgery, and the doctor charged the group only 100,000 rupees (roughly $2,200). The women in the group took the boy into their homes and cared for him after the operation. In addition to organizing medical assistance, volunteers visited the children in the orphanages regularly to give them love and physical attention. They spent much of their time just holding the children or playing with them, often without the ability to speak with them in Hindi.

The goal of the Circle of Care was "to make a difference" in the lives they touched. Some of the volunteers I spoke with were frustrated by the conditions of the orphanages and by their inability to "do anything in the nursery." One volunteer was a neonatal nurse, and she was not allowed to practice medicine on the children, some of whom had serious health problems. In one room, twenty-one iron cribs were lined up like animal cages. Children who could stand stood in their cribs; others rocked themselves, and some lay sleeping or were unresponsive. One girl had a severe case of hydrocephalus. She had an extremely large head and skinny limbs and lay on her back surrounded by a mosquito net; her prognosis was not good. She was not adoptable, and it was not likely she would survive long with her condition. My heart broke as I walked past her crib. An American nurse volunteer said, "I don't know what will happen to her." That her future was unresolved made the moment more poignant. (I was later told that she was moved to Mother Teresa's Jeevan Jyoti Home for Disabled Children.) Three of the girls were likely mentally disabled and no one wanted them. These children were the excluded, the abandoned, and the alone. One volunteer mentioned that she "forgot how hard it is to go there [to the orphanage] sometimes."

The volunteers saw themselves as giving the children love, which they thought was not being provided by the institution. Some of the volunteers had medical qualifications—one Italian doctor found herself for the first time abroad without a contract to practice medicine so she volunteered her time. An American volunteer said: "Our work is mostly for us. I think we get more out of it than anyone else. Mostly we're in the way." It was true. Circle of Care members criticized the orphanages in the same way that Mother Teresa's hospice in Kolkata had been criticized, most publicly by Christopher Hitchens in his book *The Missionary Position* (1995).[10] Hitchens condemned the Sisters of Charity for giving love instead of medical attention to the terminally sick and dying and for not attempting to overcome the structural inequalities that perpetuated the ailments of the poor. Although such criticisms are justified, they discount in prescriptive terms the actions of groups such as the Sisters of Charity and the Circle of Care as ineffectual. However, these groups are doing something positive. In addition to the surgeries, Circle of Care offered humanitarianism in the form of experience for volunteers.

The allure of this type of work was a form of service with missionary zeal. In the context of Nirmal Hriday, the issue of religious conversion did come up: the sisters who ran the orphanage were Christian, and one explained that they were happier when their children were adopted by a Christian family. The experience of volunteering, in this context, was of transcending boundaries of culture, class, language, and history toward bare, at times poignant, humanity. This was accomplished through the instrumental tasks of acquiring donations, arranging for successful surgeries, and advocating for and providing clean diapers at the orphanage.

The group at Nirmal Hriday made attempts to institutionalize change, although cultural misunderstandings often mitigated their success. For example, in India children are toilet trained at an early age, often as early as six months, and diapers, which are considered dirty and expensive, are not commonly used with older children. The American volunteers in the Circle of Care were distressed by the "unsanitary" conditions and were convinced they knew how to provide better care. The director of the group, whom I will call Mrs. C, was critical of the insufficient attention paid to the orphans. Volunteers brought toys for the children, but they often later found them broken. There was almost a complete lack of cross-cultural communication about the value of objects and representation of love.

Mrs. C knew before she arrived in Delhi that she planned on working with Nirmal Hriday, Mother Teresa's orphanage. She had always wanted to do similar volunteer work, but the other posts her husband held as a Drug Enforcement Agency employee in Pakistan and Turkey did not offer such opportunities. She adopted her fourth child in Pakistan; her husband was Pakistani-American, and they had been involved with foster care in the United States for many years. When she first got to Delhi, she put up signs at the American Embassy that said "Huggers Needed." Thirty volunteers signed up immediately, and they went to the orphanage four to five days a week in groups. The first time they went to the orphanage, they discussed the "dos and don'ts" of volunteering. Mrs. C encouraged the volunteers to be sensitive to the different culture at the orphanage:

> Don't criticize. Be accepting of things we cannot change. You can't change things. Everything is so culturally ingrained here. The kids don't need to be picked up, the kids don't need toys. Their basic needs are met. I think a lot of [the reason this is so] is Indian. If you see kids in—not an upper-class home—but if you see kids in a middle-class to a lower-class home, they don't have a lot of toys. They're not held a lot. They're carried only to transport them. . . . They're not coddled a lot. . . . A lot of it is Mother Teresa's [orphanage]. We've been to many orphanages that have brought their own cultures with them wherever they have come from, their own plans to meet their children's needs. . . . When Mother Teresa came here she said, We will become just like the culture where we are. We're not going to come in to be a separate entity.

The first thing the Circle of Care did when they started volunteering at Nirmal Hriday was to cuddle and hold the children. Then they began trying to make changes:

> [We] rediapered the place. We went out and bought 80,000 rupees worth of diapers and diaper covers and washcloths and bibs. We rediapered, bibbed, and wash-clothed the whole place. And then we saw the need for floor coverings. When we arrived there was nothing on the floor but just the cement, and kids were falling and hitting their heads and it was really just tragic. And then we were thinking, What about winter? So we went and designed these mat covers like you would see in a gymnastics place in the States. . . . Then the surgeries came around.

The baby boy she held on the first day had clubfeet, and she wanted to fix them. When she discussed with the sisters the possibility of having his feet surgically repaired, they said, "Okay, but let us show you some of the other children who need help as well." So she was introduced to a child who was born without a rectum, a child with a heart defect, and one with a cleft palate. The Circle of Care prioritized the children in terms of those who most urgently needed surgical attention and arranged for the surgeries at one of Delhi's top hospitals. Mrs. C and a friend—who was also a Circle of Care cofounder—started by funding the surgeries themselves using their credit cards. Then they went to the American Women's Association, which paid for the floor pads. Then they went to the community. A lot of women at community meetings gave them money. With regards to the poverty in India, Mrs. C said, "People were so overwhelmed with what they see, but don't know where to begin." In two years, the Circle of Care arranged for five successful surgeries to be completed.

Volunteer work was not only time-consuming, it was also emotionally consuming. Mrs. C advised volunteers not to cry and to try to "save" their emotions:

> It is depressing [work] but we ask [the volunteers] that you not cry there. It upsets the kids and it upsets the sisters. The sisters don't see anything wrong. The kids are better off than they are in the streets, etcetera, etcetera. But we've had a couple of women just get hysterical, and I've said, 'Please try to save your emotion till you get out.' A lot of times we'll go out to lunch [after volunteering], just so everyone can vent and get it out of their system. And they say we need to do this and we need to do this. And I say, Okay, we tried this and this is what happened. Everything you can imagine—wanting to change or do to better their lives—we've tried. Some of it's worked. Some of it hasn't.

Mrs. C added that "you either get in there and you love it so much you want to be there every day, or you get in there and it's so emotional you can't ever do it again."

Some volunteers can't handle work in the orphanages, so they do other work such as letter writing, purchasing, and fund-raising. I asked Mrs. C how she prepared volunteers for the taxing work at the orphanage, and she advised them not to think too much about the past or the future but to be "in the moment" with the children:

> We tell them some of the kids are very sick, some might have disfigurements that can be a little appalling. The place is not clean. The place is very run down.

> The toys are very dirty and gross and disgusting. The food is awful. But go in and do what you can do. What your job is, is to go in and hold that baby, sing songs to that baby. Take that baby out for a walk. Take that kid out for a walk. We have the older kids age group that we take in play dough and finger paints and all that kind of stuff if you're not into the baby scene. You're there to make a difference during that one to two hours that we're there. And that's all you have to think about. You can't think about what's going to happen after you leave. You can't think about what happened before you arrived and you can't think about what's going to happen tomorrow. You can make a difference *in those two hours*, and that's all that you need to focus on.

The volunteers were encouraged to focus on the experience of the moment, making this form of voluntarism a bit like impulsive philanthropy. They were told not to focus on the historical or political economy that created the moment. Part of this was the practical reality of being expatriates, strangers in the Indian cultural context. The hardest part of this was, for Mrs. C, a factor of this cultural divide:

> Having every resource to change these children's lives and not being able to. Not being able to get your point across that it is very important that a child is stimulated. That it is very important that a child has a balanced diet. It is very important if a child is on an antibiotic that you refrigerate it. And that if you do refrigerate it, you don't wait two hours to bring it to room temperature to give it to them.[11] If a medicine says ten days, you give it to him for ten days. If a child is in pain and discomfort, you need to react and take care of it.

Yet even while denying the political economy in the moment of the experience of voluntary action, Mrs. C had an understanding of inequality and of others in need that left her feeling "blessed." The best part for the volunteers was: "Making a difference. I love it. I don't see how anyone could come here and not try to do something. Even if it is going to a *jugghi* [slum] and reading to kids. If it's buying medicine for a hospital. You can't come here and not do anything. We have so much. We have been so blessed. You have to come here and you have to do something."

The Circle of Care worked exclusively with expatriate volunteers, except for the doctors, who were Indians. The Indians Mrs. C encountered could not understand why she did her volunteer work: "Most Indians are like: What are you doing? Why are you out taking care of these babies? Why do you do this? You have four kids, you have a husband, you have a nice house. Go to lunch, shop, go get your hair done. Why do you need to be out there—putting yourself not in danger but putting yourself in situations that you don't need to be in?" I wondered why people were saying this to her, and she replied: "It's people who would be at our level as far as the caste [also class] system is concerned. They just don't see why you'd want to do it, if you don't have to." Missionaries of Charity was famous for welcoming foreign volunteers, but it was not used to volunteers who arrived in groups and who periodically returned: "People come to India just to go there [India]. And they will go for one day or two days or they'll go to the Dying and Destitute [home in Kolkata] for six months . . . they're used to having people in and out. They're not used to having people come and stay as long as we have."

Mrs. C was critical of the attitude of the sisters at the Delhi orphanage. She interpreted particular cultural needs such as toys and diapers as more general, human needs. The "kids deserve to have more than the basic needs met if you can do it. And they can, they just choose not to do it." Why, I asked? "I have no idea," she said, and told another story of cultural confusion, again over the use of toys. "We have put so many toys out there, you cannot imagine. We have invested so much money in toys. Fisher-Price stuff, manipulatives," she said. "But they don't ever teach a child how to play with a toy. They never sit down and play with a child with a toy." There were two blind babies in the orphanage, and the volunteer group had purchased textured blocks so the blind babies would have special toys. The group watched as the sisters at Nirmal Hriday locked up the toys, books, and puzzles or put them on top shelves where children couldn't reach them. The sisters "don't want kids to play with them. They want to save them. I think that's a very Indian thing. . . . They don't want the kids to ruin [the toys]. You'll see them hanging from wires or from off the ceilings not to be played with." The *ayas* (maids and nannies) also tried to preserve the toys: "The minute we walk away the toys are put away in the nice little basket and they are sitting there staring at the baby . . . because everything has to be clean. It's mind boggling."

The children were abandoned by the world and then, in the eyes of the volunteers, abandoned by the people who were supposed to be looking after them. This double abandonment upset the volunteers of the Circle of Care. Yet amidst attempts to hug an orphan, to exist in the moment with a representative of "bare humanity," fissures of culture became salient. These unbearable distinctions could be transcended only through the prospect of surgeries and adoptions, which could permanently transform orphans into kin.

## Case 4: Renouncing Wealth to Find Humanity—Charity Tourism

Priya was a British volunteer who renounced materialism for volunteer work. I met her through a charitable medical clinic at a Hindu temple next to where I lived. I went to the temple to interview a doctor who was volunteering his time at the clinic. One day the doctor asked me about my research, and when I told him it was about charity, he suggested I speak to a woman who was involved in running a school in Rajasthan for disabled children, which I will call Hearts and Minds.

I visited with Priya in her office/home close to where I lived. Behind many of the doors I passed each day, someone was involved in philanthropy, charity, and dān. Perhaps my project was defined so broadly that everyone fit into it, or the practice was so widespread that one only had to tap the surface to see its depth. I was not yet sure. On that hot day, with a ceiling fan turning overhead, Priya and I talked for four hours. We were joined by a volunteer who came from the United Kingdom to work on the school's accounts and website.

Priya was critical of those who gave donations and not time. In her mind there was a moral hierarchy in giving, and volunteering was at the top:

> There are a lot more takers than givers; a hell of a lot more takers than givers. The givers then can be broken down into different categories. Those who give, that give a lot of money, and then there are those that give but give in a very small way—it could be money; it could be food out of their kitchen that morning or that afternoon. And then there are the people who really give, give part of their time. We all live in a fast world these days. We all have things to do that occupy most of our day. And to find time out of those days to do something which is not monetary—I think those kind of givers really give.

She was herself in a position of giving time to Hearts and Minds. She worked professionally in film production, and her position as executive director (and fund-raiser) for the school was unpaid. For Priya, it was a labor of love. She had lived a life of wealth and luxury and now was doing work she found meaningful. In her youth, she had been a British TV and film star. Now, she exclaimed, she wouldn't spend money on an outfit that lasted a moment. "What did it do for me internally? Nothing!" she mused. Of Indian descent, she had been born in Kenya but lived in Britain from the mid-1970s through the mid-1990s. She first came to India in 1982 but did not return to live until 1996. She was in India producing a BBC documentary for the fiftieth anniversary of India's independence when she came across Hearts and Minds outside Jodhpur in Rajasthan. It had five rooms, and 110 children with disabilities were cared for there. This was another category of society's excluded. Because many parents believed disabled children to be the result of bad deeds from a previous life, or of curses, they stayed hidden. Priya spoke of one disabled child in her neighborhood in Delhi who was wheeled around in a wheelchair after 11 p.m. at night. "Where was this child the rest of the day?" she wondered sadly.

The school was free for the children, many of whom boarded there. The aims of Hearts and Minds were to remove the stigma of disability, to provide education, and to encourage pride among the children. In 2002, Priya took ten boys to London to take part in a sports tournament. The boys had no shoes and learned the sport just five days before the competition. The children returned later for the Paralympic Games, and five received gold medals. Such stories were inspiring.

Priya tried to encourage others to volunteer at the school, and did not charge foreigners for the service. She noted that Mother Teresa's organization required payment of £2,000 to work there; another organization charged £1,200 to £1,500. Her British volunteer, Amelia, who worked at a computer as we talked, was in Delhi for six months to volunteer. In Britain, charity tourism was increasingly popular. This activity, usually undertaken by students during their "gap year" between degrees or after college before working, was becoming more common among older adults. The BBC taped an episode at Hearts and Minds of its "Grown-Up Gapper" series, which explores adults taking a year off from their lives to travel and see the world; the episode featured a volunteer, Dave, who had come there to work for a month. In an interview Dave said that he would "never forget" his time at the school in India, and it was "the bit I remember the most."[12] Asked whether he felt that working at the school was a "turning point" in his life, he replied: "Not really a turning point, more of a wake-up call. It reminded me how much fun each working day can be." Dave was woken from the slumber of his daily, unreflected, life. By stepping out of his comfortable existence, he was forced to take notice of his experience. This is something that the volunteers in the Circle of Care, Priya and her volunteers at Hearts and Minds, and Seema's Project Hope orphanage group aimed to do as well. And it was what the National Fellow program was structured to accomplish with more national effects.

As a genre (like the narratives from the National Fellows), testimonials such as Dave's document a transformation and describe an "experience." Another volunteer at Hearts and Minds wrote about the children at the school:

> So, just let me tell you about my experience of these children . . . their eyes sparkle with warmth and love. They are bright and work incredibly hard. They appreciate absolutely everything they have. They love and respect their school and their teachers. They get up at 5am for prayers, exercise and study, and go until 10pm. With only one drum and a harmonium, they put on some of the best singing and dancing performances I've ever seen. If not for this school, more than half of these kids would be begging on the streets. Coming from poor villages where their families live, the school is like a 5 star resort—running water, blankets and two meals a day. The school is free for the poor, funded partially by the government, and dependent on outside donations.

To step out of one's comfortable existence and to live in the presence of these children was transformative for volunteers.

Priya talked about why people gave, especially of their time. She thought it was in order "to tap into people's dreams." Volunteering, for Priya, was a way that giving could become a life-changing event. She did not like people simply writing checks and instead wanted them to "get involved." The website she was creating with Amelia was one example. It was not going to be a website where one could just click "donate now"; instead, it would also provide information about volunteering and testimonies from volunteers.

Priya's own history of finding the school in Jodhpur came after searching for an organization to give to. When she visited Hearts and Minds, something moved her. She was forty years old and had moved to India with her twelve-year-old son one week after having a hysterectomy. "Maybe this was the change I was looking for after surgery," she told me. Acknowledging the dynamic of charity tourism whereby members of the wealthy class visit the poor, Priya was instrumental in starting a program at Hearts and Minds that mixed disabled children from the school with able-bodied and well-to-do children in neighboring areas for team sports. In this case, the answer to the question "who is changed by charity?" was "the able-bodied children." Priya liked working with the children at Hearts and Minds because she felt she was part of their future. It was a future of possibility, not the future of a beggar on the street, who will be begging for his or her lifetime. It was a future of change. This was why she was opposed to the "donate now" buttons on websites. She wanted people to get involved to see that "the kids are not beggars." She did not see her fund-raising work as begging either. Instead, she said the kids were full of pride. They did not inspire pity; they inspired change. Begging, in contrast to the visits of volunteers and the gifts of time, which were hopeful and geared toward a future, was a derogatory term that positioned recipients as lower in dichotomous relationships: between the wealthy and the poor, those who belonged and those who were excluded, the able-bodied and the disabled.

Priya felt that organizations asking volunteers to pay, with none of the funds making it to the charity, was scandalous. One of the organizations that required volunteers to pay and of which Priya and Amelia were critical was one I will call People Tree. Its website showed some of the same contradictions that emerged in my interviews with volunteers. It is a cliché to say that India is a land of contrasts, but this is a reality that draws people to India to participate in charity work.[13] The People Tree site boasted of India's technology sector as a possible work placement (one could volunteer in any industry, including information technology, teaching, and environmentalism). It defined India as developed, an economy on the rise with opportunities to gain from participating in its zenith. The site described India as the "seventh largest Economy in the world" with "an upwardly mobile population of over 280 million people" and "the most preferred location for Information and Technology and Business process outsourcing." It noted that India's judicial and political systems were based on the same structure as Britain and asserted that it was an exciting time to be working in India's booming economy. Being a volunteer promised access to this growth business sector, to networking with management, and to being part of industry on the rise.[14] On the website, a picture of a beautiful Indian woman with a headset and microphone (a call-center worker, one would assume) was placed below an image of a man weaving on a loom, with a woman in a sari walking by. The old and the new, exotic handicrafts and the future of technology; what could be a better "experience"?

Another link on the People Tree website answered the question, "Why India?" It described India as one of the poorest countries of the world, in need of assistance, but it also described it as having "a huge depository of empathy" (see Chapter 5). Volunteering in India was defined as helping India to become part of a global culture (as if it were not already) and contributing to "building a more peaceful world." The narrative addressed foreigners coming to India to volunteer and stated that because "India is among the poorest countries of the world," it required residents of more privileged countries to help. "Most of the schools are understaffed, many projects with regards to conservation and community outreach do not have the resources to continue." It requested a contribution from readers, either of money or initiative, time, and work. It then made a rather striking plea, especially given the narrative of progress mentioned earlier: "Many Indians would never travel and your interaction with them would help us in encouraging them becoming a part of a global culture. We could through these interactions promote world peace and understanding and lessen the stereotypes and mutual distrust that is commonplace between the developing world and developed countries. We would through volunteer work help and bridge that gap. It could be your contribution to building a more peaceful world." The website listed a landscape of contrasts that a potential volunteer could fit herself or himself into, including empathy: "Beggars, destitute street children to posh nightclubs and plush hotels, over 180 languages and dialects and several religions, adversity, a great value system, a *huge depository of empathy*, vitality and a civilization of over 2000 years." The final aspect of this advertisement suggested that "you could have unique life changing experience within India."[15]

The volunteer placement organization offered placements with "elephant care projects," "turtle conservation projects," "skill learning projects," a "teaching placement," and "working holidays." One could select the volunteer experience of one's choice, as if shopping in a supermarket.[16] Like the online shopping cart provided for sponsoring a child, one could consume a prospective volunteer experience.

Amelia was critical of such organizations and instead initiated her volunteer placement without the help of any mediating institution. She was living with Priya in her flat and was at the beginning of her volunteer posting when I first met her. Like Priya, she had to do a certain amount of sacrificing material pleasures in order to get to India and volunteer. She spoke with me over the course of many months, describing her endeavors and struggles with volunteering. She was surprised at what she called "the impact on my friends back home"; she received emails from them describing how inspiring her work was for them, since it was "something outside the norm" and required a different kind of commitment. She was working, for no pay, fourteen-hour days. She had made an initial commitment to work with Hearts and Minds for three months, organizing their accounts and working on a website. It was a life of contrasts for her. But she loved her work:

> Mostly I love the fact that it feels meaningful. Even when I'm terribly sick with chicken [food] poisoning, I feel I'm doing something meaningful. When I see

> kids begging around the markets and when I hear stories of girls being abused, I compare that with the kids at the school who are standing really proudly and teaching me things. There was one girl with no use of her legs who wants to open a beauty parlor. I could help them with their English.

It had been ten years since she received her English literature degree in New Zealand and began her career in computing. For a while she wanted to be part of a more upscale lifestyle, so she worked for Goldman Sachs, flying back and forth from London to New York. The job paid well and offered considerable financial bonuses (she earned £85,000 a year and received a £33,000 annual bonus), but "it is not all about the money," she said. "I wasn't happy and now I'm just full of beans. It was the day the bonus hit my bank account that I walked into my boss's office and quit. I am very lucky that I could do this. The night I was leaving for India, I thought—even if I died on this flight I would have made an impact by having decided to do this." Her shift from working for money in investment banking to working for no pay at all was transformative. In addition to her personal transformative experience, she felt she was having an effect on her friends and on the world by doing something meaningful.

. . .

THE PORTRAITS OF THESE FOUR GROUPS organizing volunteer work contribute to our understanding of how volunteering gains value through the concept of experience. The examples acknowledge the context of the moment and encourage attention to what "the moment" means for the people involved. For volunteers, the emphasis of their actions is not on a strict teleology of outcomes. For the sake of my argument here, what is important is not what the act of assistance does, but what it means to the people who assist. It is a gift of experience from the recipient to the donor.[17]

When one looks at the act of giving time in New Delhi, with an understanding of Indian ideas of dān, the lack of emphasis on outcomes and effects begins to make sense. With dān, the inequality of the giver and recipient is understood and expected; however, the fact that dān reinforces such inequality does not negate its significance. The worthiness of the recipient, and here I mean in terms of merit or the moral worthiness of the gift (as in Parry 1994), reflects back upon the donor. It is not an exchange between equals, and it is not reciprocal, as Mauss (1990 [1950]) might have identified. It is transformative, if only for a moment. The experience of this moment—sought after and reflected upon—is how humanitarianism is, as Volunteer Now described it, "being change" and "practical dreaming." In Delhi, volunteering echoes Mahatma Gandhi's directive to "Be the change you want to see in the world." For some of the volunteers it was a temporary experience. For others, like Priya at Hearts and Minds and Mrs. C from Circle of Care, it was a way of life. This way—a form of what I call "relational empathy"—is the subject of the next chapter.

Chapter 5

# Empathy

MUCH HAS BEEN SAID about the capacity for the liberal imagination to inspire empathy, and for this to provoke altruism. Liberal philosopher Martha Nussbaum, for example, promotes the empathy-altruism thesis in her books *Poetic Justice* (1995) and *Cultivating Humanity* (1997). According to this thesis, through literature we are exposed to characters in circumstances distant from our own. We empathize with them, which leads to the capacity for the rights-based potential for social justice to be cultivated in us. Some may argue that in practice, the link between empathy and rights is a stretch, but this thesis has recently been forwarded in anthropology (Wilson and Brown 2009). Others have vehemently criticized the thesis, arguing that it ignores the politics that produce sentiments, and that literature may be good to read, but does not necessarily generate political action (Boler 1999; Laqueur 2009).

Empathy is an emotional response that involves the possibility of experiencing the feelings of others. Sometimes empathy is defined by its absence—people who lack empathy are considered social exceptions (autistic children and psychopaths, for example). A lack of empathy is sometimes termed a social disorder, whereas having empathy is considered a basic quality of being human. Some animals, such as dogs, are considered empathic and thus make good companions. Empathic feelings are nonjudgmental and can be positive or negative. Torturers can be empathic, both "feeling" for their victims and gaining pleasure from their pain. Yet torturers do not have sympathy for their victims. The empathic response does not stop torturers from committing torture (Nussbaum 2001). My point in emphasizing this aspect of empathy is that it does not guarantee benevolence. Sympathy, on the other hand, is a sensibility that entails feeling for others, being affected by their suffering to the degree of compassion, and, ultimately, being compelled to end their suffering.

My concern with empathy (not sympathy, pity, or compassion) is to interrogate liberal altruism and present a challenge to it. This challenge, which I call "relational empathy," is differentiated from liberal altruism on the basis of individual autonomy and is presented through a spectrum of four cases. The first case, a group of volunteer knitters who distributed sweaters and organized a party for slum children in New Delhi, illustrates how liberal altruism becomes a form of pedagogy. The second involves a foreigner in Delhi who attempted to fulfill her longing for community through voluntarism. However, the discourse of liberal altruism prohibited her achievement of the relational empathy she sought. The third case discusses an Indian man who started a school in his home for the children of urban laborers. As the brother of a disabled sister, he had learned firsthand how those excluded from society could suffer. Largely through his own family, he was inspired to begin his school in central Delhi. The fourth case is a British nurse who worked in a leprosy colony for fifteen years in Andhra Pradesh. Afterwards, she moved to New Delhi, lived with a family of people affected by leprosy, and ran a charity shop to market handicrafts produced by cooperatives in leprosy colonies to international consumers. While the first two cases fit within the bounds of the empathy-altruism thesis, the second two inspire a rethinking of the relationship between empathy and humanitarianism.

In New Delhi, to hazard a generalization, quotidian forms of helping are modeled on relations of kinship. This model is opposed to dān, which, as we have seen, calls for a renunciation of interest in the gift. It also contrasts liberal models of humanitarianism that assert radical and abstract notions of equality in which all humans are worthy of rights and the care of strangers is privileged to the care of kin.[1] As I will demonstrate, in New Delhi, helping asserts one's social obligations: one helps those one has relationships with, not abstract others. Webs of kinship obligations present constant demands and responsibilities; even friendship works in the same manner. One helps because one knows someone, and association is precisely what motivates this assistance. Indian ideas of relational empathy differ from those held by foreigners in India who volunteer to hold babies at orphanages, give their time and presence in slums, sit at Mother Teresa's home for the sick and dying and wash bodies, and throw parties for slum children who are not kin. When performed in the context of family, these same activities would be unmarked or unremarkable forms of action. They would be considered usual acts, even required acts. That humanitarians help others with whom they have no connection is what makes them distinctive in the Indian context. As I show in the cases that follow, foreigners who seek community through voluntarism are out of place in New Delhi, not only because they are foreign, but because of their liberal assumptions about how to perform moral "good."

## The Empathy-Altruism Thesis: Rights-Based Entitlements in Liberal Humanitarianism

What is the liberal-political relationship between humanitarianism and empathy? Richard Wilson and Richard Brown, in their introduction to *Humanitarianism and Suffering* (2009), describe humanitarianism as an "ethos that compels people to address the suffering of strangers" (2). They link this ethos historically to the emergence of a liberal political discourse of human rights in the eighteenth century and argue that both human rights and humanitarian law "share a view of humanity as a unified legal community when crimes are committed that offend not only a nation or a country, but the entire human race" (5). This "law of humanity" enforces an idea of humanity that provides legitimacy and political sovereignty that can be communicated across borders. This type of humanitarianism is based on liberal political ideals dependent on an idea of humanity, later cultivated during post–World War II efforts to rectify "crimes against humanity" (see 1949 Geneva Convention; Redfield and Bornstein 2011). Both liberal humanitarianism and liberal altruism are tied to notions of rights. In order to empathize with the plight of others, one must be aware of having rights oneself. Only then can the deprivation of the rights of others distant from oneself be understood and felt (Wilson and Brown 2009: 12). In the eighteenth century, liberal Europeans and Americans internalized the belief in the natural rights of individuals, promoting empathy with others. This understanding of rights is what some connect to the rapid rise of the novel in the late eighteenth and nineteenth centuries (Nussbaum 1995; Wilson and Brown 2009). This era also produced the abolitionist movement and the birth of what historian Thomas Haskell has called "the humanitarian sensibility" (Haskell 1985a and 1985b).

In Nussbaum's work on literature and altruism (1995), empathy assumes a power differential in which there is justice to be done on behalf of a victim with rights. This is not pity, where a reader of a tale looks down upon the suffering of others. With pity, feeling for someone is a derogatory act. Sympathy involves favorable understanding, but it does not assume the need for political action. Empathy, on the other hand, according to Nussbaum, not only involves putting oneself in someone else's shoes; it assumes they are shoes one wouldn't want to be in. One does not have empathy for the wealthy and powerful (corporate CEOs, for example); one has empathy for the poor and powerless. Humanitarianism is part of the liberal, moral imagination, and there is a causal connection to its utility. Reading about the distant suffering of others provokes sentiment and affect through a moral imagination that requires empathy. This, in the frame of liberal education, is to be cultivated as an unquestionable good. With this logic, reading about the suffering of victims of the Haitian earthquake, Darfurians, the lost boys of the Sudan, Indians starving in slums, or Sierra Leone's child soldiers produces a type of global solidarity in which one anticipates the rights of others being violated.

In *Poetic Justice* (1995), Nussbaum argues that the novel is a "morally controversial form." A novel expresses a normative sense of life; "it tells its readers to notice this and not this, to be active in these and not these ways" (2). The literary imagination is a public imagination, and as such, literary forms have a contribution to make in moral reasoning for public good. Nussbaum argues that public imagination steers judges and policymakers and influences social action. She identifies the ability to empathize with the subjects of novels—through whom readers are able to imagine what it is like to live the life of another person in circumstances radically different from their own—with this transformative social process. Through literature, we take on the experience of others. By reading literature, according to the empathy-altruism thesis, we engage in social critique, experienced and embodied by characters in novels. Novels teach us to assess life both inside and outside the narrative, helping us to become better judges of the social milieu as well as better citizens. Because the literary imagination inspires critical reason (or, as Nussbaum says, "rational emotions"), literary judgment via engagement with narrative is a form of social engagement that involves the capacity to critically engage with a world of difference.

Some contest the empathy-altruism thesis, noting that it is not moral sentiment but rather politics and law that produce the sentiment that forms the basis for humanitarian action.[2] Critics (Boler 1999; Laqueur 2009) assert that there is no reason to assume that sympathizing with a fictional character will translate directly into the humanitarian treatment of real people. By presenting the limitations of the "sentimentalist thesis," these critics posit a political understanding of empathy: how narratives of suffering "constitute, motivate, and authorize political action" (Laqueur 2009: 36). Law is the mediator in such a process, between narratives of suffering and public action. Humans are treated in certain ways because they bear rights, not because they are somehow essentially human. Thomas Laqueur (2009) traces how in the late eighteenth century the "ethical subject" was democratized in Europe. Through law, more and more people could be included in the "circle of we" (see also Stein 1964 [1917]).[3] Other critics (Boler 1999; Keen 2007) argue that the production of empathy from literature produces a romantic functionalism. The others whose lives are imagined do not want empathy; they want justice. Moreover, the production of empathy without context is dangerous because empathy without obligation allows the abdication of responsibility.[4] One can feel for people in dire circumstances without doing anything to help them.

Humanitarianism is a tool for social pedagogy in liberal education as a moral exemplar of good behavior. We may extend the topic beyond novels to other forms of narrative representation of social suffering such as newspaper accounts, documentary reports, and film. I am less concerned with whether reading literature inspires humanitarian activity, but through the cases that follow, I argue that there is an alternative to the liberal-empathic model for humanitarian action—what I call relational empathy, where humanitarian practice strives to make others relational in the model of kin. Relational empathy challenges liberal models of humanitarian activity oriented toward the needs of strangers. In the extreme form of relational empathy, humanitarians live with those whom they assist in a kinship of humanitarianism.[5]

## Kin-Based Entitlements in India

In north India, the web of kinship obligations presents constant and ongoing demands—an aging parent, a sibling, a niece or nephew can and will arrive at a doorstep with the expectation that he or she will receive hospitality and care. Because rejecting this responsibility risks potential social exile, "no" is a rare word in the vocabulary of familial relations. This is not to say that Indians abide by obligations—there are many ways to squirm out of responsibilities, but they are never direct. This may be due to the fact that the concept of a sovereign individual with rights is neither desired nor sought after. Such a structural form is seen as alienating and lonely. That one can and does depend on others in a constant sea of possible demands is the social life that sustains and rewards.

Whether or not helping others is seen as a burden, it is often done as duty, as what is proper and right.

Families have built-in inequalities. Their members have rights and entitlements of differing degrees, while strangers do not have any rights. To extend the "circle of we" to all others would be to open oneself up to unlimited demand; it is both impractical and impossible. Thus boundaries are maintained. Obligations to family enforce this web of affiliation, identified through kinship. The web is tightly maintained and highly orchestrated, a symphony directed by customs and habits. Indians who engage in service to society at times do so at the expense of family—such as the man in Chapter 4 who started the school for slum children. This theme has also appeared in the lives of famous figures such as Mahatma Gandhi, who sacrificed his family for the cause of independence. In India, sacrifice as a form of humanitarianism is acceptable when read through lives such as Mahatma Gandhi and Swami Vivekananda, who emulated reformist doctrines of social service and world renunciation.

In India, and probably other places as well, selfishness is a negative attribute. Yet there is a distinction to be made: the obligations and responsibilities that one has toward kin and friends are not considered to be humanitarian. Such obligations are not announced and they are understood as duty; they are only marked if unfulfilled. Thanks are not exchanged. Such assistance is not charitable work, as one has a vested interest. By privileging the individual at the expense of the group, or in support of an abstract group instead of a specific other, liberal political philosophy such as John Rawls's cosmopolitan version of the "Original Position" (Rawls 2005 [1971]) fails to find ground in the Indian context (see also Rawls 2001 and Rawls 1999, in an international form). The Original Position is a thought experiment that begins with the premise that one must imagine living in a reconfigured society without knowing beforehand which role one will have within it. One must operate behind what Rawls calls a "veil of ignorance," which masks arbitrary social factors (in his case these are affiliative forms such as race, age, ethnicity, income, and gender) and thus eliminates them from influencing decisions regarding how society should be structured. Because of the veil of ignorance, one does not know whether one would benefit or suffer from a particular position and thus will select institutions that benefit the least advantaged. The veil of ignorance affirms that representatives will operate as free and equal citizens and will do what is best for society. Political theorists may see the veil of ignorance as a pure moral good, but let us step back and analyze the assumptions underlying why one moral good (toward abstract society) is superior to another (toward specific others with whom one identifies via affiliation and/or group membership).

In order to understand this distinction, I contrast ideas of relational empathy with liberal altruism. The unmarked tasks that, when written about in the context of family, would be considered usual acts or required acts become heroic acts when liberal humanitarians do them for others with whom they have no connection. It is simultaneously what makes these acts humanitarian and what makes them distinctly problematic in the Indian context. "Why would you do that?" Indians will ask. A noble humanitarian act in an American context may arouse suspicion in an Indian one, implying neglected duties: "Don't you have your own family to take care of"? One can easily substitute children, parents, or others. Moreover, the question continues: "And if not, why not?" Perhaps foreigners in India who practice liberal altruism are social orphans, so they seek family with strangers. Perhaps Indians are so buried in family that they do not need more. As I mentioned earlier, foreigners who seek community through humanitarianism are out of place in New Delhi, not only because they are foreign, but because of their liberal assumptions about moral "good."[6] As I have articulated in previous chapters, Hindu conceptions of dān most clearly fit with the philanthropic mode of helping others without any expectation of a return. This model differs from relational empathy and a kinship of humanitarianism that are built through dynamics of social obligation. The four cases are shades on a spectrum between liberal ideas of humanitarianism and Indian ideas of relational empathy. First, we see how liberal altruism is put to pedagogical use, then how the desire for relational empathy exists alongside liberal altruism via a community of strangers. In the third and fourth cases, we see how humanitarian efforts manifest relational empathy and humanitarian families (or, the kinship of humanitarianism). This spectrum is not meant to be read as a moral litmus; rather, it is a diagnostic frame.

## Case 1: Liberal Altruism as Pedagogy

Through a friend, I encountered a knitting group composed of foreigners in Delhi that organized two annual events for slum children: a "kid-for-a-day" party held at a wealthy farmhouse each spring, and a knitted-sweater distribution for slum children held each fall. This group articulates how liberal altruism oriented toward strangers is, in fact, a form of pedagogy, and the case exemplifies a liberal humanitarian stance.

The kid-for-a-day party was a grand daylong event during which children were served food, played games, had their portraits taken, and received prizes. One member of the knitting group explained: "Every woman who has ever been involved in it has come away and said this has been one of the most fulfilling experiences—in terms of feeling absolutely wonderful because you know you've touched that many children that day." The children were generic "slum children" and "street children" for whom the experience of an extravagant party was intended to be both a treat and a gift. Yet this party had particular pedagogical aims. The organizer's goal was to start the slum children at a level of education so that eventually they would be admitted to government schools and would move beyond their parents' achievements. The organizer's biggest problem was "getting the parents to allow the children to go to school because the parents just want the children to beg, as they've done." The party was for the children, to expose them to possibility and to reward them for good behavior at school, but the pedagogy was also for parents. There was an insurmountable distance between the women from the knitting group and the slum children and therefore no chance for relational empathy (the term will become clearer as my discussion continues). The distance between the children and the knitters manifested itself linguistically in objectifying statements from the knitters such as:

> There's nothing nicer than a cute little kid begging on the street, you know. The only thing is someone who is really pathetic missing limbs or whatever, but most of these children are intact. Although there was one really gorgeous little child and she had clubfeet and when we were doing the dancing we hadn't realized until everyone was dancing and one of the women said, "Look at that little girl." And her feet were so deformed and she was up there dancing like Scheherazade. She was brilliant, absolutely brilliant.

Initially, the slum children were invited to the kid-for-a-day party on the basis of academic performance. Then the women decided to include other categories such as "most improved," "brightest smile," "most sociable," or "best citizen"; they also wanted to include the category of "most needy." According to the knitters, the slum children had "no chance" in life. The organizer explained: "We're not the ones giving them a chance; we are making them a kid-for-a-day, that's all. It was for them to have a memory that will mean something to them." It was extraordinary (to me) that the group aimed to give the children a fleeting and ephemeral experience. This gift of a temporary "experience" opposed the more permanent and fatalistic stance of "accepting one's lot in life," or trying to change the structural causes of impoverishment. The women were under the impression that if the children could experience a different life for a day, they would know that such a life was possible and would strive for it. As a gift and an incentive, the group of knitters framed the party as a glimmer of possibility in a sea of struggle.

A total of 150 children had attended the previous year. Their teachers, who were Indian, attended the party because the children did not speak English, and they received gifts as well. The knitters also persuaded their husbands to participate in the event. One woman's husband worked for the Amway Corporation, and, although the Amway Opportunity Foundation supported blind children as its chosen charity, it made an exception in this case and funded a small school backpack for every child filled with toys, goodies, and school supplies.

During the party, lunch was served. One woman commented, "We have the most beautiful meal and we do veg and nonveg, and some of them taste chicken for the very first time in their lives." The knitters made sure the food served at lunch was fresh and "edible." They bought the chicken, the vegetables, and the oil. "Most of the children in the slum would barely get a meal as brilliant as this—we eat the same food," a woman told me. "The women who are there for the day, we don't have a different pot of food. It's the same cook that cooks for the children; we eat that same food because we know that this is going to be the freshest, most good food that they're going to get for a very long time." The bridging of class and status through food was symbolically potent with the discourse of rights that liberal altruism propounds. In a Rawlsian turn, everyone, even slum children, could possibly be placed in the Original Position.

After the meal, the children rested and watched a magician. The knitting group organizer said:

> And they're all kind of bunched forward on top of each other: they have no concept of kind of sitting back and allowing the space. They can't believe what they're seeing, so they're all kind of crunching onto each other to see it and they participate in it. So they have this wonderful magic show, and then after the magic show quite often a few of them will get up and do a little song or dance. They love to sing or dance or do some little act, and of course throughout the day we also have brought a whole lot of prizes. . . . The [knitting-group] money pays for the food, the prizes, a lot of the contents of the backpack: we buy them a little pencil case with pencils with rubber and ruler and sharpener, a couple of exercise books,

> a few nice school supplies, one year we had some chocolates. Last year [one woman's] husband gave us Horlicks; he's with GlaxoSmithKline, so he gave us beautiful little Horlicks, and toothbrushes, and one year one of the women gave noodles—a little cup of noodles. So we fill these backpacks with just goodies.

Humanitarianism as pedagogy came in the form of gifts. I imagined the backpacks of goodies must be treasures for the children. The organizer continued, excitedly, recounting what took place: "And everything that happens, these children are sort of like—My god, something more? Wait there's more? It's just like—it's like child for a day. They don't really have the experience of childhood. I think Indian slum-living children don't really have a childhood as we know it and yet they don't seem to be jealous or covet what we have."

In previous years the knitting group had held the kid-for-a-day party at a hotel but had since switched the event to a farmhouse. One year there was a bouncy car and train, another year, races: three-legged races, spoon races, and skipping races. The event continued on the farm from 11 a.m. to 4 p.m. The knitters tried to be conscious of the children who would otherwise "go until they dropped."

After the lunch and dessert and the magician, the knitters distributed prizes, such as games, balls, and colored pencils. Almost all the children won prizes, and more than one hundred were distributed the first year. As the director and I spoke, the chatting and laughing of the women in the knitting group in the background streamed in and out of our conversation.

The second annual event organized by the group was the distribution of knitted sweaters. Started by one woman knitting jumpers, more women soon joined and formed simple patterns for vests that could fit all sizes in "cheerful colors." In 2004, the group distributed more than two hundred sweaters, after which the phenomenon kept growing. One woman had a friend in Australia, a schoolteacher, who told her students about the work of the knitters in New Delhi. The knitting group member sent the knitting pattern to the Australian children, and after her next visit to Australia, she returned to India with a bag of sweaters knitted by the schoolchildren and their parents. The effect on the project's growth was exponential. In 2005 the group distributed close to three hundred sweaters through what the women called a labor of love.

Their knitting was part of a humanitarian imagination, inspired by the social context of the women in New Delhi but fueled by connections to other places. Yet it was puzzling to my husband. About the sweater-knitting project, he asked, "Why don't people just buy the sweaters?" I explained how the act was not solely about the sweater; it was about the labor of love. The organizer of the group agreed with my assessment enthusiastically: "And not only that. These [sweaters] are special. Quite often, well, see these ones here and this one here. [She shows me a knitted poncho.] We have thought about selling them to try and raise more money, and then we thought, no, that really isn't the concept. The concept is that we're making these to keep them [the children who receive them] warm, and when we take them out, we actually put them on the children." Putting the sweaters directly on the children was essential to this form of giving. She showed me pictures, evidence, of its manifestation, pointing out a line of children and the women "popping [the sweaters] on." She added, "They are really beautiful kids and they are just so, so happy to get any little thing." Another group member showed me photos of the sweater distribution and described how grateful the children were to receive them.

Out of context, the children in their new sweaters were photogenic, picture-perfect. During the kid-for-a-day party, the children had the opportunity to experience being something other than a slum child for a day, and the knitters experienced being near slum children for a day. But after both events, everyone returned to his or her proper place. The children did not become kin; they remained human and unrelated. Like the unbridgeable distance of charity tourism (see Chapter 4; also Hutnyk 1996; Mathers 2010) or like the audiences of the 2008 film *Slumdog Millionaire* who witnessed graphic and disturbing depictions of slum life and then were able to leave the theater and return to their lives, this instance of liberal altruism remained free of obligations to specific people.

Given the success of the two annual events, I was surprised to learn that the kid-for-a-day party had not been held in 2005. Instead, the knitters supported the building of schools. How was having a party comparable to building schools? One was fun, ephemeral, a moment in time and a memory; the other was economic development. That the two were interchangeable, a choice, seemed impossible: education was a right, a party was not. The women calculated that they could build thirty temporary school structures—each to educate fifty children a day: twenty-five in the morning and twenty-five in the afternoon. However, because the structures were temporary, they would last only until the first major monsoon, when they would need to be repaired. The women debated about whether to hold the party again the following year or to continue to support the schools. In both instances, the efforts of this group of women who met monthly to knit together were an example of liberal altruism. The women felt for the children, and their empathy inspired them to perform humanitarian acts. That there was an insurmountable distance between the women and the children, a distance bridged through empathy, places this case squarely in the realm of liberal altruism.

## Case 2: A Community of Strangers

This next case explores the desire for empathy in humanitarianism and its impossibility in a liberal humanitarian context, through one woman's attempt at volunteering. While the group of knitters may represent liberal humanitarianism and the discourse of pedagogy, this case features a British woman (whom I will call Miriam) who practiced liberal empathy but who also desired relational empathy. Miriam desired relationships, but because of the temporary nature of her involvement, she could not manifest them.

Miriam sought to volunteer at an NGO that aided autistic children. Autism is a particular condition that, for our purposes, acts as a worst-case template for the topic of empathy in humanitarian work because autistic children are classically asocial and have difficulty displaying empathy. Miriam was a volunteer, and the Indian employees of the NGO could not understand why she wanted to volunteer in a school for autistic children if she did not have an autistic child herself. The concept of "good citizenship" understood by Miriam as habitus and common sense was viewed by the NGO employees as abstract love that competed with love for existing social relationships. Miriam's search for a volunteer home was also the search for a community, and this too was nonsensical in New Delhi, where community was not a matter of choice and further exaggerated her isolation in a foreign country. The humanitarian notion of a community of strangers that she held so dear to her heart was alien territory in Delhi.

Miriam raised her children in the United States and then followed her husband to India, where he was employed by the World Bank. When she first arrived in the country and was confronted by poverty and need, she wanted to volunteer, like the people profiled in Chapter 4. The American Embassy suggested that she volunteer at the American school; however, that was not where she wanted to target her efforts. "I was adamant," she said. "I've come all the way to India. There are so many places that need help. The last place I'm going to go is the American Embassy school. It's just not what I've come to India for." She wanted to "volunteer with something Indian," she said. "I really thought when I came to India there must be a thousand needs." But she soon discovered that "you can't volunteer for an organization, however much they need help, if they are not set up for volunteers."

When I met her, she was volunteering at a charity shop and at the American Women's Association. Although she eventually found a volunteer niche, arriving there had been a journey and an ordeal. First, she had attended the British group's monthly coffee, but it was, as she said, "Not my thing. It's not my comfort level. I just really wasn't that interested. I guess I found it—all of them, the first thing they say when you meet them is 'How are you, where was your last post, and how many postings?'" She felt she was in another category. Her children were grown. She had never been overseas (aside from having spent the previous twenty-five years in Washington, D.C.), and she was not comfortable with the group of British cosmopolitans. The American group, however, was more to her liking. They were "more hands on" as they "actually go to orphanages." The American volunteer group had pet projects, which they would assess to determine whether the project was "valid" and whether it should receive money. "And then they follow up to make sure it [the money] is being used correctly," Miriam said. "So it's very thorough and it does seem that each person has a special project." One project was a school. Each year the school added a new grade, up through college. The school accepted children from the slums, but it differed from other schools because it tested the children and admitted only the bright ones. She was struck by this project. She recounted: "They needed underwear because the children in the slums don't wear underwear. So they wanted money for underwear and they needed money for a computer. So it was a whole—to me that summed it up: from underwear to a computer for a school. That really covers the whole spectrum. And there was a discussion about, well, you know, the parents are going to have to learn to send their children to school."

Another project that also moved Miriam was a sign-language group of deaf women that produced a book on the body and AIDS. Literally, people with no voice gave voice to the voiceless, rights to the victims. Her desire for hands-on engagement was (as seen in Chapter 4) a desire to be closer to need. The sign-language group was led by a Ugandan woman who was working with a group of deaf Indian women in Delhi, and the American group of volunteers was involved. Miriam described the excitement of overcoming hurdles—experiencing the joy of others. Humanitarian work involved the potential empathy of witnessing success, not only suffering but also the very possibility of overcoming suffering. Miriam was struck by the fact that the deaf women could learn to speak, literally through sign language and metaphorically about taboo bodily topics of sexual contact and AIDS. An information meeting about the women had brought Miriam to tears. She was impressed with how proud and empowered the deaf women had become.

Miriam's first experience volunteering in Delhi was with the NGO that worked with autistic children. Someone told her, "Please come; the children love to be held." She thought autistic children didn't like to be he held, so this piqued her interest, especially because she knew that autistic children were not always communicative. The NGO was terribly short-staffed, and those who worked there did so in cramped conditions. As Miriam described it: "The school is some real shabby place up on the top floor, and they have this railing going around on the outside where the children would play. I mean it's fenced; it's got wire mesh all around. The conditions were definitely far from ideal."

Miriam had a difficult time feeling comfortable at the school, and felt "in the way" because she didn't know the histories of the children:

> With an autistic child, you can't just jump in and interfere. I thought I need to know the history of this child. . . . It seemed most of them there were mentally retarded . . . but there were a lot there that weren't. So you'd have maybe four in the class, and the teacher would spend the whole lesson sort of saying—it was in English, which is impressive, so they're learning two languages—"Plate—this is a plate, what is this?" And the children were looking around, doing their own thing, rocking, banging. I didn't know if I should interfere, and they'd keep saying "excuse me" to get by me. I just realized then, and talking to some other people, you can't just volunteer if they're not set up.

The temporary engagement of voluntarism interfered with Miriam's desire for social engagement.

Miriam felt that the NGO workers at the school weren't helpful or welcoming. For instance, the woman who offered to show her around the school was busy when Miriam arrived for her tour. "She never got to me, and this went on for a few times," Miriam said. "And there was no one I knew who I could ask, and it seemed that most of the people working there had an autistic child or were in some way connected, and they'd say to me, 'Well, why are you here? Are you doing an internship? Or do you have an autistic child?' Which shouldn't matter if I want to volunteer, but I just didn't feel comfortable." Eventually, the director of the school suggested that Miriam organize the library, but she ended up disappointed in the library task because she wanted more "hands-on" engagement.

The next time she went to volunteer, it was a holiday and the school was closed. Miriam was angry and insulted that the school had not informed her of the holiday and told her husband that she wasn't going back. She wanted to be useful, but they never called her. Not only could those who worked at the NGO not understand why Miriam would want to be there, but she was not needed as much as she desired to be. She took it as a personal slight that they did not call her to tell her about the closure for the holiday. "They are overwhelmed," she said. "They are. But my point is that you can't volunteer. I don't think you can just go and jump in."

Miriam was distressed trying to volunteer for this NGO and used it as an example of not being able to do hands-on work. The issue of "hands-on" was literal. She imagined going to the school to hold the autistic children, like the volunteers at the orphanage in Chapter 4. At the same time, it was difficult for Miriam to go to the school. "I found it very upsetting," she said. "In fact, I realized that was the other reason when I found it was a school holiday and they hadn't told me, my reaction was, Phew! I don't have to go back, and I thought suddenly, Whoa, I shouldn't be dreading volunteer work. I should be going because I'm really enjoying it, and that's when I realized I really wasn't enjoying it." Miriam was conflicted: she dreaded the volunteer work, yet was upset when the school did not notify her about the holiday.

After her experience at this NGO, Miriam did not give up. Her husband traveled often for his work, and she was lonely; although it was not easy to "get connected," it was the "connection" that she desired. Miriam made a statement that we spent some of our interview unraveling together. "Indians don't tend to volunteer, do they?" she said. "It's not an Indian thing. Which is why sometimes it's hard, and you think you're trying to help them, but they're not ones who are prepared to help their own." I thought about this as I spoke with Miriam. Based on her experience, she was right. Indians tended to give to charity, whether it was in terms of time or money, in situations or places where they had a personal connection (as in direct philanthropy; see Chapter 2). Those who worked and volunteered their time at the school for autistic children were connected in some personal way, and they were less likely to help someone they did not know. In the United States, children are trained at a very young age to help those in need, even when they are strangers. Why was this so? Miriam began thinking out loud: "It's so different. I mean, community service in the West. I have no idea what the schools here are like, but more and more [in U.S. public schools] . . . now in order to graduate you had to do something like sixty hours of community service." Volunteering in the United States was pedagogy for civic responsibility and global citizenship. When Miriam's children were in kindergarten in a small private school in Washington, D.C., they were already doing community service projects: "By the time you were in first grade, I think you went to the local park and you cleaned up the trash. . . . and this was twenty years ago." I could not imagine children in India going to a local park and cleaning up trash.

Volunteering required commitment; however, Miriam was ambivalent about committing her time and wanted to maintain the freedom to sometimes travel with her husband. The commitment of volunteering interfered with her flexibility and freedom. As a result, she sought volunteer opportunities that afforded her some flexibility as well as hands-on work. I found that many other expatriates required the flexibility of volunteering that wasn't full time. In fact, the volunteer work of several American groups shut down over the summer when the expats took their vacations. This differed from the professional humanitarian work of Indian and transnational NGOs.

Miriam pointed out another problem with summer volunteer work: "In the summer they don't encourage you to go to the orphanages because there's a couple of diseases the children have." One disease—cytomegalovirus, or CMV—that was supposedly carried by the children was extremely contagious and was dormant until summer. There had also recently been a meningitis scare, and I too had taken a break from my work studying voluntarism in orphanages. It was risky for both the volunteer and the ethnographer, and such risks did not outweigh obligations to family. Miriam said, "I don't want to pass it on to my children." But despite such risks, Miriam still searched for community through her volunteer efforts. She was desperate for community, and her isolation and loneliness were exaggerated by her efforts and disappointments. In Delhi, it was she who was an orphan. For Miriam, empathy was a measure of the success of her humanitarian engagement, but more often than not, she met with failure. As with the knitters, empathy as a measure distinguished her work from more formal, professional forms of humanitarian activity. In other words, empathy was the orienting discourse in both cases.

## Case 3: My Children, My Brothers and Sisters

This case, an example of what I call relational empathy, outlines how kin relations provide a model for development and social welfare, particularly through Hindu narratives of Lord Krishna and ideals of family relations. I first met Rajesh (a pseudonym) at an orientation for Volunteer Now (see Chapter 4). His presentation challenged young Delhiites to let go of their protected, air-conditioned worlds and experience the "real" India, to live like most Indians—in poverty, simply and humbly. The fear in the young college students' eyes was met by compassion in his. He had a particular love for his efforts that made his work more than a job; he seemed to live his work. When I walked upstairs to Rajesh's home on the second floor of an upscale market in central Delhi, I realized that in his home above the fancy shops was a school for local laborers, marked by a small sign.[7] Expatriates and wealthy Indians frequented the market, and I was sure most had never noticed the sign or the school for laborers it identified on the second floor.

In the market below Rajesh's home, one could find a European bakery selling pastries and bread, a chemist offering the latest cosmetic creams, grocery shops providing sundries, stores with clothing and linens in colorful block prints designed and manufactured by self-help cooperatives. There were hair salons with prices far beyond the means of average Indians. There was a stationery shop and two bookstores—one with a coffeehouse and restaurant upstairs. A McDonalds catered to the wealthy clientele, with a TV broadcasting the latest Bollywood dance numbers and cricket matches. The market was located across the street from Lodhi Gardens and was near my son's school. I frequented this area often, as it was a convenient site for interviews with diplomats and expatriates. The coffeehouse was an oasis where I could write field notes over strong cups of cappuccino. The street level was filled with hustle and bustle, and the market emanated a sense of affluence and excess. It was a particular class location that I, as an ethnographer and an academic on an American salary, could inhabit in places such as New Delhi. Yet there was a backside to the glitz, and it was not until I went to my interview with Rajesh that I learned about the other economy intertwined with this affluence. The proximal pairing of poverty and wealth, while commonplace in Delhi, may seem striking to those more familiar with urban landscapes in the United States. It is a contrast that has been the subject of countless Hindi films and novels, such as Aravind Adiga's 2008 novel *The White Tiger*, which offers a poetic commentary on the violence of desire that these disparities produce. Although many megalopolises have service industries and underbellies, one does not see the other sides of cities until one has an interpretive frame to view their signs and symbols. It is not a question of where to look, as poverty is neither hidden from view nor placed elsewhere, but a question of how to see.

As Rajesh described his work, his disabled older sister Supriya (also a pseudonym) interjected in slurred speech. Although she clearly had a handicap, she was neither shy nor demure. They verbally leapfrogged over each other in a competitive way, their stories interspersed with sibling banter. Supriya's disabilities began when she was three years old and a fall at home caused a head injury. After an operation, her right side was paralyzed and she lost vision in one eye. Rajesh grew up alongside this sister with special needs. During her school years, Supriya faced teasing and discrimination. She heatedly told me of an early incident when she was boarding the bus to school; as her mother helped her onto the bus, it started to move away. This kind of insensitivity, a lack of empathy to special needs combined with stigma, made school difficult for Supriya. Supriya and Rajesh's mother was a housewife and their father ran a shop. Their mother took Supriya to hospitals and advocated for her care. Driven by her love for her daughter, she sought treatment and schooling for her. Their mother went to public hospitals that were crowded and required long waits to see a doctor. Their father, on the other hand, thought that not much could be done for his daughter. The doctors said she would not be able to speak—which caused us now to laugh, given how garrulous Supriya was. For his mother, Rajesh said, "It didn't make a difference what she would do. Her love for her [Supriya] was so great that she had to do something; she couldn't just sit and see her sort of wither." A mother's love was the driving force behind the particular type of humanitarianism that evolved in this family—first practiced by the mother and then by Rajesh himself.[8]

Supriya's affliction made their mother extroverted. Soon she was teaching embroidery and needlework in her home to other children. Although at that time special-needs children were hidden in homes, Supriya's mother did not hide her daughter. Rajesh explained:

> Even now but then even more, a lot of families that had special-needs kids just hid them. So they didn't come out so much. At that time she [his mother] had, without thinking, without anyone telling her, just very normally she did something which is very, I don't know, brave in the sense that Supriya was always openly meeting everyone, going to all the family gatherings. Everywhere she was put in front. Go ahead do this, go ahead do this. In the sense that usually special children have a lack of confidence. They won't go to new situations; they will just stay back. Some of them speak very softly because they are afraid. . . . With Supriya it is just the opposite. If there is a chance of doing something, she will rush headlong into it. She is not scared of anything. Even what she cannot do she says I can do and goes ahead and does it.

Rajesh was not always involved in humanitarian and development work. He finished his MBA and then traveled in Canada and Europe. When his father was diagnosed with cancer, Rajesh returned to Delhi to help with his care. At that time, his mother began volunteering in Supriya's school. When Supriya grew too old for the school, their mother volunteered in order to keep her there, out of a selfish motive. In contrast to Miriam's efforts in the previous case, this particular type of volunteering was not disinterested. Rajesh's mother had a vested interest in helping Supriya, and this in turn brought her to volunteer at the school. By 1998, their mother had been volunteering for almost twenty years. She developed a relationship with the school's principal, who eventually paid her a small honorarium. Their mother went on to study and receive qualifications for employment with the mentally handicapped.

Supriya and Rajesh's mother's involvement emerged from a combination of self-interest and empathy. That she had a special-needs child made it possible for her to do work that others might call humanitarian or development work. Empathy appears here in the distinction between professional teaching and volunteering. Their mother was volunteering because, as Rajesh explained, "she had developed a bond for special children. She wanted to work for them; she wanted to help them, and she felt, being a parent, there was a kind of *an empathy*." The professional teachers did not have this bond. For most of them, it was a job at a public school, and they were satisfied to keep the children in a corner while they talked. The teachers felt threatened by Supriya and Rajesh's mother and considered her haughty because she was committed to the children and worked with them during recess. Eventually, their mother was able to start a school of her own with the financial support of a friend. Some of the teachers from their mother's school were drawn from Rajesh's school for laborers that he started in their home.

The model of humanitarian work emulated by Rajesh's mother, and Rajesh, differed from the model followed by those who volunteered in order to earn prestige. Rajesh was critical of those who did such work "to get credit," as he put it, referring to spiritual credit as well as honor. Recall that in Hinduism, dān earns spiritual merit. Rajesh's and his mother's schools were both funded by small monthly receipts of dān. He described how his mother gathered donations by telling "all and sundry" about the school:

> [She] doesn't have the concept of [a] funding agency and finding some big chunk [of money]. She would just talk to everybody. And people in [the] market, some people from amongst our relatives, somebody else who heard, would pay small

> donations. Some people said, "Okay, we'll give you 100 rupees every month," so that added up. At one time there twenty such people paying 20 rupees every month, so paying 2,000 [rupees]. And the costs were very low. We kept the costs very low, and the entire thing runs on less than 5,000 rupees a month.

The school was still run partly on monthly donations. "Partly monthly, partly somebody gives," Rajesh said. "It is not like a fixed [thing]. We don't know exactly where it will be from. The intent is that we have at least a year's honorarium in reserve a year ahead because we don't know—some year this can stop, there is no commitment."

Despite the donations that kept the school running, Rajesh was critical of dān, particularly of the way his mother shamed donors into contributing:

> [There are] many kinds of dān and [reasons] why they are doing it. I think most of the time, here it is because they are partly embarrassed into it, so I am not very happy my mother is collecting this kind of money. My mother really embarrasses them. I can't do it, so I try to stop her. . . . Someone is giving 100 rupees a month but these are the people. They would spend 100 rupees on just a phone call. It's really nothing. I'm not denigrating it. What I'm saying is if they make an issue of giving the dān, if they make any issue of it, it is because many of them really don't want to give, but they are embarrassed into doing it.

During our interview, to my surprise, Rajesh repeatedly referred to his students as his "children," although he was not married and had no children of his own. "My children, meaning students," he said, "I see them more as younger brothers and sisters. . . . They call me elder brother [*bhaiya*]." In India, known others are immediately brought into a kinship model through such terms as bhaiya, *didi* (a term for sister), and uncle. Even in colloquial speech with strangers, one turns them into particular kin relations in order to reduce social distance. In India, kin relations engender obligations—to social relationships and resources. As already mentioned, marriage is sacred in Hinduism, as is having a child. It is seen as a duty, or part of dharma. Not to have one's own children is to make a social statement and to open oneself to the opinions of others regarding correct social action. But Rajesh did not see the need to have his own children because "there is no shortage of that connection or those relationships especially in India."

That Rajesh did not have his own children was unusual in the middle-class family that he inhabited. He defended his childless position to others who critiqued it with a religious story, of the godly example of Krishna and his foster mother. The mother of Krishna is often referred to as the exemplar of motherly love. However, the mother whom people refer to is not Krishna's biological mother, Devaki, but the woman who raised him, his adoptive mother Yashoda. Rajesh said: "I like to ask this question to people: who was Krishna's mother? And invariably the answer is Yashoda." Krishna's childhood is a popular topic of folklore, poetry, songs, and dance. Stories of his pranks and naughtiness—such as stealing butter, lying to his mother—are emblematic of the love between mother and child. Rajesh emphasized that it was the love between Krishna and his adoptive mother that is "such a part of our language, that [when] we just want to talk of it, we say Yashoda and Krishna. . . . So it's still alive and so our culture is replete with songs about Yashoda and Krishna and not a single song about Devaki. Not even one. Not even recognizing that she's the biological mother. Everybody knows the story, but people will not remember the name of Devaki." I asked Rajesh, "When you mention this story as justification for your caring for the children of laborers, what do people say?" "They have no answer," he replied. "They cannot respond." They could not challenge his decision not to have his own children when given a sacred Hindu example. This story from Hinduism provided an explanatory frame for those who questioned Rajesh's helping strangers instead of family, although he saw adoption as very different from what he was doing because he considered adoption a kind of ownership. He said, "Even adoption is treating a child like property."

## Case 4: Humanitarian Families, or, the Circle of We

This last case is also tied to the idea of humanitarian families. In the heat of Delhi in late April, I sat with a British woman I'll call Jane in her charity shop as she joked about having recently installed an air-conditioner. In Delhi, charity embraces discrepancies between the lives of the disadvantaged and those who provide assistance. Yet Jane was somewhat of an anomaly with regards to the divide; she lived with a leprosy-affected family and ran an NGO that sold handicrafts made by leprosy-afflicted and other disabled people. In order to market goods to people "who live in the lap of luxury," air-conditioning was a necessity. "It would be nice to put a notice on the door that says we don't have air-conditioning in here because we think you should all experience what it feels like [to not have it]," Jane explained, "but the reality is that people won't come in and do the shopping." The charity shop was a buffer zone for humanitarian engagement without messy interaction. Despite this amenity, we sat in an un-air-conditioned back room as a ceiling fan feebly moved the hot air above us.

In homes where I interviewed diplomats, expatriates, and prosperous Indians, the air-conditioner's whisper emanated from doorways and ceilings, delimiting chasms between the extremely wealthy and the extremely poor. The distance between social spaces was marked by the movement of silent, cooled air.

Trained in Britain as a nurse, Jane, who was a Christian, had lived and worked in the leprosy colony in Andhra Pradesh for fifteen years before moving to Delhi to run Helping Hands. She first came to India in 1978 as a hospital nurse on a three-year contract with the Salvation Army, seeking an adventure and a break from the British National Health Service. She "got involved" with a family, and it became difficult to leave because they had become her friends. She knew when she began her work with leprosy-affected people that she needed to spend a whole year, "to see the seasons. To see how it is." After two and a half years, she "wanted to be stretched a bit as an individual." She wanted to stay in India, but she "was looking for something more." An Australian monk working at a neighboring leprosy colony adjacent to the hospital where Jane worked asked her to work in the colony. Her mother did not understand, saying to Jane, "I could understand that you wanted to be fulfilled and you went for three years for this adventure, but why would you want to live uncomfortably?"

She started a weaving program in the colony after a pregnant woman had a negative reaction to the medicine she was taking for the disease and was unable to beg. Jane's work expanded beyond leprosy-affected people to include people who, because of their disability, learned an income-generating skill as a form of development, as well as traditional crafts artisans. Although charity was marketed in Jane's shop as being about those receiving skills training in weaving, it was also about relationships between those who wanted to give and those who needed assistance. When Jane first moved to Delhi, it was hard for her to navigate the great distances between affluence and poverty, between the pleasure of her work and the pain of empathy. Her job in Delhi forced her to traverse such crevasses. While in the leprosy colony in Andhra Pradesh, she had lived with the afflicted, so she was not accustomed to having to cross the divide between need and abundance, although this was what she tried to bridge with her shop.

Through her charity shop, Jane facilitated the production of goods produced by the handicapped and their consumption by foreign clients. One leprosy group was raising chickens for sale to expatriates. An expatriate volunteer told me she discovered the charity shop through the chickens; at the time, it was one of the few places to buy decent broilers in Delhi. However, Jane noted, they did not advertise where the chickens were raised: "We never told them that our chickens come from leprosy colonies. We never talked to about it. . . . Only now people are asking questions like, 'Are they organic?' Or are they, you know, 'What's the feed?' Still they're not asking who is producing them." We laughed together at the contrast between expats and lepers, brought together unknowingly through the production of chickens. Despite this obvious social distance, exemplified by the wealthy expats in search of tasty chickens and the lepers as producers, Jane's approach to development differed from liberal altruism.

Development, for Jane, was about relationships, and these relationships brought Jane pleasure. She used a Christian example from her experience with the leprosy colony in Andhra Pradesh. Members of a church used nylon stockings to knit bandages for the colony, which were particularly useful for holding dressings on chronic ulcers. People from a Canadian church saved their nylon stockings and sent them in large shipments. Some of the bandages were knitted and women through Canadian Lutheran World Relief sent quilts. At some point, the churches decided it was not cost effective to send the stockings, bandages, and quilts to India. "The old ladies were very upset," Jane said. "For them it was a contribution that they could make. Far away, they cared about those people; they didn't have the money to give, or if they did they already allotted that, but they did have this time they could spend [knitting and making quilts]." Jane had seen the women quilting: "The women don't know how to contribute to this world of need and poverty. This is what they knew how to do, and it was a social event." This relational aspect of development—and here it was relations between the knitters and quilters, not with those in need—could not be calculated in reports. This other realm of meaning making, representing both the social and the intangible realm of possibility and hope, was also, for some, a spiritual realm (as in Durkheimian social solidarity, Durkheim 1995 [1912]).

In the leprosy colony in Andhra Pradesh, Jane also participated in child sponsorship schemes. Alongside dān and direct philanthropy, child sponsorship is a form of charity popular in India with both foreigners and Indians precisely because it involves relationships (see Chapter 3 and Bornstein 2001). Jane noted that Indians gave "direct to this little Raju with a face, a real person," or "Neha and paying for Neha's education, and I can visit her on her birthday!" She said that this kind of giving "attracted people in the West, too," because it was helping "a real person." She felt it was "interesting" that in the leprosy colony she and her colleagues also found sponsorship for elderly people. HelpAge International, an organization based in Britain, had an adopt-a-granny scheme. And Jane sourced leprosy-affected people in the colony for elderly British to sponsor. This sponsorship program, however, which was also relational, could not bridge the distance it aimed to unite. Jane explained:

> It took up too much time, and it cost too much in post and all that. And it was absurd! Imagine this situation where we get very, very sweet letters from delightful old ladies in England saying, you know, "Dear Ethanamma, the spring is here and the daffodils in my garden are quite the most beautiful we've ever had." And you have to, I mean, . . . your conscience would not allow you not to translate that, so then you say, "Oh you know, she has very nice spring flowers this year," and this woman [in India] doesn't have a garden . . . in many ways her life is really wretched. . . . We had one in which a woman sent us a photograph of her cat wearing a bowtie at her son's wedding. Sweet woman, a lovely woman who wanted to share her joy with this woman she was sponsoring or this man she was sponsoring in India. So, she wrote that letter. And that for her, giving in that way, nobody was siphoning anything along the way. . . . But one had to respond to this letter!

I asked her what she did in this circumstance, and she said, "I showed her the picture of the cat and said, 'Oh, isn't this funny, she's dressing her cat up because it was her daughter's wedding!' But it wasn't supposed to be a joke. . . . But that's where that kind of thing can be taken, to absurdity. But it was popular because a person felt they were really giving to another person."

At one point during our interview Jane began speaking as if she herself were afflicted with leprosy. In the dialogue that follows, I emphasize the shifts in pronoun use Jane made between third person, "they," to second person, "you," and eventually to first person, "I." This discourse creates intimacy and collapses distance on a spectrum, from "they," located over there, to "you," being a bit closer, to I, being right here. This linguistic shift may be instrumental, for dramatic effect, as is the case with much discourse on humanitarianism where viewers are encouraged to empathize with victims in order to *feel* their circumstances and *experience* their suffering. The empathic linguistic turn is a core strategy of humanitarian discourse (see Boltanski 1999; Sontag 2003). In the quotation that follows, Jane was talking about long-term hospital care for leprosy-affected people versus community-based care. She described why people with leprosy preferred to live in leprosy colonies and not stay in their homes with community-based development schemes (emphasis added):

> But then a lot of *these people* were discharged when, after this, treatment changed from long-term asylum to sending people home when *they* finished a

> course of some kind of treatment or on *their* treatment. And then *most people* didn't go home, *they* went and formed a little leprosy colony or something. 'Cause if *you've* been in an institution a long time and suddenly *you* turn up back in *your* home, first of all they're not used to feeding *you*. So it's expensive economically. But especially if *you* come home and *you* can't—clearly *you're* not the guy who's going to do any work. Nobody's going to want to employ *you*. So here we have this sulking bloke just sitting around the house. So most people knew *they* wouldn't be very welcome for economic reasons.

Later, Jane shifted from third and second person, "they" and "you," to first person, "I." Through linguistic empathy, she herself became affected with leprosy:

> Very, very often there are many activities here in India when you think, "Why do *they* do that?" and then you think about it a bit harder and you realize it's because there's nothing to fall back on here, there's no social security program. Often *people* are kept partly for those reasons to build up a little nest egg for *your* family, all that kind of stuff. And then, this case, if *I* go home, first of all they may not want *me* at all because *I'm* leprosy infected, but sure as heck they're not going to want me if *I'm* going to start eating them out of house and home. So *they* just went and settled on land adjacent to the hospitals, most of them, forming these leprosy colonies.

Jane's approach to her humanitarian work in Delhi mirrored the structure of the leprosy colony—membership in a family of outsiders. The colony was united by leprosy. Although the leprosy colony did not have family relationships to keep people in check, people invented family relationships. In the colony there was also a high level of political organization. Since the 1950s, the members of the colony had formed themselves into a group that fought for their rights. This was only possible when they formed a separate leprosy community and went against the dominant discourse of community-based self-help that kept people affected with leprosy at home with their families. Jane called the members of the leprosy colony her friends, but she also discussed how they were like her family. When we met, she was living with a family from that community in Delhi.

When Jane decided to leave the leprosy colony, members of the community were shocked because they had come to consider her family. "They just couldn't believe that I would go," she said. "And it was this mother relationship, and it was like, you can go as far as you like with your mother." They had taken her for granted, as a mother would love them despite their illness. Jane moved to

Delhi with a leprosy-affected family, near a leprosy colony where the family had friends. This family had adopted her: the children called her "Ma" (to others, she was "Special Auntie"); she considered this a privilege. Jane did not have any children of her own, and she considered the children of her adopted family to be her children. As a nurse, she had been present when the children were born and they had since become part of her family. Her mother in Britain included pictures of the two children of Jane's Indian adopted family with pictures of her grandchildren. To work with a group in a humanitarian capacity, and to build relationships with that group, was part of belonging to a humanitarian family in the kinship of humanitarianism.

. . .

THROUGH THESE FOUR CASES we can see a challenge to the liberal empathy-altruism thesis, which assumes that altruistic behavior emerges from the overcoming of distance through empathy and then maintains this distance by interpolating others as liberal bearers of rights. The first case fits squarely in the liberal empathy-altruism thesis: the group of volunteer knitters embodied a liberal-empathic approach through their pedagogy. In the second case of Miriam, who desired relationships but was unable to attain them through her temporary volunteer work—a challenge emerges. Miriam is not satisfied with the distance that liberal altruism maintains. The final two cases elaborate the practice of relational empathy: Rajesh and Jane offer Hindu and Christian accounts of how humanitarian relationships approach belonging to kin. In New Delhi, helping others posits humanitarians as relational and as kin. Only then, through a relational prism, does humanitarian activity make social sense. In short, humanitarians that practice liberal altruism eschew the relational model by turning to abstract others in need, while those who practice relational empathy turn strangers into kin.

# Epilogue

AT FIRST IT MAY APPEAR that there is a fundamental contradiction at work between humanitarianism, in which recipients may enjoy abstract human rights but cannot make claims on a donor's time and money, and social welfare systems, in which claimants are entitled to certain benefits. Yet as the cases in this book have depicted, the two forms are not as distinct as they might initially seem. In practice—in orphanages, in tsunami relief, in literacy programs for the poor, and in many other settings in New Delhi—the fleeting impulse to assist those who are suffering and in need may be institutionalized, ritualized, and made a regular and required act. In such settings, social relations that mediate expectations of the gift transform the gift into an entitlement.

A final parable—of a request for "donations forever"—illustrates this point. Once, a young man completed his treatment in a leprosy hospital and returned to his village in Andhra Pradesh, India. Over the years the disease relapsed, and he returned to the hospital. Filled with fear that his home community would learn of his disease, he debated moving to a leprosy colony located near the hospital. Jane, the nurse we met in Chapter 5, did her best to persuade him otherwise as he was a single man who lived with his mother, whom he loved very much. One of the symptoms of this man's disease was that he would sweat profusely, which made him self-conscious while he worked in the fields. Eventually, he decided to move to the leprosy colony where he found support and freedom because he no longer had to hide his condition. In the colony, he received humanitarian assistance through the philanthropy of well-meaning donors.

However, he was also a claimant with rights to some state-supported welfare services. People affected with leprosy came together as an identified group to fight for state-sponsored roads and electricity in the colony. The community, which consisted of 341 families, amounted to the bulk of the votes in one ward (between six hundred and seven hundred votes). Their numbers compelled local political counselors to provide resources for the colony as a constituency. The local counselor could not ignore these people, for if he did, he would not get elected the following year. This is an example of liberal rights and entitlements at work, with leprosy-affected individuals as claimants demanding welfare provisions from the state.

The colony was supported primarily through the begging of its members. They had neither stable patrons nor donors (aside from those who gave them alms) until Jane and other humanitarians moved in and addressed the colony's requests for medical care and education for their children. Through the efforts of these humanitarians, money was soon gathered from international charities and philanthropists to provide the welfare services that the state could not. The state provided roads and electricity, but it did not provide medical care. However, because donations are not rights (they are gifts), at one point Jane told members of the colony that there was a risk that international donors would stop giving funds because of perceived instability in the colony. One of the leaders of the colony asked her, "If [one particular donor] stops supporting us, can we take him to court?" Members of the colony saw funds from donors as their right and considered those funds equivalent to their demands of the state. Because of their disability, the colony members felt that donations were *their* money. "They believed that money is raised for them," Jane said. "It has their name on it, that money, it's theirs." The donation had become (in their minds) an entitlement, and members of the leprosy colony wanted to stop begging in favor of permanent donations. They asked: "Could everybody have 500 rupees per month? Can you get us a donation from somewhere, forever? Five hundred rupees, for life, to stop begging?"

That donations are capricious and temporary is a functional reality of both dān and humanitarianism. It is also their beauty, power, and limitation. Impulsive philanthropy does not offer rights to recipients; it offers help and sustenance according to the will of the donor. For donors, gifts may provide merit, meaning, and in some cases even a transformative experience. But in the language of humanitarianism, "donations forever" is absurd. The rights-based critique of charity, which privileges entitlements, is articulated within a discourse of social justice in which every individual is the bearer of potentially enforceable rights. It is against the charity model of alms and dān. According to this logic, freedom is an attribute of individuals. But, as we have seen, there are other frames of reference in humanitarian practice. When freedom is redefined as a form of relationality—freedom in relation to groups to whom one belongs and to whom one is obligated—only then can "donations forever" be entertained. Through relational association, donor-recipient dynamics can begin to resemble kin-based entitlements.

The kinship of humanitarianism is the affective and meaningful arena to which this book has been devoted. The members of the leprosy colony could conceive of "donations forever" from the philanthropist because they had a long-term relationship that the group envisioned continuing in the future. From the perspective of liberal social welfare, this may be judged negatively as a form of dependence. Other forms of humanitarian assistance may, in contrast, accept this as sought-after evidence of relationships built and of trust.

Throughout this book I have emphasized the topic of relatedness in humanitarianism. I posed the act of giving as problematic—where releasing oneself from the gift (in ideal forms of dān) articulated the liberating potential of giving. The impulse of the gift existed in dynamic tension with forms of regulation that reined in the gift. While the impermanence of the gift in the Derridean sense was its beauty, as soon as it was manifest in the social realm, relations of obligation fettered its purely liberating potential. We saw how the desire to see one's gift go to good ends was met with a form of direct philanthropy in which links of affiliation fueled the practice of giving—whether to a group defined by religion, regional association, gender, or social interest. The prism of accountability and audit practices rendered this practice "corrupt," and I argued that suspicion itself became an audit for the gift, a form of questioning that articulated issues of trust. To answer questions of trust, corruption, and self-interest, we saw how certain people were "better" to give to, and certain places were more ideal sites for giving. Orphans, for example, were valuable in humanitarian discourse precisely because they were not kin (which ensured no self-interest). For donors, orphanages became sacred sites for giving. That orphans had the potential to become kin through adoption garnered protection, as citizens with rights, from the state in the global political economy. At orphanages, and elsewhere, the experience of volunteering was a sought-after phenomenon, and volunteers went to great lengths to find meaningful connections to strangers in foreign lands through their humanitarian work. The experience of volunteering brought foreigners closer to each other and to suffering. Though volunteering did not fulfill the desire for membership in a group, it addressed membership in an abstract "global humanity." Empathy toward strangers in circumstances widely different from one's own is a desirable attribute promoted by liberal altruism, which promises to garner a capacity for human rights. Yet in practice, we saw how empathy was a discourse that humanitarians used to measure the success of their work. Some humanitarians employed a type of relational empathy modeled on kin relations. Through relational empathy one could "be with" others in need, unconditionally, in a manner that translated humanitarianism into a more permanent status—a way of life.

Humanitarianism, as a viable solution to the crisis of meaning in a giver's life, is a disquieting endeavor. Giving to a beggar on the street, volunteering at an orphanage, sponsoring an orphan child, or sending a donation to an NGO are all activities that produce meaning for people. Giving challenges people to think relationally about their place in the world. In this age of abundance and scarcity, models of renunciation and giving away are powerful reminders of the relations that make us members of groups. Although humanitarianism makes headlines in the short term with dramatic narratives of victims and heroes, people continue to address human suffering and need, even as the headlines fade, in manners that differ widely in their motivations, habitus, and frames of understanding. An impetus of this book has been to show how certain frames of giving are under judgment: impulsive philanthropy (versus social development), direct philanthropy (versus accountability), and relational empathy (versus liberal altruism). Liberal forms of welfare are not the only solutions to suffering and need; neither is the welfare state. Various shades of play occur between varieties of humanitarian forms, which are often practiced in dynamic interaction. Unlike the large-scale humanitarianism that makes headlines, a great deal of humanitarianism is spontaneous, informal, unmediated, and habitual. That it is not rational and institutional does not make it invalid. These small gestures are social gestures to strangers and to distant kin, to a kinship of humanitarianism that brings small, often utopian, solutions to an unjust world.

# Reference Matter

# Notes

## *Prologue*

Parts of this prologue have been adapted from Bornstein (2007).

1. Since Schneider's critiques of kinship (1980, 1984), recent works have reconfigured kinship and belonging through an analysis of "cultures of relatedness" (Carsten 2000; Franklin and McKinnon 2001), "families we choose" (Weston 1991), and families that choose others (see cross-cultural studies of adoption, Bowie 2004; Dorow 2006; Howell 2006; Modell 1994, 2002; Volkman 2005; Yngvesson 2002, 2004). One might also consider studies of families we flee (Passaro 1997) and friendships we maintain (Grindal and Salamone 2006).

2. Cf. Beteille (1992) on the importance of family in urban India.

3. Dyck (2000) and Pink (2000) write of fieldwork at home.

4. Feminist ethnography set the groundwork for questions of multiple subjectivities in field research. Books such as *Women in the Field* (Golde 1986) and *Children in the Field* (Cassell 1987) present narratives of trials and ordeals, some due to gendered contexts. The field has been, and continues to be, reconfigured in our changing world, where one no longer attempts to write a general ethnography of a culture.

5. Families demarcate groups of obligation and membership, the boundaries of which can determine whom one assists and whom one ignores. For middle- and upper-class urban Indians, these demarcations can also direct spheres of humanitarian effort. Unlike caste, which was not a category mentioned much in my ethnographic work, families were meaningful rubrics of care. That caste and its correlative realms of purity and pollution were not relevant categories for my research on giving may strike some readers as odd. Some of those familiar with earlier anthropological literature on India may assume that caste is a central orienting rubric for any understanding of religion and politics—particularly Hindu inflected practices (see Dumont 1980; for critiques of this paradigm, see Beteille 1979; Appadurai 1988; and Dirks 2001). Let there be no misunderstanding: I am not describing India as traditional, religious, and hierarchical in relation to a modern, secular, and egalitarian West. Today, as in earlier eras, what may seem like distinct practices—of Indian dharmic dān and Western philanthropy or humanitarianism—are co-constituted. See van der Veer (2001) for an analysis of co-constitution in colonial eras; also see Bornstein (2012) for a historical-legal analysis of the category of religion in charitable work in India. See Haskell (1985a, 1985b) on colonial humanitarianism as constituted by British abolitionists in relation to the slave trade in British colonies.

## *Introduction*

1. For an analysis of scriptural directives of dān in South Asia, see Agarwal (2011), Heim (2004), and Nath (1987).

2. I have oversimplified the distinction for the sake of brevity here; a more elaborate exegesis follows in Chapter 1. Since Mauss, the anthropological literature on "the gift" has become extensive. See Coleman (2004) and Elisha (2008) on giving in Christianity. Silber (1998: 134–45; 2001) writes eloquently against a unified theory of the gift. On blood and ova donation in light of the gift, see Copeman (2005) and Konrad (2005), respectively. On gift economies, see Godelier (1999), Gregory (1982), and Rupp (2003). On time, honor, and the gift, see Bourdieu (1977). On the gift in Melanesia, see Malinowski (1922), Miyazaki (2005), Strathern (1988), and Weiner (1992). On the anthropology of the gift in India, see Dusenbery and Tatla (2009), Laidlaw (1995, 2000, 2002), Parry (1986, 1989, 1994), Raheja (1988), Reddy (2007), Simpson (2004), Snodgrass (2001), and Trautmann (1981).

3. The realm of religious donation is not an informal economy, but a formal economic realm segregated from secular charity by law and governed through Personal Law (Bornstein 2012). The Indian constitution offers a *unique* case of secularism that integrates religious law in civil personal law. Personal Law, which governs donations to religious endowments, also regulates (for Hindus, Muslims, Parsis, Christians, and Jews) marriage, dowry, divorce, parentage, legitimacy, guardianship, wills, inheritance, and succession (see Larson 2001; Williams 2006).

4. Today, humanitarian aid agencies also encourage "self-reliance" and "autonomy." Development has not completely gone away. Now it is bundled in discourses of philanthropy.

## *Chapter 1*

An earlier version of this chapter was published in *Cultural Anthropology*; see Bornstein (2009).

1. Laidlaw (2002) urges anthropological attention to the concept of freedom and of ethical projects that involve freedom, particularly, how freedom is exercised in different social contexts.

2. Maimonides specified eight degrees of charity, which served as a code of benevolence for giving.

3. According to Kochuyt's (2009) analysis of zakat, wealth is a gift from God, and one gives back to God by giving zakat, but the gift is not direct: it is given to the poor on behalf of God. The countergift (in exchange for wealth given by God) is zakat to the poor. Allah has made the poor his beneficiary. This interaction is what produces solidarity, linking the giver (God) and the recipients (the faithful who give and receive zakat). The Qur'an articulates specific recipients for zakat: (1) the poor and needy, (2) those who administer zakat, (3) people who have recently converted to Islam, (4) debtors, (5) slaves and captives, (6) mujahidin who fight for Islam (most recently interpreted as through "mosques, religious foundations, schools, charitable trusts, hospitals, social projects or emergency relief programs around the globe"), and (7) travelers (Kochuyt 2009: 103; Benthall 1999, 2010).

4. Some Jewish humanitarian organizations, such as the American Jewish World Service, don't limit their work to helping Jews.

5. This articulation of dharma is in a strictly religious context of proper conduct. It should not be confused with the Hindu nationalist use of this term, for which, in the case of female renunciants, see Menon (2010).

6. See also Maharaj (1972), Miller (1986), and Gandhi (2000) for other translations. The passage is an interpretation of chapter 17, verses 20–21, in the *Bhagavad Gita* (Miller 1986: 140):

Given in due time and place
to a fit recipient
who can give no advantage,
charity is remembered as lucid.
But charity given reluctantly,
to secure some service in return
or to gain a future reward,
is remembered as passionate.

Verse 22 is also relevant for the current discussion (Miller 1986: 140):

Charity given out of place and time
to an unfit recipient,
ungraciously and with contempt,
is remembered for its dark inertia.

7. Each issue of the newsletter covers a topic related to NGO regulation or accounting and is mailed to about twenty-seven hundred people working in NGOs, agencies, and audit firms.

8. Quotation from the *Mahabharata*.

9. From the journal of Madame Drinette Verdier, quoted in *New Discoveries*, vol. 1, pp. 487–88, cited in Vivekananda 1997: 322–23.

10. It has also provided a shelter for high-tech companies that do not have to pay taxes. See India's Special Economic Zone policy at Special Economic Zones in India, http://www.sezindia.nic.in/index.asp.

11. Van der Veer (2002) proposes that instead of seeing the religious fervor of migrant communities as traditional or conservative (or terrorist), we should consider them as expressions of transnational cosmopolitan diasporic communities. The Vishva Hindu Parishad is both a vehicle for Hindu nationalism that is antisecular and anti-Muslim and a vehicle for the globalization of Hinduism. Hindu and Muslim global social movements are both part of transnational religious movements and forms of non-Western cosmopolitanism.

12. The appeal differs from that oriented toward Hindu nationalists *in India*. Menon (2010), for example, documents how female religious renunciants mobilized for Hindu nationalist causes—and how the concept of dharma was utilized for political mobilization. The mythic referents of religious nationalism were fueled by female renunciants who were perceived as representing the body of the nation, fighting for moral order. In this case, in India, religious sentiment and imagery combined with nationalist politics to foster violence.

13. Philanthropic giving by the Indian diaspora is facilitated by Indian-American umbrella groups (occupational, ethnic, religious) and through Indian organizations based in India, U.S.-based NGOs, U.S.-based affiliates of Indian NGOs, high-tech and other businesses that operate in India, and American venture philanthropists (Sidel 2004b).

14. *Shradh* is an annual ritual performed for the dead on the anniversary of their death to ensure *moksh* (salvation).

15. See Copeman (2009) and Dupont, Tarlo, and Vital (2000) on the matter of Delhi's supposed lack of conscience.

16. My intent is not to evaluate whether philanthropy is effective; this has been, and continues to be, well done by others (particularly by those engaged in its practice; see CAF India 2000; Dadrawala 2004; and Tandon 2003).

17. Biksha requires the humility of the recipient.

18. With food as well as with blood, see Copeman (2009) for a direct connection and Reddy (2007) for an inferred one.

19. See Sundar (1997b) for a history of post-Gandhian philanthropy by women.

20. Stirrat was a volunteer advisor for a British agency involved in relief efforts in Sri Lanka after the 2004 tsunami when, in the landscape of development, NGOs were competing for beneficiaries, for local partners, and for relief opportunities that manifest visible results of effectiveness—all exacerbated by extensive media coverage. It was not only beneficiaries who competed for the resources of donors, but donors who competed for suitable recipients for humanitarian aid.

21. Some religious philanthropy does involve account books (Bayly 1973; Haynes 1987; Laidlaw 1995) although it may still exist outside regulation by the state.

22. In gupt dān "the donor tries to avoid revealing his or her identity in order to earn extra spiritual merit" (Asia Pacific Philanthropy Consortium 2007: 21).

23. The seven-country project, part of "Investing in Ourselves: Giving and Fund-raising in Asia," included baseline surveys of fund-raising and giving in the Philippines, Indonesia, Thailand, Pakistan, Bangladesh, Nepal, and India and was sponsored by the Asia Pacific Philanthropy Consortium. It explored the nature of giving, the definition of giving, and measures of giving (including the percentage of people giving, the average amount given per household, and the average amount given per capita). The country-wide study focused on large urban areas and utilized stratified, systematic random sampling to select households; a total of 6,499 households were interviewed (Sampradaan Indian Centre for Philanthropy 2001: 25).

24. At the time of this writing, the Government of India was working to implement a new tax code. See Direct Taxes Code, at Ministry of Finance, http://www.finmin.nic.in/DTCode/index.asp.

25. Applicable to different states in India. The Bombay Trusts Act of 1950 is applicable in the states of Maharashtra and Gujarat; the Rajasthan Public Trusts Act of 1959 is applicable in the state of Rajasthan; the Madya Pradesh Public Trusts Act of 1951, is applicable in the state of Madhya Pradesh.

26. All-India national legislation with each state adopting modifications. The Indian Companies Act and the Income Tax Act are national legislation.

27. Requires a minimum of two trustees. The board does not legally require rotation of its members. Trustees are held personably liable.

28. Requires a minimum of seven individuals for registration. A society requires the rotation of board members, and the liability of members is limited.

29. "They would now attract tax at the maximum marginal rate (presently 33.66%). However, religious and religious–charitable organizations have presently been exempted from this in view of [the] widely prevailing practice among devotees of *gupt daan*, or confidential donation, where the donor tries to avoid revealing his or her identity, in order to earn extra spiritual merit" (Asia Pacific Philanthropy Consortium 2007: 21, also see above in relation to scriptural dān). The government later revoked this imposed tax. See "Taxing NPOs—The Proposed Tax Code," *AccountAble*, No. 144 (February 2009–March 2009), http://uttardayee.freewebspace.com/AccountAble_India/144%20-%20Taxing%20NPOs%20-%20The%20Proposed%20Tax%20Code.pdf.

30. Which does not mean it does not exist (Laidlaw 1995, and the life of ascetic Jains, who live with impossible ideals).

31. This sūkti was recited to me by a scholar of Hindi literature who organized donations for public literary charitable causes, such as libraries and publishing in north India.

## Chapter 2

1. This ensemble of distrust exists without paralyzing the social body.

2. At the time of this writing the FCRA was being revised. See Government of India (2006, 2010), Puri (2008), and Sundar (2010) for details, history, and debates surrounding the act.

3. There is an extensive literature on witchcraft in Africa; for examples relevant to this chapter see Bornstein (2005) and Englund (2006).

4. Like those analyzed by Cohen (1999, 2004, 2007) regarding organ donation in India and Englund (2006) regarding the illegal sale of body parts in Africa.

5. For a related but contrasting study, see Copeman (2005) on blood donation in India: directed donation is intended to go to many. The gift is split into parts and not directed to specific others.

6. They estimated to have imparted education and training to approximately 1,840 students from "the weaker sections." Future plans included targeting approximately 120,000 women and children for help "by cooperating with the Government and Corporate Sectors."

7. This legislation is detailed in the Societies Registration Act (1860).

8. On a website listing organizations involved in tsunami relief in Nagapattinam (NGO Co-Ordination Centre, Nagapattinam), of the 235 organizations working in Nagapattinam, only one, a U.S.-based NGO, did not list an Indian contact address. The rest were Indian individuals; NGOs; religious organizations, such as the Chinamaya Mission; schools; corporations; hospitals; Bhoodan associations; education societies;

GOI agencies; and international NGOs, such as CARE and Catholic Relief Services. The Bhoodan movement, translating roughly as "land gift movement," is a form of dān initiated by Vinoba Bhave, who was influenced by Gandhi. The slum school was listed on the roster.

9. Mr. A was well versed in Indian scripture, and much of our discussion revolved around his exegesis of ancient texts. For example, he listed the history of dān, the different types of dān: "In my heart I never feel anything at someone who is asking, and neither do I regret when I have given money. In ancient Indian law, you could sue to receive a promise of a donation. As soon as a promise is made, you have alienated it [the gift]. After giving, I do not speak of it over and over again. By describing what you have given, is self-destruction."

10. From NGO Credibilty Forum, IndianNGOs.com at http://www.indianngos.com/ngosection/ngocredibility/anilbaranwal/fullinterview.htm (page no longer available).

## Chapter 3

This chapter was originally published in a slightly different form in Bornstein and Redfield, *Forces of Compassion* (see Bornstein 2011). Reprinted by permission of the author and the publisher.

1. See Aryasamja Gandhidham, "Charity for Children—Children Profile" at http://www.aryagan.org/aryasamaj/profile.php, accessed 8 February 2008.

2. At the time of writing, the conversion rate was roughly 40 rupees to $1.

3. "Child Welfare," GiveIndia, at http://www.giveindia.org/c-51-children.aspx.

4. In UNICEF's subsequent annual reports on the state of the world's children, titles shift from a focus on orphans and vulnerable children—"Excluded and Invisible" (2006) to "Women and the Double Dividend of Gender Equality" (2007) and "Child Survival" (2008).

5. Statistics are from an adoption advocacy organization called Catalysts for Social Action (CSA) (http://www.csa.org.in as well as IndianNGOs.com at http://www.indianngos.com/issue/child/adoption/statistics/index.html, accessed 6 December 2006 [no longer available]). Other statistics I have found give only a slightly different picture. Jamal (2005) states that 17,403 children were adopted through CARA in 2001; 7,377 of these adoptions were intercountry adoptions. These numbers do not include illegal adoptions.

6. In the 2005 Day of General Discussion for the U.N. Committee on the Rights of the Child on the issue of children without parental care, NGOs submitted supporting documents and reports (see India Alliance for Child Rights [IARC] 2005[a] and 2005[b]; Child Relief and You [CRY] 2005: 3).

7. CRY defines advocacy as follows: "Advocacy is done through the facilitation of a network of individuals, NGOs, teaching institutions and academics, professionals with specialized knowledge such as lawyers, and managers of homes for children. Constructive engagement with the State is seen as an essential ingredient of the advocacy process" (Child Relief and You [CRY] 2005: 3). Also see U.N. General Assembly Resolution No. 64/142, "Guidelines for the Alternative Care for Children," at http://www.crin.org/

docs/guidelines-english.pdf (accessed 18 March 2011). This document outlines how, when parents can't care for children, the state is responsible. The guidelines cover kinship care, foster care, family-like placements, residential care (including adoption and family reintegration guidelines), and care through agencies (including public, private, state, and NGOs).

8. Only CARA oversees in-country adoption and regulates intercountry adoption. CARA has sixty-nine placement agencies throughout India. The process for adoption is governed by the Guardians and Wards Act (Jamal 2005).

9. Creedal and secular definitions apply in the current law (1956). The creedal definition is based on religion—defined by the religion of the adopting parents. It also applies to any child abandoned by parents and brought up in that religion, as well as converts and "reconverts" to that religion. The secular definition of who is Hindu is "persons who are not Christians, Parsis, Muslims, or Jews." It includes atheists.

10. Although dowries are illegal in India, the practice continues as "gifts."

11. An additional distinction is drawn between the adoption of a son and the appointment of an heir who does not have kin relations.

12. In old Hindu law, the shastras prescribed two sets of ceremonies: one religious and the other secular. Religious ceremonies included the recital of certain prayers and Vedic hymns (*dattak-homa*, or the oblation of fire) that involved ceremonies of gift and acceptance and burnt sacrifice to procure good fortune for the adoptee. Caste had its place in the scriptural hierarchy of humanity: in the case of Sudras (the lowest of the four varnas, or castes), neither dattak-homa nor any religious ceremony was essential. In the shastras, the secular ceremony of giving and taking was mandatory for the validity of adoption. The ceremony made the transfer of the child complete, final, and irrevocable. "The ceremony of giving and taking has to be performed by the person who gives the child in adoption, whether he is father, mother, or guardian, and by the person who takes the child in adoption. According to Baudhayana: 'One should go to the giver of the child, and ask him saying "Give me thy son!" The other answers "I give him!" He receives him with these words: "I take these for the fulfillment of my religious duties; I take these to continue the line of my ancestors"'" (Manu cited in Diwan 2000: 89).

13. The Hindi word for orphan is *anāth*, which translates literally as "without lord, without God, or without protector." Hindu conversion is one of acceptance into a community. It is not a product of individual choice, such as being "born again" in Christianity. There is no formal ceremony of purification or expiation to effect conversion. Conversion, in other words, is a matter of *belonging*. The bare declaration of Hinduism is not enough to convert; one must be accepted by members of the community as such and recognized socially.

14. In contemporary postcolonial, secular India, each community has its own family law governed under Personal Law. While Hindu and Muslim law are claimed to be of divine origin, no such claim is made by the other religious communities. Some communities are governed by custom. For example, Jewish family law in India is "customary law." Ancestral and customary law are relevant to the legislation of joint property in some places. "Scheduled tribes" are governed by "custom," and Hindu law does not ap-

ply; thus there are many exceptions to instances in which Hindu family law is applied to family disputes. In addition, Personal Law differs from state to state within India. Each community is governed by a single system of law, yet within the community (for example, along divisions of caste, subcaste, and subsect) there are regional distinctions. Different "schools" of Hindu and Muslim law are also regionally specific. However, all adoptions are governed by the codified law of the Hindu Adoptions and Maintenance Act of 1956. Only Hindu law recognizes adoption. Adoption is not recognized under any other Indian Personal Law with the exception of Parsi Personal Law, which has two forms of recognized adoption. See Diwan (2000).

15. Many other specific conditions must be present for a valid adoption: (1) If adoption is of a son, the adoptive parents must not already have a son, son's son, or son's son's son; (2) if it is of a daughter, then parents must not have a Hindu daughter or a son's daughter; (3) if a man is adopting a girl, he must be at least twenty-one years older than the girl to be adopted; (4) if a woman is adopting a boy, she must be twenty-one years older than the boy she is adopting; (5) the same child cannot be adopted simultaneously by two or more people; (6) the child to be adopted must be given and taken by parents or guardians in order to be adopted. Before the 1956 law, the ceremony of giving and taking was mandatory and considered enough for a valid adoption.

16. A study by the Committee for Legal Aid to Poor (CLAP) (2005) examines cases and causes of child abandonment in India. The causes it cites include illegitimacy, death of parents, migration and exodus, working parents, single parents, religious fundamentalism, children in conflict with the law (juvenile delinquents), exploitation through trafficking, child labor, street children, kidnapping, and children in armed conflict. The study concludes that poverty and the absence of parental care are interwoven. Personal Law in India does not accommodate illegitimate children. The CLAP publication cites a 1992 statistic from the National Institute of Public Cooperation and Child Development documenting thirty million orphans in India as a category of risk in children at risk (100).

17. Caste does not seem be a significant aspect in Siddiqui's study. She notes that of her 157 respondents, 72 percent belonged to the upper or middle caste of Hindus, Jains, and Sikhs. Only 2 percent of the girls belonged to scheduled castes. The rest of the girls (41 percent) belonged to the Muslim community. Only one girl was Christian (Siddiqui 1997: 43).

18. "Father Questions Madonna Adoption," BBC News online, 22 October 2006, http://news.bbc.co.uk/2/hi/entertainment/6075476.stm.

19. "An Adoption Gone Wrong," 24 July 2007, National Public Radio, Morning Edition, http://www.npr.org/templates/story/story.php?storyId=12185524.

20. Maintenance refers to (1) "provision for food, clothing, residence, education and medical attendance and treatment"; and (2) in the case of an unmarried daughter, the reasonable expense of her marriage (Diwan 2000: 23).

21. *Frontline*, May 2005, "Complaints from Foreign Adopters."

22. See *Laxmikant Pandey vs. Union of India*, 1984.

23. In the case of willful relinquishment by the birth mother, she is given two

months to reconsider and then the child is put up for adoption. In the case of abandoned children, they are considered free for adoption after forty-five days of being found (Jamal 2005: 2).

## *Chapter 4*

1. Narratives of experience can be compared with narratives of sacrifice and religious transformation as in mysticism and conversion (James 1982 [1902]). In the Indian context, such narratives also evoke reference to narratives of renunciation in relation to the gift (Laidlaw 1995).

2. For a comparison of Durkheim and James, see Jones (2003).

3. Joan Scott (1991) has written about the use of experience as evidence and the dangers of its uncritical use. Instead of assuming that experience is an essential and uncontested truth (connected to particular identities and groups), I follow Durkheim (1995 [1902]) to emphasize how it is mediated by institutions. Experience is always represented socially, and its representation reifies collective identities. As Scott notes, "It is not individuals who have experience but subjects who are constituted through experience" (1991: 779).

4. See Watt (2005) and also Tandon (2003) for background on Gandhian ideas of service in the nonprofit sector in India.

5. This name is a pseudonym for the organization.

6. Of the 230 student applicants who were recruited to apply from Delhi's top universities, 161 were short listed for interviews. Out of those short-listed, 18 were disqualified because they did not show up to the interview, 36 were rejected, 40 were selected, and 23 were wait-listed. There were 20 slots available at 10 NGOs.

7. See Turner (1986) on the relationship between experience and social drama.

8. The orphanage was established in 1995.

9. This may be tied to neoliberal reforms. See Sen (1993), Sharma (2006), Sooryamoorthy and Gangrade (2001), and Tandon (2003).

10. Also see Prashad (1997), Redfield and Bornstein (2011), and Farmer (2003) for the social justice critique more broadly. See Hutnyk (1996) for a political economic critique of charity tourism in Kolkata and representation produced by it.

11. Many Indians believe that cold drinks exacerbate illness.

12. Interview was at http://www.bbc.co.uk/holiday/tv_and_radio/grown_up_gappers/traveller_dave.shtml, but the site is no longer available.

13. Hutnyk (1996) writes of charity tourism as a leisure activity of the global bourgeoisie, as the soft edge of capitalist exploitation, and as a form of plunder.

14. From http://www.gapyearindia.com/prog_work.htm (no longer available), accessed 31 October 2006.

15. http://www.gapyearinindia.com/why.htm. Emphasis added.

16. The People Tree website advertised that the organization provided the following: a T-shirt and certificate with the volunteer's name and project, an Indian fact file, a language conversion dictionary and basic phrasebook, a recommended reading list about India, a visit to a local restaurant, a visit to a cultural event, a lecture about India,

train and air schedules, a map of India, travel information within India, a visit to a local bazaar, and regular meetings with an advisor to solve any problems that the volunteer might be facing. Part of the contribution from the volunteer went toward various conservation projects that were supported by the "People Tree Trust" in India (despite Priya and Amelia's assertions to the contrary that nothing went to charity).

17. This stance is most likely to be controversial in circles of humanitarian practitioners. See the excellent collection by Barnett and Weiss (2008) on this topic, Rieff (2002), and Calhoun (2008) on the distinction between value rationality and instrumental rationality in humanitarianism. See Hutnyk (1996: 214–23) and Mathers (2010: 155–80) for critiques of charity tourism in Kolkata and Africa, respectively. Both Hutnyk and Mathers argue that American-ness gains meaning after an American returns from travel, and American identity is formed through its encounter with humanitarianism in Kolkata and Africa.

## Chapter 5

1. For liberal models of helping strangers, see Rawls (2001) and Ignatieff (1984). Calhoun (2003) has critiqued extreme liberal cosmopolitanism for its inherent assumption that world citizenship is morally superior to local solidarities, particularly when the worldly belonging of liberal cosmopolitanism is made to contrast supposedly illiberal local affinities.

2. The emergence of the novel points to a larger historical shift in social imagination that evokes Benedict Anderson's (1991) idea: how the printed paper (not necessarily the novel) led to an understanding of abstract others—the co-readers.

3. Laqueur (2009) writes about how the practice of naming graves for pauper deaths contributed to the identification of ethical subjects worthy of rights. The Truth and Reconciliation Commission in South Africa is a contemporary, similar process. These are narratives that "expand the circle of we." Laqueur points out how dignity for the living was connected to a new dignity for the dead. Affect and the productivity of sentiment can also produce problems for those in need (as in Brauman 2009). Brauman (2009) uses the case of Médecins sans Frontières during the 2004 tsunami to show that affective appeals for humanitarian aid, fueled by the electronic media, can do more harm than good. Such appeals in turn produced a "funding bonanza" that was unwarranted given the circumstances of the disaster and that hurt appeals a few months later following the earthquake in Kashmir. Emotional appeals produced so many donations that Médecins sans Frontières announced, with great controversy, that it would not longer accept donations for the tsunami only one week after the disaster (110). This work and others demonstrate that we must look critically at how sentiments are produced, and their effects (see Fassin and Rechtman 2009). Humanitarianism is not untouchable and beyond critique (see Fassin 2011).

4. Here, Sontag (2003) and Boltanski (1999) are relevant.

5. Missionaries and anthropologists also do this, and hence they consider their endeavors humanitarian.

6. For an analysis of American ideas of voluntarism, see Allahyari (2000), Elisha (2008), Putnam (2000), and Wuthnow (1993).

7. The Hindi name of this NGO translates as a combination of "destination" and "goal." It also means "stages" or "aspired destinations" and is used in colloquial speech to refer to the floor or story of a building.

8. As with other cases in this book, the mother's attention to Supriya caused a rift in the family. Humanitarian efforts were conducted at the expense of other family members, particularly Rajesh. He recounted that his mother "wasn't looking after what was happening in the house; she wouldn't know what is happening, if the food is being cooked or not. Luckily we had a servant who was with us for forty years so he was like the housewife. I like to call him the housewife anyway because he took care of everything. Including not just doing work that was required of him. But if some guests came, he would extend our hospitality in a way that somebody from the house would—insisting that they stay for lunch, in every way. He was kind of my parent, my support. I could turn to him for anything."

# Bibliography


*AccountAble.* 2006 (April 2005, released January 2006). No. 112. Accountability and Hindu Dan. http://uttardayee.freewebspace.com/AccountAble_India/112%2-%20Accountability%20and%20Daan.pdf.

Agarwal, Sanjay. 2005. Sampradaan, Bi-monthly Bulletin of Sampradaan Indian Centre for Philanthropy. Delhi: Sampradaan Indian Centre for Philanthropy.

———. 2011. *Daan and Other Giving Traditions in India.* New Delhi: AccountAid India.

Agarwal, Sanjay, and Noshir Dadrawala. 2004. Philanthropy and Law in India. In *Philanthropy and Law in South Asia,* edited by M. Sidel and I. Zaman. Pp. 115–81. Manila: Asia Pacific Philanthropy Consortium.

Allahyari, Rebecca Anne. 2000. *Visions of Charity: Volunteer Workers and Moral Community.* Berkeley: University of California Press.

American Civil Liberties Union. 2009. Blocking Faith, Freezing Charity: Chilling Muslim Charitable Giving in the "War on Terror Financing." New York: ACLU.

Anderson, Benedict. 1991. *Imagined Communities: Reflections on the Origins and Spread of Nationalism.* London: Verso.

Anderson, Leona. 1997. Generosity among Saints, Generosity among Kings: Situating Philanthropy in South Asia. In *Philanthropy and Cultural Context: Western Philanthropy in South, East, and Southeast Asia in the 20th Century,* edited by S. Hewa and P. Hove. Pp. 185–202. Lanham, MD: University Press of America.

Appadurai, Arjun. 1985. Gratitude as a Social Mode in South India. *Ethos* 13 (3): 236–45.

———. 1988. Putting Hierarchy in Its Place. *Cultural Anthropology* 3 (1): 36–49.

———. 2006. *Fear of Small Numbers: An Essay on the Geography of Anger.* Durham, NC: Duke University Press.

Apparao, Hansa. 1997. International Adoption of Children: The Indian Scene. *International Journal of Behavioral Development* 20 (1): 3–16.

Asia Pacific Philanthropy Consortium. 2007. Philanthropy and Law in South Asia: Recent Developments in Bangladesh, India, Nepal, Pakistan, and Sri Lanka. http://www.asiapacificphilanthropy.org/node/8.

Barnett, Michael N., and Thomas George Weiss. 2008. *Humanitarianism in Question: Politics, Power, Ethics.* Ithaca, NY: Cornell University Press.

Bayly, C. A. 1973. Patrons and Politics in Northern India. *Modern Asian Studies* 7 (3): 349–88.

Benthall, Jonathan. 1993. *Disasters, Relief and the Media.* London: I. B. Tauris.

———. 1997. The Red Cross and Red Crescent Movement and Islamic Societies, with Special Reference to Jordan. *British Journal of Middle Eastern Studies* 24 (2): 157–77.

———. 1999. Financial Worship: The Quranic Injunction to Almsgiving. *Journal of the Royal Anthropological Institute* 5 (1): 27.

———. 2005. Confessional Cousins and the Rest: The Structure of Islamic Toleration. *Anthropology Today* 21 (1): 16–20.

———. 2011. Islamic Humanitarianism in Adversarial Context. In *Forces of Compassion: Humanitarianism between Ethics and Politics,* edited by E. Bornstein and P. Redfield. Pp. 99–121. Santa Fe, NM: School for Advanced Research Press.

———. 2012. "Cultural Proximity" and the Conjuncture of Islam with Modern Humanitarianism. In *Sacred Aid,* edited by M. Barnett and J. G. Stein. Oxford: Oxford University Press.

Benthall, Jonathan, and Jerome Bellion-Jourdan. 2003. *The Charitable Crescent: Politics of Aid in the Muslim World.* London: I. B. Tauris.

Beteille, Andre. 1979. Homo Hierarchicus, Homo Equalis. *Modern Asian Studies* 13 (4): 529–48.

———. 1992. Caste and Family in Representations of Indian Society. *Anthropology Today* 8 (1): 13–18.

Bharadwaj, Aditya. 2003. Why Adoption Is Not an Option in India: The Visibility of Infertility, the Secrecy of Donor Insemination, and Other Cultural Complexities. *Social Science and Medicine* 56: 1867–80.

Bharat, Shalini. 1993. *Child Adoption Trends and Emerging Issues: A Study of Adoption Agencies.* Bombay: Tata Institute of Social Sciences.

Birla, Ritu. 2009. *Stages of Capital: Law, Culture, and Market Governance in Late Colonial India.* Durham, NC: Duke University Press.

Boler, Megan. 1999. *Feeling Power: Emotions and Education.* New York: Routledge.

Boltanski, Luc. 1999. *Distant Suffering: Morality, Media, and Politics.* Cambridge: Cambridge University Press.

Bornstein, Erica. 2001. Child Sponsorship, Evangelism, and Belonging in the Work of World Vision Zimbabwe. *American Ethnologist* 28 (3): 595–622.

———. 2005 [2003]. *The Spirit of Development: Protestant NGOs, Morality, and Economics in Zimbabwe.* Palo Alto, CA: Stanford University Press.

———. 2006. No Return: A Brief Typology of Philanthropy and the Sacred in New Delhi. In *The Politics of Altruism: Caring and Religion in Global Perspective,* edited by K. Inaba and R. Habito. Pp. 165–79. Cambridge: Cambridge Scholars Press.

———. 2007. Harmonic Dissonance: Reflections on Dwelling in the Field. *Ethnos* 72 (4): 483–508.

———. 2009. The Impulse of Philanthropy. *Cultural Anthropology* 24 (4): 622–51.

———. 2011. The Value of Orphans. In *Forces of Compassion: Humanitarianism between Ethics and Politics*, edited by E. Bornstein and P. Redfield. Pp. 123–47. Santa Fe, NM: School for Advanced Research Press.

———. 2012. Religious Giving Outside the Law in New Delhi. In *Sacred Aid*, edited by M. Barnett and J. G. Stein. Oxford: Oxford University Press.

Bornstein, Erica, and Peter Redfield, eds. 2011. *Forces of Compassion: Humanitarianism Between Ethics and Politics.* Santa Fe, NM: School for Advanced Research Press.

Bourdieu, Pierre. 1977. *Outline of a Theory of Practice.* Cambridge: Cambridge University Press.

Bowie, Fiona, ed. 2004. *Cross-Cultural Approaches to Adoption.* New York: Routledge.

Brauman, Rony. 2009. Global Media and the Myths of Humanitarian Relief: The Case of the 2004 Tsunami. In *Humanitarianism and Suffering: The Mobilization of Empathy*, edited by R. A. Wilson and R. D. Brown. Pp. 108–17. Cambridge: Cambridge University Press.

CAF India. 2000. Dimensions of the Voluntary Sector in India. New Delhi: CAF India.

Calhoun, Craig. 2003. "Belonging" in the Cosmopolitan Imaginary. *Ethnicities* 3 (4): 531–68.

———. 2008. The Imperative to Reduce Suffering: Charity, Progress, and Emergencies in the Field of Humanitarian Action. In *Humanitarianism in Question: Politics, Power, Ethics*, edited by M. Barnett and T. Weiss. Pp. 73–97. Ithaca, NY: Cornell University Press.

Carsten, Janet, ed. 2000. *Cultures of Relatedness: New Approaches to the Study of Kinship.* Cambridge: Cambridge University Press.

———. 2005. Images of "Waiting Children": Spectatorship and Pity in the Representation of the Global Social Orphan in the 1990s. In *Cultures of Transnational Adoption*, edited by T. A. Volkman. Pp. 185–90. Durham, NC: Duke University Press.

Cassell, Joan, ed. 1987. *Children in the Field: Anthropological Experiences.* Philadelphia: Temple University Press.

Child Relief and You (CRY). 2005. Because Tomorrow Should Not Be Like Yesterday. http://www.cry.org/resources/pdf/GDD2005.pdf.

Cohen, Lawrence. 1999. Where It Hurts: Indian Material for an Ethics of Organ Transplantation. *Daedalus* 128 (4): 135–66.

———. 2004. Operability: Surgery at the Margin of the State. In *Anthropology in the Margins of the State*, edited by V. Das and D. Poole. Pp. 165–90. Santa Fe, NM: School of Advanced Research Press.

———. 2007. Song for Pushkin. *Deadalus* (Spring) 136 (2): 103–15.

Coleman, Simon. 2004. The Charismatic Gift. *Journal of the Royal Anthropological Institute* (10): 421–42.

Committee for Legal Aid to Poor (CLAP). 2005. Children without Parental Care: A Socio-Legal Analysis from Indian Perspective. http://www.crin.org/docs/resources/treaties/crc.40/GDD_2005_CLAP.pdf.

Copeman, Jacob. 2005. Veinglory: Exploring Processes of Blood Transfer between Persons. *Journal of the Royal Anthropological Institute* (11): 465–85.

———. 2009. *Veins of Devotion: Blood Donation and Religious Experience in North India.* New Brunswick, NJ: Rutgers University Press.

Dadrawala, Noshir. 2003a. The Legal and Fiscal Framework. In *Working with the Nonprofit Sector in India*, edited by C. India. Pp. 52–68. New Delhi: Charities Aid Foundation, India.

———. 2003b. *Merchants of Philanthropy: Profiles in Good Corporate Citizenship.* Mumbai: Centre for Advancement of Philanthropy.

———. 2004. *The Art of Successful Fund Raising.* Mumbai: Centre for Advancement of Philanthropy.

Das, Veena. 1995. National Honour and Practical Kinship: Of Unwanted Women and Children. In *Critical Events: An Anthropological Perspective on Contemporary India.* Delhi: Oxford University Press.

Derrida, Jacques. 1992. *Given Time: I. Counterfeit Money.* Translated by P. Kamuf. Chicago: University of Chicago Press.

De Waal, Alexander. 1997. *Famine Crimes: Politics and the Disaster Relief Industry in Africa.* London: African Rights and the International African Institute, in association with James Currey, Oxford and Indiana University Press, Bloomington.

Dirks, Nicholas B. 2001. *Castes of Mind: Colonialism and the Making of Modern India.* Princeton, NJ: Princeton University Press.

Diwan, Paras. 2000. *Law of Adoption, Minority Guardianship, and Custody.* 3rd ed. Delhi: Universal Law Publishing.

———. 2007. *Modern Hindu Law.* Delhi: Allahabad Law Agency.

Dorow, Sara K. 2006. *Transnational Adoption: A Cultural Economy of Race, Gender, and Kinship.* New York: New York University Press.

Douglas, Mary. 1994 [1966]. *Purity and Danger: An Analysis of the Concepts of Pollution and Taboo.* London: Routledge.

Duffield, Mark R. 2001. *Global Governance and the New Wars: The Merging of Development and Security.* London: Zed Books.

Dumont, Louis. 1980. *Homo Hierarchicus: The Caste System and Its Implications.* Chicago: University of Chicago Press.

Dupont, Véronique, Emma Tarlo, D. Vital, 2000. *Delhi: Urban Space and Human Destinies.* New Delhi: Manohar.

Durkheim, Émile. 1995 [1912]. *The Elementary Forms of Religious Life.* Translated by K. E. Fields. New York: Free Press.

Dusenbery, Verne A., and Darshan Singh Tatla. 2009. *Sikh Diaspora Philanthropy in Punjab: Global Giving for Local Good.* New Delhi: Oxford University Press.

Dyck, Noel. 2000. Home Field Advantage? Exploring the Social Construction of Children's Sports. In *Constructing the Field: Ethnographic Fieldwork in the Contemporary World,* edited by V. Amit. Pp. 32–53. London: Routledge.

Ebrahim, Alnoor, and Edward Weisband. 2007. *Global Accountabilities: Participation, Pluralism, and Public Ethics.* Cambridge: Cambridge University Press.

Elisha, Omri. 2008. Moral Ambitions of Grace: The Paradox of Compassion and Accountability in Evangelical Faith-Based Activism. *Cultural Anthropology* 23 (1): 154–89.

Englund, Harri. 2006. *Prisoners of Freedom: Human Rights and the African Poor.* Berkeley: University of California Press.

———. 2008. Extreme Poverty and Existential Obligations: Beyond Morality in the Anthropology of Africa. *Social Analysis* 52: 33–50.

Farmer, Paul. 2003. *Pathologies of Power: Health, Human Rights, and the New War on the Poor.* Berkeley: University of California Press.

Fassin, Didier. 2005. Compassion and Repression: The Moral Economy of Immigration Policies in France. *Cultural Anthropology* 20 (3): 362–87.

———. 2007. Humanitarianism as a Politics of Life. *Public Culture* (19): 3.

———. 2008a. The Humanitarian Politics of Testimony: Subjectification through Trauma in the Israeli-Palestinian Conflict. *Cultural Anthropology* 23 (3): 531–58.

———. 2008b. Aids Orphans, Raped Babies, and Suffering Children: The Moral Construction of Childhood in Post-Apartheid South Africa. In *Healing the World's Children: Interdisciplinary Perspectives on Health in the Twentieth Century,* edited by G. Weisz. Pp. 111–24. Montreal: McGill Queens University Press.

———. 2011. Noli Me Tangere: The Moral Untouchability of Humanitarianism. In *Forces of Compassion: Humanitarianism between Ethics and Politics,* edited by E. Bornstein and P. Redfield. Pp. 35–52. Santa Fe, NM: School for Advanced Research Press.

Fassin, Didier, and Estelle D'Halluin. 2005. The Truth from the Body: Medical Certificates as Ultimate Evidence for Asylum Seekers. *American Anthropologist* 107 (4): 597–608.

Fassin, Didier, and Mariella Pandolfi. 2010. *Contemporary States of Emergency: The Politics of Military and Humanitarian Interventions.* New York: Zone Books–MIT Press.

Fassin, Didier, and Richard Rechtman. 2009. *The Empire of Trauma: An Inquiry into the Condition of Victimhood.* Princeton, NJ: Princeton University Press.

Feher, Michel. 2007. *Nongovernmental Politics.* New York: Zone Books–MIT Press.

Feldman, Ilana. 2007. Difficult Distinctions: Refugee Law, Humanitarian Practice, and Political Identification in Gaza. *Cultural Anthropology* 22 (1): 129–69.

———. 2011. The Humanitarian Circuit: Relief Work, Development Assistance, and CARE in Gaza 1955–67. In *Forces of Compassion: Humanitarianism between Ethics and Politics*, edited by E. Bornstein and P. Redfield. Pp. 203–26. Santa Fe, NM: School for Advanced Research Press.

Feldman, Ilana, and Miriam Iris Ticktin. 2010. *In the Name of Humanity: The Government of Threat and Care.* Durham, NC: Duke University Press.

Fisher, William. 1997. DOING GOOD? The Politics and Antipolitics of NGO Practices. *Annual Review of Anthropology* 26: 439–64.

Foucault, Michel. 1973. *The Order of Things: An Archaeology of the Human Sciences.* New York: Vintage.

———. 1991. Governmentality. In *The Foucault Effect: Studies in Governmentality*, edited by G. Burchell, C. Gordon, and P. Miller. Pp. 87–104. Chicago: University of Chicago Press.

Franklin, Sarah, and Susan McKinnon, eds. 2001. *Relative Values: Reconfiguring Kinship Studies.* Durham, NC: Duke University Press.

Franklin, Sarah, and Helena Ragone, eds. 1998. *Reproducing Reproduction: Kinship, Power, and Technological Innovation.* Philadelphia: University of Pennsylvania Press.

Friedman, Lawrence. 2003. Philanthropy in America: Historicism and Its Discontents. In *Charity, Philanthropy, and American Civility in American History*, edited by L. Friedman and M. D. McGarvie. Pp. 1–21. Cambridge: Cambridge University Press.

Gandhi, Mohandas K. 2000. *The Bhagavad Gita According to Gandhi.* Berkeley, CA: Berkeley Hills Books.

Godelier, Maurice. 1999. *The Enigma of the Gift.* Translated by N. Scott. Cambridge: Polity Press.

Gold, Ann Grodzins. 1988. *Fruitful Journeys: The Ways of Rajasthani Pilgrims.* Berkeley: University of California Press.

Golde, Peggy, ed. 1986. *Women in the Field: Anthropological Experiences.* Berkeley: University of California Press.

Goodhand, Jonathan. 2006. *Aiding Peace?: The Role of NGOs in Armed Conflict.* Boulder, CO: Lynne Rienner.

Goody, Jack. 1969. Inheritance and Descent: Adoption in Cross-Cultural Perspective. *Comparative Studies in Society and History* 11 (1): 55–78.

Government of India. 2002. High Level Committee on Indian Diaspora. The Indian Diaspora. New Delhi: Ministry of External Affairs, Non Resident Indians and Persons of Indian Origin Division..

———. 2006. Foreign Contribution Regulation Bill, 2006. Ministry of Home Affairs. http://mha.nic.in/pdfs/fcmc-bill-06.pdf

———. 2007. Voluntary Action Cell, Planning Commission. National Policy on the

Voluntary Sector. Government of India. http://planningcommission.nic.in/data/ngo/npvol07.pdf.

———. 2010. Foreign Contribution Regulation Act, 2010. Ministry of Home Affairs, Foreigners Division. http://mha.nic.in/fcra.htm.

Greenough, Paul R. 1982. *Prosperity and Misery in Modern Bengal: The Gamine of 1943–1944.* New York: Oxford University Press.

Gregory, C. A. 1982. *Gifts and Commodities.* London: Academic Press.

Grindal, Bruce T., and Frank A. Salamone, eds. 2006. *Bridges to Humanity: Narratives on Fieldwork and Friendship.* Long Grove, IL: Waveland.

Gross, Robert A. 2003. Giving in America: From Charity to Philanthropy. In *Charity, Philanthropy, and Civility in American History,* edited by L. J. Friedman and M. D. McGarvie. Pp. 29–48. Cambridge: Cambridge University Press.

Gupta, Akhil. 1995. Blurred Boundaries: The Discourse of Corruption, the Culture of Politics, and the Imagined State. *American Ethnologist* 22 (2): 375–402.

Gupta, Akhil, and Aradhana Sharma. 2006. Globalization and Postcolonial States. *Current Anthropology* 47: 277–93.

Hancock, Graham. 1989. *Lords of Poverty: The Power, Prestige, and Corruption of the International Aid Business.* New York: Atlantic Monthly Press.

Hanlon, Joseph, Armando Barrientos, and David Hulme. 2010. *Just Give Money to the Poor: The Development Revolution from the Global South.* Sterling, VA: Kumarian.

Haskell, Thomas. 1985a. Capitalism and the Origins of Humanitarian Sensibility—Part 1. *American Historical Review* 90 (2): 339–61.

———. 1985b. Capitalism and the Origins of Humanitarian Sensibility—Part 2. *American Historical Review* 90 (3): 547–56.

Haynes, Douglas E. 1987. From Tribute to Philanthropy: The Politics of Gift Giving in a Western Indian City. *Journal of Asian Studies* 46 (2): 339–60.

Heim, Maria. 2004. *Theories of the Gift in South Asia: Hindu, Buddhist, and Jain Reflections on Dāna.* New York: Routledge.

Henderson, Patricia. 2007. South African AIDS Orphans: Examining Assumptions around Vulnerability from the Perspective of Rural Children and Youth. *Childhood* 13 (3): 303–27.

Hitchens, Christopher. 1995. *The Missionary Position: Mother Teresa in Theory and Practice.* London: Verso.

Hoffman, Peter J., and Thomas George Weiss. 2006. *Sword and Salve: Confronting New Wars and Humanitarian Crises.* Lanham, MD: Rowman and Littlefield.

Howe, Barbara. 1980. The Emergence of Scientific Philanthropy 1900–1920: Origins, Issues and Outcomes. In *Philanthropy and Cultural Imperialism: The Foundations at Home and Abroad,* edited by R. F. Arnove. Pp. 25–54. Boston: G. K. Hall.

Howell, Signe. 2006. *Kinning of Foreigners: Transnational Adoption in a Global Perspective.* New York: Berghahn.

Hutnyk, John. 1996. *The Rumour of Calcutta: Tourism, Charity, and the Poverty of Representation.* London: Zed Books.

Ignatieff, Michael. 1984. *The Needs of Strangers.* London: Chatto and Windus.

INCITE!, Women of Color against Violence, ed. 2007. *The Revolution Will Not Be Funded: Beyond the Non-Profit Industrial Complex.* Cambridge: South End Press.

Indian Alliance for Child Rights (IARC). 2005a. Children without Parental Care. The Indian Context—2005. Report from Indian NGOs. http://www.crin.org/docs/resources/treaties/crc.40/GDD_2005_IACR_Indian_Context.pdf.

———. 2005b. Children's Right to Parenting Care and Support. http://www.crin.org/docs/resources/treaties/crc.40/GDD_2005_IACR.pdf.

Jamal, Mayeda. 2005. Child Trafficking in India. Child Rights International Network document. http://www.crin.org/docs/resources/treaties/crc.40/GDD_2005_Jamal_Mayeda.pdf.

James, William. 1982 [1902]. *The Varieties of Religious Experience: A Study in Human Nature.* New York: Penguin.

Jones, Sue Stedman. 2003. From Varieties to Elementary Forms: William James and Emile Durkheim on Religious Life. *Journal of Classical Sociology* 3 (2): 99–121.

Jordan, Lisa, and Peter van Tuijl. 2006. *NGO Accountability: Politics, Principles, and Innovations.* London: Earthscan.

Jurgensmeyer, Mark, and Darrin McMahon. 1998. Hindu Philanthropy and Civil Society. In *Philanthropy in the World's Traditions*, edited by W. F. Ilchman, S. N. Katz, and E. L. Queen. Pp. 263–78. Bloomington: Indiana University Press.

Kapur, Devesh, Ajay S. Mehta, and R. Moon Dutt. 2004. Indian Diaspora Philanthropy. In *Diaspora Philanthropy and Equitable Development in China and India*, edited by P. Geithner, P. D. Johnson, and L. C. Chen. Pp. 117–213. Cambridge, MA: Harvard University Press.

Keen, Suzanne. 2007. *Empathy and the Novel.* Oxford: Oxford University Press.

Khan, Ajaz Ahmed. 2012. The Impulse to Give: The Motivations of Giving to Muslim Charities. In *Sacred Aid*, edited by M. Barnett and J. G. Stein. Oxford: Oxford University Press.

Kochuyt, Thierry. 2009. God, Gifts and Poor People: On Charity in Islam. *Social Compass* 56 (1): 98–116.

Konrad, Monica. 2005. *Nameless Relations: Anonymity, Melanesia and Reproductive Gift Exchange between British Ova Donors and Recipients.* New York: Berghahn.

Koshi, George. 2004. *Taxmann's Law and Practice Relating to Foreign Contributions and Donations: Under Foreign Contribution (Regulation) Act with FAQs.* New Delhi: Taxmann Allied Services.

Kothari, Rajni. 1986. NGOs, the State and World Capitalism. *Economic and Political Weekly* 21 (50): 2177–82.

Kristof, Nicholas D., and Sheryl WuDunn. 2009. *Half the Sky: Turning Oppression into Opportunity for Women Worldwide.* New York: Alfred A. Knopf.

Lacey, Marc. 2006. Guatemala System Is Scrutinized as Americans Rush in to Adopt. *New York Times.* 5 November. http://www.nytimes.com/2006/11/05/world/americas/05guatemala.html.

Laidlaw, James. 1995. *Riches and Renunciation: Religion, Economy, and Society among the Jains.* New York: Clarendon.

———. 2000. A Free Gift Makes No Friends. *Journal of the Royal Anthropological Institute* (6) 4: 617.

———. 2002. For an Anthropology of Ethics and Freedom. *Journal of the Royal Anthropological Institute* (8): 311–32.

Lakoff, Andrew, ed. 2010. *Disaster and the Politics of Intervention.* New York: Columbia University Press.

Laqueur, Thomas W. 2009. Mourning, Pity, and the Work of Narrative in the Making of "Humanity." In *Humanitarianism and Suffering: The Mobilization of Empathy,* edited by R. Wilson and R. D. Brown. Pp. 31–57. Cambridge: Cambridge University Press.

Larson, Gerald James. 2001. *Religion and Personal Law in Secular India: A Call to Judgment.* Bloomington: Indiana University Press.

Libal, Kathryn. 2001. Children's Rights in Turkey. *Human Rights Review* (October–December): 35–44.

Lobo, Aloma, and Jayapriya Vasudevan. 2002. *The Penguin Guide to Adoption in India.* New Delhi: Penguin.

Maharaj, Dnyaneshwar. 1972. *Gita the Mother.* Translated by M. Subedar. Ludhiana: Kalyani.

Malinowski, Bronislaw. 1922. *Argonauts of the Western Pacific.* London: Routledge.

Malkki, Liisa H. 1995. *Purity and Exile: Violence, Memory, and National Cosmology among Hutu Refugees in Tanzania.* Chicago: University of Chicago Press.

———. 1996. Speechless Emissaries: Refugees, Humanitarianism, and Dehistoricization. *Cultural Anthropology* 11 (3): 377–404.

———. 2010. Children, Humanity, and the Infantilization of Peace. In *In the Name of Humanity: The Government of Threat and Care,* edited by I. Feldman and M. Ticktin. Pp. 58–85. Durham, NC: Duke University Press.

Manu. 1991. *The Laws of Manu.* Translated by W. Doniger. New Delhi: Penguin.

Marren, Michael. 1997. *The Road to Hell: The Ravaging Effects of Foreign Aid.* New York: Free Press.

Mathers, Kathryn Frances. 2010. *Travel, Humanitarianism, and Becoming American in Africa.* New York: Palgrave Macmillan.

Mathew, Biju, and Vijay Prashad. 2000. The Protean Forms of Yankee Hindutva. *Ethnic and Racial Studies* 23 (3): 516–34.

Mauss, Marcel. 1990 [1950]. *The Gift: The Form and Reason for Exchange in Archaic Societies.* Translated by W. D. Halls. New York: W. W. Norton.

Mead, George H. 1969 [1930]. Philanthropy from the Point of View of Ethics. In *Intelligent Philanthropy*, edited by E. Faris, F. Laune, and A. J. Todd. Pp. 133–48. Montclair, NJ: Patterson Smith.

Meintjes, Helen, and Sonja Giese. 2007. Spinning the Epidemic: The Making of Mythologies of Orphanhood in the Context of Aids. *Childhood* 13 (3): 407–30.

Menon, Kalyani Devaki. 2010. Living and Dying for Mother India: Hindu Nationalist Female Renouncers and Sacred Duty. In *Everyday Life in South Asia*, edited by D. P. Mines and S. Lamb. Pp. 343–53. Bloomington: Indiana University Press.

Miller, Barbara Stoller. 1986. *The Bhagavad-Gita: Krishna's Counsel in Time of War.* Translated by B. S. Miller. New York: Bantam.

Minear, Larry. 2002. *The Humanitarian Enterprise: Dilemmas and Discoveries.* Bloomfield, CT: Kumarian.

Minn, Pierre. 2007. Toward an Anthropology of Humanitarianism. *Journal of Humanitarian Assistance*, 6 August. http://sites.tufts.edu/jha/archives/51.

Miyazaki, Hirokazu. 2005. From Sugar Cane to "Swords": Hope and the Extensibility of the Gift in Fiji. *Journal of the Royal Anthropological Institute* (11): 277–95.

Modell, Judith. 1994. *Kinship with Strangers: Adoption and Interpretations of Kinship in American Culture.* Berkeley: University of California Press.

———. 2002. *A Sealed and Secret Kinship: The Culture of Policies and Practices in American Adoption.* New York: Berghahn.

Mosse, David, and David Lewis. 2005. *The Aid Effect: Giving and Governing in International Development.* London: Pluto.

Murdoch, Lydia. 2006. *Imagined Orphans: Poor Families, Child Welfare, and Contested Citizenship in London.* New Brunswick, NJ: Rutgers University Press.

Mustsonen, Pekka. 2005. Volunteer Tourism: Postmodern Pilgrimage? *Journal of Tourism and Cultural Change* 3 (3): 160–77.

Nabhi. 2004. *Nabhi's Handbook for NGOs: An Encyclopaedia for Non-Governmental Organisations and Voluntary Agencies.* Delhi: Nabhi.

Nagi, Saroj. 2005. Why India Refused Global Aid. *Hindustan Times*, 4 January, 4.

Narayan, Kirin. 1993. How Native Is a "Native" Anthropologist? *American Anthropologist* 95 (3): 671–86.

Nath, Vijay. 1987. *Dana: Gift System in Ancient India (c. 600 BC–c. AD 300) A Socio-Economic Perspective.* New Delhi: Munshiram Manoharlal.

Nussbaum, Martha Craven. 1995. *Poetic Justice: The Literary Imagination and Public Life.* Boston: Beacon.

———.1997. *Cultivating Humanity: A Classical Defense of Reform in Liberal Education.* Cambridge, MA: Harvard University Press.

———. 2001. *Upheavals of Thought: The Intelligence of Emotions*. Cambridge: Cambridge University Press.

Odendahl, Teresa Jean. 1990. *Charity Begins at Home: Generosity and Self-Interest among the Philanthropic Elite*. New York: Basic Books.

Oxfam. 2007. *Impact Measurement and Accountability in Emergencies: The Good Enough Guide*. Oxford: Oxfam GB.

Pandolfi, Mariella. 2003. Contract of Mutual Indifference: Governance and the Humanitarian Apparatus in Contemporary Albania and Kosovo. *Indiana Journal of Global Legal Studies* 10 (1): 369–81.

Pandolfi, Mariella. 2011. Humanitarianism and Its Discontents. In *Forces of Compassion: Humanitarianism between Ethics and Politics*, edited by E. Bornstein and P. Redfield. Pp. 227–48. Santa Fe, NM: School for Advanced Research Press.

Parry, Jonathan. 1986. The Gift, the Indian Gift and the "Indian Gift." *Man* 21: 453–73.

———. 1989. On the Moral Perils of Exchange. In *Money and the Morality of Exchange*, edited by J. Parry and M. Bloch. Pp. 64–93. Cambridge: Cambridge University Press.

———. 1994. *Death in Banaras*. Cambridge: Cambridge University Press.

———. 2000. The "Crisis of Corruption" and "The Idea of India": A Worm's Eye View. In *Morals of Legitimacy: Between Agency and System*, edited by I. Pardo. Pp. 27–55. New York: Berghahn.

Passaro, Joanne. 1997. "You Can't Take the Subway to the Field!" "Village" Epistemologies in the Global Village. In *Anthropological Locations: Boundaries and Grounds of a Field Science*, edited by A. Gupta and J. Ferguson. Pp. 147–62. Berkeley: University of California Press.

Pink, Sarah. 2000. "Informants" Who Come "Home." In *Constructing the Field: Ethnographic Fieldwork in the Contemporary World*, edited by V. Amit. Pp. 96–119. London: Routledge.

Power, Michael. 1997. *The Audit Society: Rituals of Verification*. Oxford: Oxford University Press.

Prashad, Vijay. 1997. Mother Teresa: Mirror of Bourgeois Guilt. *Economic and Political Weekly* 32 (44/45): 2856–58.

Puri, V. K. 2008. *FCRA Guide: Law, Practice and Procedure*. New Delhi: JBA.

Putnam, Robert D. 2000. *Bowling Alone: The Collapse and Revival of American Community*. New York: Simon and Schuster.

Ragone, Helena. 1994. *Surrogate Motherhood: Conception in the Heart*. Boulder, CO: Westview.

Ragone, Helena, and France Winddance Twine, eds. 2000. *Ideologies and Technologies of Motherhood: Race, Class, Sexuality, Nationalism*. New York: Routledge.

Raheja, Gloria Goodwin. 1988. *The Poison in the Gift: Ritual, Prestation, and the Dominant Caste in a North Indian Village*. Chicago: University of Chicago Press.

Raheja, Gloria Goodwin, and Ann Grodzins Gold. 1994. *Listen to the Heron's Words: Reimagining Gender and Kinship in North India*. Berkeley: University of California Press.

Rahnema, Majid, and Victoria Bawtree. 1997. *The Post-Development Reader*. London: Zed Books.

Rajagopal, Arvind. 2000. Hindu Nationalism in the US: Changing Configurations of Political Practice. *Ethnic and Racial Studies* 23 (3): 467–96.

Rajaratnam, S., M. Natarajan, and C. P. Thagaraj. 2004. *Charities: An Exhaustive Treatise for Tax and Other Matters Relating to Charitable Trusts and Religious Institutions*. 4th ed. Mumbai: Snow White.

Ramani, Venkat Ramanujam. 2010. Gifts without Dignity? Gift-Giving, Reciprocity, and the Tsunami Response in the Andaman and Nicobar Islands, India. Thesis in Geography, University of Cambridge, Cambridge, UK.

Ramanujan, A. K. 1989. Is There an Indian Way of Thinking? An Informal Essay. *Contributions to Indian Sociology* 23 (1): 41–58.

Rawls, John. 1999. *The Law of Peoples; with, The Idea of Public Reason Revisited*. Cambridge, MA: Harvard University Press.

———. 2001. *Justice as Fairness: A Restatement*. Cambridge, MA: Harvard University Press.

———. 2005 [1971]. *A Theory of Justice*. Rev. ed. Cambridge, MA: Harvard University Press.

Reddy, Deepa. 2007. Good Gifts for the Common Good: Blood and Bioethics in the Market of Genetic Research. *Cultural Anthropology* 22 (3): 429–72.

Redfield, Peter. 2005. Doctors, Borders and Life in Crisis. *Cultural Anthropology* 20 (3): 328–61.

———. 2006. A Less Modest Witness: Collective Advocacy and Motivated Truth of a Medical Humanitarian Movement. *American Ethnologist* 33 (1): 3–26.

———. 2011. The Impossible Problem of Neutrality. In *Forces of Compassion: Humanitarianism between Ethics and Politics*, edited by E. Bornstein and P. Redfield. Pp. 53–70. Santa Fe, NM: School for Advanced Research Press.

Redfield, Peter, and Erica Bornstein. 2011. An Introduction to the Anthropology of Humanitarianism. In *Forces of Compassion: Humanitarianism between Ethics and Politics*, edited by E. Bornstein and P. Redfield. Pp. 3–30. Santa Fe, NM: School for Advanced Research Press.

Rieff, David. 2002. *A Bed for the Night: Humanitarianism in Crisis*. New York: Simon and Schuster.

Rupp, Katherine. 2003. *Gift-Giving in Japan: Cash, Connections, Cosmologies*. Palo Alto, CA: Stanford University Press.

Sachs, Wolfgang. 1992. *The Development Dictionary: A Guide to Knowledge as Power*. London: Zed Books.

Sampradaan Indian Centre for Philanthropy. 2001. *Investing in Ourselves: Giving and Fundraising in India.* New Delhi: Sampradaan Indian Centre for Philanthropy.

Schneider, David. 1980. *American Kinship: A Cultural Account.* 2nd ed. Chicago: University of Chicago Press.

———. 1984. *A Critique of the Study of Kinship.* Ann Arbor: University of Michigan Press.

Scott, Joan. 1991. The Evidence of Experience. *Critical Inquiry* 17 (Summer): 773–97.

Sen, Siddhartha. 1992. Non-Profit Organizations in India: Historical Development and Common Patterns. *Voluntas* 3 (2): 175–93.

———. 1993. Defining the Nonprofit Sector: India. In *Working Papers of the Johns Hopkins Comparative Nonprofit Sector Project No. 12,* edited by L. M. Salamon and H. K. Anheir. Pp. 1–33. Baltimore: Johns Hopkins Institute for Policy Studies.

———. 1999. Globalization and the Status of Current Research on the Indian Nonprofit Sector. *Voluntas* 10 (2): 113–30.

Sharma, Aradhana. 2006. Crossbreeding Institutions, Breeding Struggle: Women's Empowerment, Neoliberal Governmentality and State (Re)Formation in India. *Cultural Anthropology* 21 (1): 60–95.

Sharma, Sanjay. 2001. *Famine, Philanthropy, and the Colonial State: North India in the Early Nineteenth Century.* New Delhi: Oxford University Press.

Shiveshwarkar, Shyamala. 2004. *Mapping for Diaspora Investment in the Social Development Sector in India.* New Delhi: Charities Aid Foundation, India.

Siddiqui, Noor Jahan. 1997. *Adolescent Girls in Delhi: A Sociological Profile.* New Delhi: Regency.

Sidel, Mark. 2004a. States, Markets, and the Nonprofit Sector in South Asia. *Tulane Law Review* 78 (5): 1611–70.

———. 2004b. Diaspora Philanthropy to India: A Perspective from the United States. In *Diaspora Philanthropy and Equitable Development in China and India,* edited by P. Geithner, P. D. Johnson, and L. C. Chen. Pp. 215–57. Cambridge, MA: Harvard University Press.

———. 2010. *Regulation of the Voluntary Sector: Freedom and Security in an Era of Uncertainty.* New York: Routledge.

Sidel, Mark, and Iftekhar Zaman. 2004. Philanthropy and Law in South Asia: Key Themes and Key Choices. In *Philanthropy and Law in South Asia,* edited by Mark Sidel and Iftekhar Zaman. Pp. 15–47. Asia Pacific Philanthropy Consortium. http://www.asiapacificphilanthropy.org.

Silber, Ilana. 1998. Modern Philanthropy: Reassessing the Viability of a Maussian Perspective. In *Marcel Mauss: A Centenary Tribute,* edited by W. James and N. J. Allen. Pp. 134–50. New York: Berghahn.

———. 2000. Beyond Purity and Danger: Gift-Giving in the Monotheistic Traditions. In *Gifts and Interests,* edited by A. Vandevelde. Pp. 115–32. Leuven: Peeters.

———. 2001. The Gift-Relationship in an Era of "Loose" Solidarities. In *Identity, Culture, and Globalization*, edited by E. Ben-Rafael and Y. Sternberg. Pp. 385–400. Leiden: Brill.

———. 2002. Echoes of Sacrifice? Repertoires of Giving in the Great Religions. In *Sacrifice in Religious Experience*, edited by A. I. Baumgarten. Pp. 291–312. Leiden: Brill.

Simmel, Georg. 1971 [1908]. The Stranger. In *On Individuality and Social Forms: Selected Writings*. Chicago: University of Chicago Press.

Simpson, Bob. 2004. Impossible Gifts: Bodies, Buddhism and Bioethics in Contemporary Sri Lanka. *Journal of the Royal Anthropological Institute* (10): 839–59.

Snodgrass, Jeffrey G. 2001. Beware of Charitable Souls: Contagion, Roguish Ghosts and the Poison(s) of Hindu Alms. *Journal of the Royal Anthropological Institute* (7): 687–703.

Sontag, Susan. 2003. *Regarding the Pain of Others*. New York: Farrar, Straus and Giroux.

Sooryamoorthy, R., and K. D. Gangrade. 2001. NGOs in India: A Cross-Sectional Study. *Contributions in Sociology*. Vol. 136. Westport, CT: Greenwood.

Stein, Edith. 1964 [1917]. *On the Problem of Empathy*. Translated by Waltraut Stein. The Hague: M. Nijhoff.

Stein, Janice Gross. 2008. Humanitarian Organizations: Accountable—Why, to Whom, for What, and How? In *Humanitarianism in Question*, edited by M. Barnett and T. Weiss. Pp. 124–42. Ithaca, NY: Cornell University Press.

Stephens, Sharon. 1995. *Children and the Politics of Culture*. Princeton, NJ: Princeton University Press.

Stirrat, R. L. 2006. Competitive Humanitarianism: Relief and the Tsunami in Sri Lanka. *Anthropology Today* 22 (5): 11–16.

———. 2008. Mercenaries, Missionaries and Misfits. *Critique of Anthropology* 28 (4): 406–25.

Stirrat, R. L., and Heiko Henkel. 1997. The Development Gift: The Problem of Reciprocity in the NGO World. *Annals of the American Academy of Political and Social Science* 554: 66–80.

Strathern, Marilyn. 1988. *The Gender of the Gift: Problems with Women and Problems with Society in Melanesia*. Berkeley: University of California Press.

———. 1996/7. From Improvement to Enhancement: An Anthropological Comment on the Audit Culture. *Cambridge Anthropology* 19 (3): 1–21.

———. 2000. *Audit Cultures: Anthropological Studies in Accountability, Ethics, and the Academy*. London: Routledge.

Sundar, Pushpa. 1997a. Charity for Social Change and Development: Essays on Indian Philanthropy. In *Occasional Papers*. New Delhi: Indian Centre for Philanthropy.

———. 1997b. Women and Philanthropy in India. In *Occasional Papers*. New Delhi: Indian Centre for Philanthropy.

———. 2000. *Beyond Business: From Merchant Charity to Corporate Citizenship*. New Delhi: Tata McGraw-Hill.

———. 2002. Religious Giving in Delhi. In *For God's Sake: Religious Charity and Social Development in India*, edited by P. Sundar. Pp. 157–77. New Delhi: Sampradaan Indian Centre for Philanthropy.

———. 2010. *Foreign Aid for Indian NGOs: Problem or Solution?* New York: Routledge.

Sundar, Pushpa, ed. 2002. *For God's Sake: Religious Charity and Social Development in India*. New Delhi: Sampradaan Indian Centre for Philanthropy.

*Sunday Express*. 2005. India Giving. 9 January, 1–2.

*Sunday Hindustan Times*. 2005. Does Delhi Have a Conscience? 9 January 9, 2.

Tandon, Rajesh. 2002. *Voluntary Action, Civil Society, and the State*. New Delhi: Mosaic.

———. 2003. Overview of the Non-Governmental Sector in India. In *Working with the Non-Profit Sector in India*, edited by C. India. Pp. 114–19. New Delhi: Charities Aid Foundation, India.

Tarlo, Emma. 2003. *Unsettling Memories: Narratives of the Emergency in Delhi*. Berkeley: University of California Press.

Terrell, John, and Judith Modell. 1994. Anthropology and Adoption. *American Anthropologist* 96 (1): 155–61.

Terry, Fiona. 2002. *Condemned to Repeat? The Paradox of Humanitarian Action*. Ithaca, NY: Cornell University Press.

Thapar, Romila. 1984. Dana and Daksina as Forms of Exchange. In *Ancient Indian Social History: Some Interpretations*, edited by R. Thapar. Pp. 105–21. New Delhi: Sangham.

Ticktin, Miriam. 2006. Where Ethics and Politics Meet: The Violence of Humanitarianism in France. *American Ethnologist* 33 (1): 33–49.

Trautmann, Thomas R. 1981. *Dravidian Kinship*. Cambridge: Cambridge University Press.

Turner, Victor. 1969. *The Ritual Process: Structure and Anti-Structure*. Ithaca, NY: Cornell University Press.

———. 1986. Dewey, Dilthey, and Drama: An Essay in the Anthropology of Experience. In *The Anthropology of Experience*, edited by V. Turner and E. M. Bruner. Pp. 33–44. Urbana: University of Illinois Press.

UNICEF. 2006. State of the World's Children 2006. Excluded and Invisible. UNICEF. http://www.unicef.org/sowc06/.

———. 2007. State of the World's Children 2007. Women and Children: Double Dividend of Gender Equality. UNICEF. http://www.unicef.org/sowc07/.

———. 2008. State of the World's Children 2008. Child Survival. UNICEF. http://www.unicef.org/sowc08/.

van der Veer, Peter. 2001. *Imperial Encounters: Religion and Modernity in India and Britain*. Princeton, NJ: Princeton University Press.

———. 2002. Transnational Religion: Hindu and Muslim Movements. *Global Networks* 2 (2): 95–109.

Viswanath, Priya. 2003. *Diaspora Indians—On the Philanthropy Fast-Track.* Mumbai: Centre for Advancement of Philanthropy.

Viswanath, Priya, and Noshir Dadrawala. 2004. Philanthropic Investment and Equitable Development: The Case of India. In *Diaspora Philanthropy and Equitable Development in China and India,* edited by P. Geithner, P. D. Johnson, and L. C. Chen. Pp. 259–89. Cambridge, MA: Harvard University Press.

Vivekananda, Swami. 1997. First Meeting with John D. Rockefeller [As told by Madame Emma Calvé to Madame Drinette Verdier]. In *The Complete Works of Swami Vivekananda.* Kolkata: Advaita Ashrama, 2002.

Volkman, Toby Alice, ed. 2005. *Cultures of Transnational Adoption.* Durham, NC: Duke University Press.

Watt, Carey Anthony. 2005. *Serving the Nation: Cultures of Service, Association, and Citizenship.* New York: Oxford University Press.

Weber, Max. 1978. *Economy and Society.* Vol. 1. Edited by Guenther Roth and Claus Wittich. Berkeley: University of California Press.

———. 1993. *The Sociology of Religion.* Boston: Beacon.

Weiner, Annette B. 1992. *Inalienable Possessions: The Paradox of Keeping-While-Giving.* Berkeley: University of California Press.

Weiner, Myron. 1991. *The Child and the State in India: Child Labor and Education Policy in Comparative Perspective.* Princeton, NJ: Princeton University Press.

Weiss, Thomas George, and Cindy Collins. 1996. *Humanitarian Challenges and Intervention: World Politics and the Dilemmas of Help.* Boulder, CO: Westview.

Weston, Kath. 1991. *Families We Choose: Lesbians, Gays, Kinship.* New York: Columbia University Press.

Williams, Rina Verma. 2006. *Postcolonial Politics and Personal Laws: Colonial Legal Legacies and the Indian State.* New York: Oxford University Press.

Wilson, Richard, and Richard D. Brown. 2009. *Humanitarianism and Suffering: The Mobilization of Empathy.* Cambridge: Cambridge University Press.

Wuthnow, Robert. 1991. *Acts of Compassion: Caring for Others and Helping Ourselves.* Princeton, NJ: Princeton University Press.

Yngvesson, Barbara. 2002. Placing the "Gift Child" in Transnational Adoption. *Law and Society Review* 36 (2): 227–56.

———. 2004. National Bodies and the Body of the Child: "Competing" Families through International Adoption. In *Cross-Cultural Approaches to Adoption,* edited by F. Bowie. Pp. 211–26. London: Routledge.

Zelizer, Viviana A. 1985. *Pricing the Priceless Child: The Changing Social Value of Children.* New York: Basic Books.

# Index

## Stanford Studies in Human Rights

*Mark Goodale, editor*



Stanford Studies in Human Rights brings together established and emerging voices from the interdisciplinary field of human rights studies. The series publishes work from a range of perspectives, including ethnographic studies of human rights in practice, critical reflections on the idea of human rights, new proposals for a more effective international human rights system, and historical accounts of the rise of human rights as a globalized moral discourse.

*Values in Translation: Human Rights and the Culture of the World Bank*
**Galit A. Sarfaty**
**2012**

*Stones of Hope: How African Activists Reclaim Human Rights to Challenge Global Poverty*
**Edited by Lucie White and Jeremy Perelman**
**2010**

*Localizing Transitional Justice: Interventions and Priorities after Mass Violence*
**Edited by Rosalind Shaw and Lars Waldorf, with Pierre Hazan**
**2010**

*Surrendering to Utopia: An Anthropology of Human Rights*
**Mark Goodale**
**2009**

*Human Rights Matters: Local Politics and National Human Rights Institutions*
**Julie A. Mertus**
**2009**

*Human Rights for the 21st Century: Sovereignty, Civil Society, Culture*
**Helen M. Stacy**
**2009**